What Readers Are Sayi

"Many who suffered through the S
heavy scars may think there is not much more which needs to be said about it. If you are among those, I suggest that you at least take a little time to read this belated but informative indictment of inerrantists who engineered the 'takeover' or 'reformation' of the Southern Baptist Convention by a career Southern Baptist missionary and appeal to the churches to take back their convention and to restore it to its original purpose—to discharge the Great Commission.

"John Merritt, with his wife Elizabeth a missionary for 34 years and General Secretary of the European Baptist Convention from 1972 until 1996, is well-qualified to speak out. I will confess here that I have more than casual interest in what he has to say because he has anchored his cause in the SBC Foreign Mission Board's precipitious defunding of the Baptist Theological Seminary at Rüschlikon, Switzerland, in 1991, ostensibly because my teaching there at the invitation of the faculty 'proved' their suspicion that the seminary faculty were 'liberal.' As one would expect given his role at the time, Merritt was not a detached bystander in all of this. As General Secretary of the EBC, he made a strong effort to have the FMB reverse its decision and, afterwards, he went to great lengths to help restore the FMB's relationship with the European Baptist Federation. Unfortunately, the Board not only refused to change their initial decision; led by Paul Pressler, they also repudiated an apology for it made by their representatives in a meeting with representatives of the EBF.

"As the title itself suggests, *The Betrayal* is not simply a history of the defunding incident. John Merritt wants to get Southern Baptist churches to realize how severely the present leaders of the SBC have damaged the mission work of the convention. Watching the continuing swing to the far right in both political and religious realms in the United States, I'm not as optimistic as he that the churches will pay heed to his pleas, despite the near reverence many Southern Baptists have for missionaries. His book, however, has lasting value in his documentation of the defunding of Rüschlikon, the reaction of European Baptists, and fundamentalists insider correspondence about the decision."

—E. Glenn Hinson, *Professor Emeritus,*
Baptist Theological Seminary at Richmond

"A 34-year missionary veteran, Merritt recounts with frankness the impact of the fundamentalist takeover of the Southern Baptist Convention on foreign missions. Writing as a participant rather than an observer, he traces in great detail those developments that have forever changed the face of denominational missions.

"In the course of reporting events and actions, Merritt takes the reader on an autobiographical journey of his missionary service in Europe. His passion for missions and his love for the church are evident not only in this personal account, but also in the informational sections.

"From the introductory chapter, 'Southern Baptist Roots,' to the final chapter, 'A New Vision for A New Future for Southern Baptists,' readers will note the author's dedication to fulfilling the Great Commission even in the midst of great disappointment and hurt within his denomination."

—*Baptists Today*

"John Merritt provides a missionary and international perspective for the Southern Baptist Convention's controversy. His insight brings into focus radical changes that have occurred in the SBC and tragic consequences for missions in general and missionaries in particular. Since missions was the generative and cohesive force of the Convention before the 'ultra-conservative takeover,' this viewpoint is extremely important.

"Merritt has strong credentials, bringing a lifetime of commitment to Jesus Christ as Lord and unquestioned belief and practice. This book is not pleasant to read because it deals with unpleasant matters. It is instructive and should be read by those wanting to understand how the controversy has impacted not only the very nature of the SBC and its mission program, but also the perception that others have about both the Convention and its mission efforts."

—R. Keith Parks, *President of the Foreign Mission Board, SBC, 1980–1992*

"I have finished reading your excellent book. It is a tremendous work you have done and while reading it I thought, 'Oh, many should read this and not block off their minds.' Thank you for writing this courageous book which will belong to the libraries as an historic document."

—Karl Heinz Walter, *General Secretary, European Baptist Federation, 1989–1999*

"John Merritt describes the Southern Baptist Convention amid a quarter century of struggle. Its experience is not unique, but another sad installment in a centuries-long conflict that has plagued the Church Universal: the conflict between freedom and authority.

"The Church must outgrow the tendency to turn on and consume itself with doctrinal rancor. The starting point for restoration to wholeness is humility. We are all human beings with limited knowledge. We look to Scripture for guidance. Once a group sets in stone the idea that its interpretation of Scripture is the sole authoritative one, and denies the validity of any conflicting interpretation, then it has entirely abandoned freedom and enshrined authority in the heart of the Temple.

"The Church, if it is to carry out its high calling as an agent of reconciliation, must abandon rigid legalism. We are called to give a free response to God's grace in Christ. That response begins by acknowledging that we are limited in our ability to understand fully the divine will.

"Merritt's depth and breadth of experience bring perspective to the current Southern Baptist controversy between authoritarianism and liberty. His long association with Baptist institutions, historical perspective, and deep, personal involvement place him as an eye witness to this struggle. The depth of feeling and conviction he displays enhance the sound of his voice, which rises to the level of prophetic calling."

— Edward L. Bleynat, Jr., *author of* The First Three Gospels: A Journey into the Kingdom, Volume I: From Bethlehem to the River Jordan, *and* Volume II: From the Desert to the Mount, *which is scheduled for publication in spring, 2005*

"I have just finished reading your spell-binding book. I could not put it down. It is so well written and documented."

—Jasper McPhail, *former SBC missionary doctor in India*

"I was an IMB missionary in Togo 1985–1994. I have suffered many personal losses as a result of the controversy and I am also interested in other people's perspectives on the situation."

—Paula Settle, *former SBC missionary in Togo*

"I've just finished reading your book. I want to go back and re-read some of the chapters. It has really enlightened me about the controversy that has been going on for some years and I would only hear bits and pieces and never really know the whole story. The book is really a masterpiece and so well written."

—Jimmie Mason, *school teacher, retired*

"The book tells a sad story ... but I am pleased that someone of John's wide experience and gracious character has put on record the tragic happenings of recent years."

—Bernard Green, *former General Secretary of the Baptist Union of Great Britain and author of* Crossing the Barriers: A History of the European Baptist Federation

"The 'takeover' has been covered by other books, but none have dealt with the controversy from the unique perspective of European Baptists and missionaries. The way the SBC has distanced itself from its former overseas ties and from the Baptist World Alliance through hurtful accusations and outright falsehood is an amazing chronicle of merciless tactics and un-Christian behavior. I was a loyal Southern Baptist for 45 years. It is hard to break ties such as these but to do otherwise would be to compromise both faith and reason."
—Richard L. Atkins, *aeronautical engineer, retired*

"The truth does shine. Baptists need to hear this story. Since this book comes from an eye-witness, it will carry even greater weight. Thank you for capturing these events in print."
—James Heflin, *former General Secretary, European Baptist Convention, now professor of preaching, Logsdon Theological Seminary*

"The book was informative and upsetting. Thanks for your candor, courage and integrity."
—Eldridge Brock, LTC, *U.S. Army, retired*

"We've finished the book and found it worth passing on to our friends. Since we know most of the players, we expected it to be interesting but found it to be deeply spiritual also. May God use it to wake up the people in the pew!"
—Doylene and John Wilkes, *former Southern Baptist missionaries in Europe*

"You've done a great job with your book. It's hard-hitting and right on target."
—Landrum Salley, *pastor and college teacher, retired*

"Based on my interpretation of your comments in the book, you have been scorched far more often and deeply than I. I applaud you for taking the stand you have taken down through the years in your missionary work as well as the stand you have taken in the book. Thanks, too, for offering constructive criticism and your suggestions for improvement concerning SBC leadership. In my opinion you did it fairly, lovingly, honestly and from your heart."
—B.J. Hankins, *crop physiologist and voluntary missionary in Europe*

THE BETRAYAL

The hostile takeover of the Southern Baptist Convention and a missionary's fight for Freedom in Christ

John W. Merritt

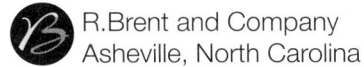

R.Brent and Company
Asheville, North Carolina

The Betrayal: The hostile takeover of the Southern Baptist Convention and a missionary's fight for Freedom in Christ © 2005 by John W. Merritt. All rights reserved.

Published in Asheville, North Carolina
by R. Brent and Company
50 Deerwood Drive
Asheville, NC 28805
828-299-0977
E-mail: robbin@rbrent.com

Publisher: *Robbin Brent Whittington*
Editor: *Joanne Johnston, Ph.D.*, Asheville, North Carolina
Cover and Interior Photography Pages Design: *Jane Ware*, jb graphics, Asheville, North Carolina
Interior Design: *R. Brent and Company, jb graphics, and Electronic Publishing Services, Inc.*
Compositor: *Electronic Publishing Services, Inc.*, Jonesborough, Tennessee
Cover design on first book: *Phil Merritt*, Hattiesburg, Mississippi

The background on the cover is text from the Gospel of John from the Gutenberg Bible.

First published in the United States in 2004 under the title: *The betrayal ... of Southern Baptist Missionaries by Southern Baptist Leaders 1979-2004.*

No part of this publication may be reproduced or transmitted in any form or by any means, electronic or mechanical, including photocopy, recording, or any information storage and retrieval system now known or to be invented, without permission in writing from the copyright holder, except by a reviewer who wishes to quote brief passages in connection with a review written for inclusion in a magazine, newspaper, broadcast, or internet site.

Library of Congress Cataloging-in-Publication Data

Merritt, John W.
The Betrayal: The hostile takeover of the Southern Baptist Convention
and a missionary's fight for Freedom in Christ—1st ed.
  p. cm.
  ISBN 978-0-9678061-6-7
  ISBN 0-9678061-6-X
  1. Religion 2. Southern Baptist 3. European Baptist Convention
  Title
                        2005902869 LCCN

14 13 12 11 10 09 08 07 06 05   1 2 3 4 5

Printed in the United States of America

In gratitude to Southern
Baptists and their churches
for their support during
thirty-four years of
missionary service

Acknowledgements

The encouragement of numerous friends to write this book has been a source of strength. My family has lived with me and "the book" for several years. They deserve a medal for patience. No one has been more patient than my wife, Elizabeth, or asked more often, "When will it be finished?" than she. She has contributed much in reading manuscripts and making insightful suggestions.

Several colleagues have read and critiqued manuscripts in their various stages and made valuable suggestions. I am deeply grateful for the contributions these outstanding Baptist leaders have made to the manuscript: Dr. Isam Ballenger, Dr. David Currie, Dr. Alan Gragg, Dr. Keith Parks, Dr. Herbert Reynolds, Dr. Guy Sayles, Dr. Walter Shurden, and Dr. Charles Wade.

I am indebted also to Dr. Eugene W. Baker for formatting the manuscript for publication and to my son, Phil, for the cover design of the book.

Being an active member of a congregation that is serious about following Jesus is an ongoing inspiration. The First Baptist Church of Asheville, North Carolina, and its pastor, Dr. Guy Sayles, are pursuing its stated Mission : *At the intersection of our culture and the Kingdom of God, the First Baptist Church of Asheville is a community of faith in which people* **experience life in the body of Christ and transformation into the image of Jesus.**

My deep gratitude goes to the editor, Dr. Joanne Johnston. The daughter of a Baptist pastor and an experienced editor, she has helped me stay focused on the objective of the book and has made many invaluable suggestions regarding content, process and wording. Equally important, she has affirmed the content and encouraged me to finish the book.

I am grateful that the book has sold well and that a new printing is needed. Selling out of books is a good thing. It gave me an opportunity to rework and improve several things about the book and I am very pleased with the outcome. I am indebted to my new publisher, Robbin Brent Whittington of R. Brent and Company, for her excellent ideas and suggestions, both for the cover and interior design, and her great interest in publishing and marketing the book. This book features a new cover, added reader comments, photograph section, interior design, and an index. Much-deserved credit for the new title, cover design and interior photograph pages goes to Jane Ware of jb graphics. I appreciate Rick Soldin's great contribution, working against a very tight deadline, to produce attractive book pages. Many thanks to Jane and Rick.

Numerous people have read the book and written unsolicited comments of appreciation for it. Others have bought multiple copies for distribution to friends and others who do not support the current fundamentalist leaders of the Southern Baptist Convention.

I am grateful to all who are engaged in the battle for truth.

Contents

Acknowledgements viii
Abbreviations xv
Foreword xvi
Introduction xvii

CHAPTER 1
Southern Baptist Roots 1

  A. 1845–1900
    Southern Baptist Convention Established 1
    Foreign and Home Mission Boards 3
    European Baptist Mission Expansion 5
    Christian Education 5
    Role of Women in Foreign Missions 7
    State Conventions 8
    Civil War Impact 8
    Women's Missionary Societies 9
    Resistance to Role of Women in Missions 10
    Lottie Moon Christmas Offering 11
  B. 1900–Present
    Sunday School Board 12
    Baptist World Alliance 13
    Brotherhood 13
    Baptist Student Movement 14
    Annuity Board 15
    Early Fundamentalist Issues 15
    Confession of Faith (1925) Versus a Creed 16
    Cooperative Program 17
    Great Depression Impact 18
    Post World War II European Developments 19
    Baptist Faith and Message (1963) 22
    Conservatives versus Moderates in the Modern Era 23
    Patterson's—Pressler's Plot 24

Chapter 2
Impact of Fundamentalist Takeover 27
About The Bible 27
Purpose of the Bible 32
Inerrancy 34
Conference on Biblical Inerrancy 36
Language in the Marketplaces 40
Accusations Against Others for Not Believing the Bible 41
The Bind: A Crisis of Conscience............................. 42
Early Efforts Toward Reconciliation.......................... 44
Call for Parity 44
Peace Committee.. 45
Responses to Fundamentalism 48
Authority Over Information 49
Exclusion of Women... 50
Exclusion of Lay Leadership 50
Further Baptist Developments in Europe 52
Changes in SBC Leadership 53
Further Responses to Fundamentalism 54

Chapter 3
Changes In Foreign And Home Missions 57
FMB Trustees Pressure Rüschlikon Seminary 58
FMB Trustees Defund Rüschlikon Seminary 59
Fundamentalist Communication 64
Fundamentalist World Vision 69
False Accusations Against Missionaries 70
FMB Trustees Reconsider Defunding............................ 71
FMB Trustees Refuse to Reverse Defunding 81

Chapter 4
The (non) Apology... 85
Birth of the Cooperative Baptist Fellowship in Europe 85
Dorfweil Statement... 87
International Baptist Church of Brussels Defunds European
    Baptist Convention 88
CBF Supports Rüschlikon...................................... 92
EBF—FMB Consultation 94
Peter Barber's Statement 96
The Hamburg Agreement 101

Full Text of the Apology 105
Denial of the Apology. 106
The Meaning of An Apology 107
Authority Over Truth 107

Chapter 5
One Missionary's Journey 109

Education, Evangelism and Missions in Church 110
Education 111
My First Pastorate 111
Sneads, Florida 112
Beginning a Missionary Career 112
Vicenza, Italy 113
Language Study 114
Milan, Italy 114
European Baptist Convention 115
Unity in Diversity 117
Membership in European Baptist Federation and
    Baptist World Alliance 117
First Visit To A Communist Land 118
Growth and Expansion 119
Partnerships in the Gospel 119
A Vision for the Nations 120
New EBF Leadership 120
Building Churches Where Walls Stood 121
EBF Presidency. 122
FMB's New Policy in Europe 123
Unity In EBF Threatened Over Role of Women in Leadership 123
Authority Over Church Offerings 138
1994 Interlaken Baptist Assembly 140
The Ultimatum: Like It Or Get Out!. 140
Renewed Resolve 142

Chapter 6
The Gospel of Jesus Christ. 145

The Voice of Jesus Christ 146
The Authority of Jesus Christ 147
The Authority of Jesus Christ in Scripture 147
Love: The Greatest Test of Christians 149

Love and Christian Leadership 150
Warnings Against Presenting Another Gospel 151
Unity in Christ. 152
State of the Southern Baptist Convention 153
Deceptive Unity in Annual SBC Meetings 154
The 1997 Southern Baptist Convention Annual Meeting 154
The 1999 SBC: Declaration of Complete Victory! 155
The 2000 SBC: Authority Over Jesus Christ 156
Partiality Toward Men. 160
Authority Over Missionaries and Their Message 162
SBC Fundamentalist Leaders Preach and Practice
    Another Gospel. 163

Chapter 7
Appeal to the Churches. 165

Aspects of Another Gospel in SBC Fundamentalist Movement. 166
  1. Rebellion Against God's Greatest Commandments 166
  2. Commitment of Evil Against Others, Especially
     Christian Leaders 167
  3. Failure to Live by the Truth 168
  4. Rejection of the Ministry of Reconciliation 170
  5. Quenching the Spirit and his Gifts in Themselves and Others . . 171
  6. Closing the Door of Freedom Opened by God 171
  7. Establishment and Enforcement of Partiality 173
  8. Refusal to Listen to the Church 173
  9. Self Exaltation 174
  10. Ignoring Biblical Warnings Against Disobedience to God 174
The Only Legitimate Division 175
Conflicts of Accountability 176
The Coming Crash 176

Chapter 8
Actions for Churches 179

Study and Ask Questions About the Bible 179
Study and Ask Questions About Your Church 182
Hold Church Leaders Accountable to the Church 183
Study and Ask Questions About Your Church and the
    Cooperative Program 184
Create Open Forums of Discussion 185

Chapter 9
A New Vision for a New Future for Southern Baptists 187
    Potential in Ourselves 188
    New Southern Baptist Convention Leadership. 189
    Unity in the Southern Baptist Convention 190
    Potential Destinies. 191
    Inclusiveness of Genders and Generations 193
    Gender Barriers. 195
    A Vision for the Nations of Love and Inclusion 198
    IMB Fires Missionaries 200
    2003 SBC Defunds Baptist World Alliance 201
    Baptist World Alliance Accepts CBF into Membership 201
    SBC Votes to End Membership in Baptist World Alliance. 202
    Rebuilding Relationships with Baptist Partners 204
    Relationships with Other Christians 206
    Sharing Resources. 210
    Hear What the Spirit Is Saying to the Churches 211
Epilogue 213

Appendix A
Consortium of New Baptist Seminaries 219

Appendix B
Letter to IMB Missionaries 220

Notes 223

Additional Recommended Reading 226

Index 227

Abbreviations

BBI	Baptist Bible Institute—later New Orleans Baptist Theological Seminary
BSSB	Baptist Sunday School Board—renamed LifeWay Christian Resources
BWA	Baptist World Alliance—a fellowship of 211 Baptist unions and conventions comprising a membership of more than 47 million baptized believers in 193,000 churches in more than 200 countries worldwide.
CBF	Cooperative Baptist Fellowship
CEBTS	Consortium of European Baptist Theological Schools
CIS	Euro-Asiatic Federation—Baptist Unions in areas formerly part of the All Union Council of Evangelical Christians-Baptists of the Soviet Union
CSI	Cooperative Services International Committee of the IMB
EBC	European Baptist Convention—renamed International Baptist Convention—a convention of more than 65 churches and missions in Europe, the Middle East and Africa
EBF	European Baptist Federation—a fellowship of more than 50 Baptist unions and conventions in Europe and the Middle East
EBPS	European Baptist Press Service
EBWU	European Baptist Women's Union
FMB	Foreign Mission Board—named changed to International Mission Board
GAs	Girls Auxiliary, a Southern Baptist missions education program for girls
GBU	German Baptist Union
Highlights	Newsjournal of the European Baptist Convention.
HMB	Home Mission Board, later the North American Mission Board
IBC	International Baptist Church, Brussels, Belgium
IBTS & BTS	International Baptist Theological Seminary—formerly located in Rüschlikon, Switzerland, now located in Prague, the Czech Republic
IMB	International Mission Board—formerly Foreign Mission Board
NAMB	North American Mission Board, formerly Home Mission Board
NOBTS	New Orleans Baptist Theological Seminary—formerly BBI—New Orleans, Louisiana
SBC	Southern Baptist Convention
SWBTS	Southwestern Baptist Theological Seminary, Fort Worth, Texas
RAs	Royal Ambassadors, a Southern Baptist mission education program for boys
WMU	Woman's Missionary Union of the Southern Baptist Convention

Foreword

John Merritt provides a missionary and international perspective for the Southern Baptist Convention's controversy. His insight brings into focus radical changes that have occurred in the SBC and tragic consequences for missions in general and the lives of missionaries in particular. Since missions was the generative and cohesive force of the Convention from its inception until "the ultra-conservative takeover," this viewpoint is extremely important.

Much of his observation came while serving in Europe as a missionary under appointment by the Foreign Mission Board, SBC. His role enabled him to work with Baptist and other Christian leaders across the continent. Since the controversy focused on Europe when it erupted internationally, he was at the center of those most affected.

Merritt has strong credentials, bringing a lifetime of commitment to Jesus Christ as Lord and unquestioned biblical belief and practice. He and his wife Elizabeth served 34 years as Southern Baptist missionaries. He has the confidence of European Baptists, members of numerous international churches and fellow missionaries as well as many of us who formerly served as FMB staff.

He combines passion for fulfilling the Great Commission, careful research and biblical insight in expressing anguish over what has happened. He details the dismay and regret of strong European Baptist leaders as well as missionary colleagues. He provides informative material that has not been generally available until now.

Merritt writes with candor about actions and events he feels were wrong. He also outlines high biblical principles he feels would lead Southern Baptists out of the controversy. He longs for a time when the SBC would once again be known for commitment to cooperating with others in missions rather than excluding others by requiring doctrinal conformity.

This book is not pleasant to read because it deals with unpleasant matters. It is instructive and should be read by those wanting to understand how the controversy has impacted not only the very nature of the SBC and its mission program, but also the perception that others have about both the Convention and its mission efforts.

—R. Keith Parks, *President,*
Foreign Mission Board, 1980–1992

Introduction

The writing of this book has been a work in progress for several years, during which time it has developed in some exciting and sometimes surprising ways. I have intended for many years to write a history of the European Baptist Convention (EBC, now International Baptist Convention), which I served as General Secretary from 1972 to 1996. No comprehensive history has been written on the EBC in more than thirty years. The EBC story is important both to those who have given brief periods of time and to those who invested many years in ministry in EBC churches or on the EBC staff. It is also important to Southern Baptists, because it is largely the result of the dedicated service of Southern Baptist lay persons, men and women, who planted their Christian faith, life and love in English language Baptist churches overseas.

However, the story of the EBC cannot be written apart from the story of the Southern Baptist Convention (SBC), the European Baptist Federation (EBF) and the Baptist World Alliance (BWA). From the founding of its first churches in the late 1950s, the EBC has cherished close ties with the SBC. In the 1970s it became a member of the EBF and BWA.

The primary problem which I am compelled to address in the book is the rise of the fundamentalist movement in the SBC and the subsequent impact on Baptist mission work. The surge of this movement throughout the SBC and into all aspects of Convention life has had a major impact on our missionary work. It affected the EBC and the relationships of the EBC with the BWA, EBF and SBC.

I learned a great deal about some of the dynamics and strategies of how the fundmentalist leaders' objectives were accomplished. I believe it will be beneficial for Southern Baptists to understand the strategies used because they have profound effects on our churches, our Convention, our missionaries and our mission work throughout the world.

My understanding of the movement has been progressive. At first, the acquaintance was from afar, as a concerned and interested observer. The most obvious symptoms of the movement were continuous strife, controversy and division. Throughout Scripture these symptoms are presented as the result of evil and immaturity in Christians.

I was born in Mississippi and served as pastor of Southern Baptist churches in Mississippi and Florida. Throughout my years as a pastor of churches before appointment and as a missionary after appointment, whoever was elected president of the SBC, or presidents of SBC seminaries, boards or agencies, or trustees of these was of little concern to me. I believed everybody who was elected to these positions had the kingdom of God and the best interests of our Convention at heart and were dedicated servants of Jesus Christ. When the controversy arose in the Convention in 1979, I believed that wise leaders who were led by the Holy Spirit could lead to a resolution of the controversy and thus to peace and unity in our Convention. Whether my faith in Convention leaders of the past was justified, I do not know. In any case, my faith in all Convention leaders ended when the fundamentalist leaders gained dominance in our Convention.

When the fundamentalist movement asserted itself in full force overseas through the trustees of the FMB in 1991, my experiences with the movement were up close and personal. They were jolting and shocking. I witnessed personally the evil of deception in the movement. The deception took on many forms, including false accusations, lies and slander. These sins of Christian leaders who do not live by the Spirit have resulted in Christians betraying other Christians. Jesus told his followers that they would suffer various forms of persecution. *"At that time many will turn away from the faith and will betray and hate each other, and many false prophets will appear and deceive many people. Because of the increase of wickedness, the love of most will grow cold, but he who stands firm to the end will be saved."* (Matt. 24:10-13) **I am a witness to the betrayal of Southern Baptist missionaries by Southern Baptist leaders!**

How the fundamentalist leaders achieved dominance in our Convention and betrayed other Christians, including missionaries, should be understood by all Southern Baptists who love Christ, love our Convention, believe in the Great Commision and send missionaries in obedience to Christ.

Ultimately, the missionaries sent by churches are ambassadors for Christ and from the churches to the world. They carry the beliefs, doctrines, mission and vision of the churches. Jesus said, *"As the Father has sent me, I am sending you,"* (John 20:21) *"You will be my witnesses,"* (Acts 1:8) and *"Make disciples of all nations ... teaching them to obey everything I have commanded you ..."* (Matt. 28:19-20). It is important that churches and missionaries understand their primary mission. This book is written to clarify who sends missionaries and under whose authority they live and work.

Unless otherwise indicated, Scriptures are quoted from the New International Version of the Bible. Spellings follow American English (program) unless in quotes by those who follow British spelling (programme).

CHAPTER 1

Southern Baptist Roots

*Listen to me, you who pursue righteousness and who seek the Lord:
Look to the rock from which you were cut and to the quarry from which
you were hewn . . . (Isaiah 51:1)*

The dawn of a new century finds Southern Baptists perplexed and divided. Although perplexity and division are painful, it can be of some consolation to remind ourselves that the Southern Baptist Convention was birthed in similar circumstances.

A. 1845–1900
Southern Baptist Convention Established

The 293 messengers from nine states who met for five days in Augusta, Georgia, in May 1845, gathered with the intention to divide from the Triennial Convention and to embark by faith in a new direction. The Triennial Convention, so named because it met once every three years, was organized in 1814 and was the first national Baptist organization in the United States. Even before the Triennial Convention, Baptist churches organized themselves into associations of churches, patterned after Baptist associations in England.

> By 1800 Baptists in America had at least forty-two associations. . . . Historians have named the Philadelphia Association as the first Baptist association in America and dated its origin as 1707. . . . The second Baptist association in America, and the first in the South, was formed at Charleston, South Carolina, by Oliver Hart in 1751. . . . The Charleston Association sponsored two major projects in the eighteenth century: ministerial education and home missions.[1]

In the years before 1845, the issue that would engulf the entire nation in the Civil War in 1861 divided the Triennial Convention. The main issue was the "peculiar institution" of slavery. Many northern Baptists in the Triennial Convention were militant abolitionists. Many, but not all Baptists in the South at that time defended and practiced slavery.

> Climate, geography, and King Cotton dictated the concentration of slaves below the Mason-Dixon line. The mountain sections of the South were relatively free of slavery, but the large plantations of the eastern seaboard and other southern states apparently could not prosper without slave labor.[2]

The collective conscience of the churches in the South had not developed the conviction that it was wrong for some people to enslave other people. Such a conviction would develop over time. An impasse was reached when militant Baptists from the North, who controlled the appointment procedure for sending missionaries, refused to appoint slave owners as missionaries.

A fundamental issue, which has characterized Baptist beliefs since their beginnings in Europe in the early 1600s, was soul freedom, often defined as "competency of the soul." It is the belief that an individual and groups of individuals (churches) are competent and have the right to study the Bible and obey their conscience before God without other individuals or groups, whether civil or religious, interfering by passing laws or otherwise prohibiting their religious freedom. Many Baptists in Europe were put to death and others were imprisoned by state and church authorities who were intolerant of full religious freedom as understood by Baptists.

Numerous Baptists were among the early settlers from England and Holland who immigrated to the American colonies in pursuit of religious freedom. Other Puritan immigrants, such as Roger Williams, John Clarke, Obadiah Holmes and Thomas Gould, became Baptists after arriving. They fought against church tyranny and for religious freedom. Although many Baptists in the colonies were imprisoned and otherwise harassed for their faith, they won their point in practice and in courts.

> Baptists like Isaac Backus and John Leland influenced later Presidents Thomas Jefferson and James Madison in critical issues of religious liberty. As early as 1776 their efforts paid off when Virginia guaranteed religious liberty in its constitution and achieved full fruition when an amendment forbidding the establishment of religion was ratified by the states of the young nation. Baptists had not only won the battle for the most cherished principle but, in the process, secured a new degree of social acceptability and respect.[3]

One of the most dominant leaders in the 1845 Augusta meeting was W. B. Johnson, president of the South Carolina Baptist Convention. He was asked to summarize why Baptists of the South felt it necessary to form a separate convention. His summary included the following:

> ... He described what was happening as a 'painful division.' he 'sought to minimize the extent of the disunity' ... At the present time it involves only the Foreign and Domestic Missions of the denomination. Northern and Southern Baptists are still brethren. They differ in no article of the faith.
>
> They are guided by the same gospel order ... We have constructed for our basis no new creed; acting in this matter upon a Baptist aversion for all creeds but the Bible ... Our objects, then, are the extension of the Messiah's kingdom, and the glory of our God ... We have shaken ourselves from the nightmare of a six years' 'strife about words to no profit,' for the profit of these poor, perishing and precious souls.[4]

Foreign and Home Mission Boards

In addition to slavery, missions was a critical issue in the minds of most leaders of the South at that time. "While it is undeniable that the primary cause of the division between the Northern and Southern Baptists was the slavery issue, it is also evident that the missionary spirit was the new convention's breath of life."[5] They had been inspired by the vision and work of English missionary to India William Carey and the work of the Baptist Missionary Society, founded in Kettering, England, October 2, 1792. Support for American Baptist missionaries Adoniram Judson and Luther Rice and the expansion of foreign missions were the catalysts for the work of the convention.

The new Southern Baptist Convention established both the Foreign Mission Board and the Board of Domestic Missions and established basic requirements for missionaries who sought appointment by either board. "Missionaries appointed by any of the Boards of this Convention, must, previous to their appointment, furnish evidence of genuine piety, fervent zeal in their Master's cause, and talents which fit them for the service for which they offer themselves."[6] The new Convention elected J. B. Jeter to lead the Foreign Mission Board and decided to locate its office in Richmond, Virginia. Basil Manly was elected to lead the Domestic Mission Board, which was located in Marion, Alabama. One of its initial tasks was to establish Baptist work in New Orleans.

Among the delegates who gathered in Augusta were numerous capable men who had distinguished themselves in preaching, education, and Christian statesmanship. Besides W. B. Johnson, another prominent leader in Augusta was Richard Fuller of Beaufort, South Carolina.

Fuller had achieved some fame for defending the institution of slavery from a scriptural point of view in a debate with a northern Baptist, Francis Wayland. Their debate was published in a book called *Domestic Slavery Considered as a Scriptural Institution*. Two years later, Fuller became pastor of the Seventh Baptist Church in Baltimore, where he helped those on both sides of the issue try to understand each other. Since Maryland would remain in the Union, Fuller's views must have modified enough to allow him a significant hearing. The fact that they did so reflects the ambivalence that ran up and down the borders toward the issue that was beginning to divide the fledgling United States of America.[7]

The missionary thrust that was central to the developments in Augusta was a clear victory over the anti-mission beliefs of some Baptists. The sacrifices of Adoniram Judson and his family in missionary service remained an inspiration to all who loved missions. "His heroism caught the imagination of Baptists in the South and gave them a passionate missionary conviction that steadfastly resisted the radical anti-missions sentiments still plaguing many churches."[8]

Some missionaries were employed and others appointed during the first year of the Convention's existence.

> The Foreign Mission Board's (FMB) initial actions were to contact existing missionaries. Three of them, I. J. Roberts, J. Lewis Shuck and his wife Henrietta Hall Shuck, Southerners under appointment to China with the Triennial Convention, agreed to transfer their support to the new Board. The first appointees of the Foreign Mission Board were the S. C. Cloptons, who went to China in the fall of 1845.[9]

The vision of the delegates was for an inclusive convention of churches. A major objective was to elicit, combine and direct the resources of the churches to support the missionary work.

> A measure of just how committed Southern Baptists were to the missionary task is evident in the fact that receipts to the Foreign Mission Board doubled between 1846 and 1849 and almost doubled again by 1853. They reached their high-water mark in 1859, after which the war devastated support.[10]

> Much has been written about who was at that first meeting and what they did . . . No women registered for these proceedings. Neither were any black members of the churches at the meeting. This is significant because on the rolls of their various congregations both groups probably outnumbered the white males who were there. Women played a serious role in Baptist life and had for many years. But history paid scant attention to the role of Catherine Scott in Roger Williams' Baptist decision, Martha Stears Marshall's role as a frontier preacher in the Sandy Creek movement,

Mary Webb's role in establishing America's first Baptist missionary society in Boston, or even Lydia Turner's role in the conversion of W. B. Johnson, who later presided over this organization. It was obvious that though Baptists in the South represented a union of the regular and separate traditions of its American heritage, the Separates' openness to women's ministries had been largely overcome by the Regulars' practice of denying the same. Yet Judson College in Alabama and what became Mary Hardin-Baylor College in Texas were even then being founded by Baptists to encourage literacy and leadership among women . . . Nor were any black Baptists present. This should provoke little surprise since in all but a few significant instances their status was that of a slave. While the First African Baptist Church of Richmond, Virginia, which J. B. Jeter had helped bring into existence, was being replicated in other places, for the most part blacks were members of southern Baptist churches.[11]

European Baptist Mission Expansion

Baptist work was also spreading during this period in Europe, led by Johann Gerhard Oncken, a young German evangelical preacher.

(Oncken) sought believers' baptism from an American missionary in Hamburg in 1834 and formed the first Baptist church in Germany. His missionary influence spread far and wide, until he was described as the father of German and Continental Baptists. The pioneering work of Oncken and his colleagues led to the growth of Baptist congregations from the North Sea eastwards to the Ural Mountains, and from the North Cape southwards to the Balkans. There were, of course, other influences in the development of Baptist life throughout Europe, such as the Anabaptists of the sixteenth century, the Dutch Mennonites and British Baptists of the seventeenth century, and American, German, Swedish and British missionaries working with Baptist groups which came to birth in the nineteenth century.[12]

Christian Education

There were other issues besides missions in the vision of the leaders in Augusta. Some resolutions urged taking "all prudent measures for their religious instruction of our colored population . . . and instructions to the Domestic Board to direct their effective attention to aid the present effort to establish the Baptist cause in New Orleans . . . and urged the churches to sustain the Indian Mission Association with zeal and liberality."[13]

They believed in and promoted education for ministers and all Baptists. Baptist colleges had already been established in Georgia (Mercer), Kentucky (Georgetown), Mississippi (Mississippi College), South Carolina (Furman) and Virginia (Richmond). Most of these institutions included theological departments that actively trained ministers.

> Many Southern Baptist leaders, however, envisioned a seminary dedicated to the professional training of ministers. . . . The Southern Baptist Theological Seminary (SBTS) opened its doors in rent-free quarters in Greenville, South Carolina (later to move to Louisville, Kentucky), in the fall of 1859, with James P. Boyce as president (then called chairman of the faculty) and John A. Broadus, William Williams, and Basil Manly, Jr., as faculty. Boyce and Broadus, especially, would be the founders of this pioneering institution which again and again became the focus of controversy, both from those who were essentially anti-institutional and anti-intellectual and those who felt violated by theological or historical positions advocated by its professors.[14]

Just as there were anti-mission beliefs among Baptists, there were also anti-education beliefs among them. Since Baptist churches are automous in calling pastors and in electing other leaders, no entity outside the local church sets educational standards that are binding on any other entity. The result of this freedom is that in all Baptist entities, whether local church, association, state Baptist convention or Southern Baptist Convention, the disparity in education is often very wide.

Many controversies over ethical, gender, social and theological issues would follow. Despite such controversies, the vision for missions, education, no creed but the Bible and governance by consensus that resulted in the organization of the Southern Baptist Convention in 1845 would guide and inspire further development of this organization of Baptists and their work nationally and internationally for many years into the future.

Landmarkism caused much controversy and provided strong opposition to the Southern Baptist concept and practice of local churches joining each other in associations and conventions to accomplish what individual churches could not do alone. Landmark leaders, such as J. R. Graves, denied that Baptist churches traced their history to Anabaptists or Baptists in England, insisting instead on a succession of Baptist churches dating all the way back to Jesus. Graves insisted also that Baptist churches were the only true churches and opposed the practice of some Baptist pastors who exchanged pulpits with non Baptist ministers. Fletcher wrote that "Graves taught that only Baptist churches were authorized to baptize and serve the Lord's Supper. Thus, Landmarkers railed out at what they called 'alien immersion' and insisted upon a 'closed communion.' The frontier environment was ripe for Graves."[15] Although the strength of Landmarkism declined in the 1860s, its influence in Southern Baptist life remained a force to be reckoned with for years to come.

> Africa was the second field of work of the Foreign Mission Board. Various considerations combined to urge upon our sympathies, her spiritual interest. Many of her sons are among us, and from them we may hope, in the process of time, to select those who become immanently qualified to preach to their countrymen 'the unsearchable riches of Christ.' . . . Apparently the board assumed that the financial outlay of sending missionaries to Africa would be minimized since they would be African-American and bi-vocational missionaries, who would go to Liberia, where English could be spoken and the necessity of acquiring another language would be unnecessary.[16]
>
> In 1847, an American Negro missionary, John Day, serving in Liberia under the Triennial Convention, agreed to work under the new convention. And in 1848 another black American, B. J. Dayton of the First African Baptist Church in Richmond, sailed for Liberia to join him. Liberian work had been established in 1821 by a freed slave, Lott Carey, backed by Baptists in Richmond . . . The Board formally committed itself to another African field when Thomas J. Bowen was sent to what is now Nigeria in 1849.[17]

In both China and Liberia, the first churches established by Baptist missionaries were English language churches. "On 5 May 1842, Shuck led in constituting the Queen's Road Baptist Church with five members, which was the first Protestant church established in China. . . . Lewis preached regularly in English at Queen's Road and three times a week in Chinese at the Bazaar Chapel."[18]

In Liberia, "a little church of only seven members, with Lott Carey as pastor, was organized in an upper room of a private dwelling in this city. That church is now the First Baptist Church in Monrovia. It has been the mother of some seven to ten other churches, and also of the Providence Baptist Association in Liberia."[19]

Role of Women in Foreign Missions

The first woman was appointed as a foreign missionary in 1849.

> Southern Baptists' first, and for a long time only, single woman missionary sailed for China in 1850. Harriet A. Baker from Powhatan, Virginia, received reluctant appointment the year before to 'establish a school for female children.' The goal was to ensure that young men emerging from the existing missionary schools should find suitable mates. Baker immediately found I. J. Roberts so hostile to her presence that she moved from Canton

to Shanghai. The Board broke ties with the difficult Roberts in 1851, but Harriet Baker became ill and resigned in 1854, terminating a pioneering role that was all but forgotten for many years.[20]

State Conventions

By the time the Convention was organized in 1845, nine state Baptist conventions had already been established in southern states. State conventions in Arkansas, Louisiana and Texas were organized in 1848 and in Florida in 1854.

Civil War Impact

The Civil War began in April, 1861, and ended in April, 1865. The war was devastating to the entire nation and to Christian cooperation and fellowship. When the Southern Baptist Convention met in Savannah, Georgia, in 1861, messengers were feeling the effects of the war. Feelings ran strong, as the rhetoric in the report of a special committee reveals.

> With astonishment and grief, we find churches and pastors of the North breathing out slaughter and clamoring for sanguinary hostilities with a fierceness which we have supposed impossible among the disciples of the Prince of Peace. A resolution urged prayer for their foes and another urged them to keep the 'spirit of Jesus in the face of the North's lawless reign.'[21]

During the war, every aspect of Christian work was affected and serious financial problems were common. One positive factor was the superb leadership of James B. Taylor, who served as Corresponding Secretary of the Foreign Mission Board for twenty-five years.

> Taylor continued to travel throughout the devastated South often going into occupied territories or behind lines trying to raise money. In addition, to help defray his salary, Taylor worked as a chaplain and colporteur in hospitals and as an employee of the Virginia Sunday School and Publication Board. Nevertheless, when the war was over and despite the faithful support of the churches in Kentucky and Maryland, the Foreign Mission Board faced a staggering $10,000 debt . . . In 1870, four missionaries, including W. D. Cote, M.D.; and George B. Taylor, son of James B. Taylor, were appointed to Rome, Italy. In 1872 the Foreign Mission Board elected Henry Allen Tupper of South Carolina as corresponding secretary, succeeding Taylor, who had suffered from failing health and died in December, 1871.

Estep wrote of the contrasts between Taylor and Tupper.

> The contrast between James B. Taylor and H. A. Tupper as far as personal backgrounds are concerned could hardly have been greater. Taylor was the son of an artisan, a cabinetmaker; Tupper, the son of a wealthy businessman. Taylor, born to poverty, was largely self-taught with no formal education beyond elementary school, while Tupper had the advantages that wealth affords, including the finest theological education available in the United States. Yet both were fitted uniquely for the challenges that demanded their best.[22]

Tupper was a man of deep faith and a broad vision for missions. His vision was:

> to formulate a plan for the support of foreign missions that would enlist Baptists in every church and every state convention. He called for each state association or convention to establish a missions committee in cooperation with the Foreign Mission Board . . . Information, adequate financing, and the involvement of women in every aspect of the work were indispensable in his mind for the future of the Southern Baptist foreign mission effort.
>
> All would be coordinated by the Foreign Mission Board in cooperation with the Central Committee of each state. Tupper's 'cherished plan,' however, would not be fully implemented until another fifteen years when the Woman's Missionary Union was organized.[23]

Women's Missionary Societies

Women's missionary societies were being formed, notably in Georgia, Maryland, South Carolina and Virginia. They were well organized and highly motivated to provide leadership and money in support of missions.

Tupper took the issue of the involvement of women in missions to the Southern Baptist Convention in 1872, where he addressed for the first time in the Convention's history the role of women.

> . . . The necessity of Christian women to carry the word of God as men cannot do it, to the women of heathen lands, is increasingly felt. Women societies are organizing to support Bible-women at our Missionary stations. God helping them, our sisters, on the way, will do good work. The sisterhood of our Southern Zion should be aroused to the grand mission of redeeming their sister-woman from the degrading and destroying thraldom of Paganism.[24]

Southern Baptist Roots

In 1872 Edmonia Moon, a younger sister to Charlotte (Lottie) Moon, was appointed to China. In 1873 Lottie Moon received notice of her appointment to the Shantung Province in China. The Moon sisters, born in Virginia, were well educated, intelligent and highly motivated to be obedient to Christ. They served together briefly in China, until a feud between missionaries and Edmonia's fragile mental health led to their return to the United States in 1876. Lottie returned to China and resumed a missionary career as evangelist, builder of relationships and fund raiser among Southern Baptists.

Resistance to Role of Women in Missions

Raising the level of women's service in home, church and missionary service met strong resistance among many Southern Baptists who believed that all women should be subordinate to men in all aspects of life.

> Though not coming as messengers, women attended the Southern Baptist Convention as early as 1868. Only in 1872 did the Convention's Committee on Women's Work endorse the appointment of unmarried women as missionaries. But ten years later only ten women had been appointed by the Foreign Mission Board, including Lottie Moon. Further underscoring their conviction that women should be denied leadership roles in religious life, Southern Baptists changed Article III of their constitution from the word 'messengers' to 'brethren' in 1885. The change was precipitated by the arrival of messengers from Arkansas including two women. The women were not seated, and Article III was changed to make sure the men were not embarrassed again. The frustration engendered may have, according to historian Leon McBeth, helped bring about the organization of Woman's Missionary Union just three years later.[25]

Women active in missionary societies began meeting while men met in Southern Baptist Convention meetings.

> While the Southern Baptist Convention was meeting in the First Baptist Church of Richmond, the women met in the Broad Street Methodist Church. Present were duly elected delegates from twelve Central Committees and representatives from three other states. On 11 May 1888, The Executive Committee of the Woman's Missionary Union (WMU: Auxiliary to the Southern Baptist Convention) was formally organized. Annie Armstrong, who had emerged as the most forceful leader of the Southern Baptist woman's missionary movement, was elected corresponding secretary and Martha McIntosh of South Carolina, president.[26]

Women did not gain messenger status in the Southern Baptist Convention until 1918. Texas Baptists were well ahead of most Southern Baptists on this issue. The editor of the Texas *Baptist Standard* had written in 1901:

> We are bigger than the Southern Baptist Convention in numbers, but that is not as distinguishing as the fact that we are bigger than our great Southern Baptist Convention on the woman question. Our women are messengers to our conventions—to all of them. This is as it ought to be.[27]

Lottie Moon Christmas Offering

The organization of women to support missions was just in time to respond to an urgent request that came from Lottie Moon in China. She had written to Tupper in 1887 suggesting that an offering for missions be taken during the Christmas season.

> Another letter from the lonely missionary of P'ingtu, dated 24 May 1888, spelled out the urgent need for more women missionaries. Tupper sent the letter on to Armstrong with the suggestion that 'your Executive Committee might give special attention to this matter, until it should be accomplished.
> What do you think?'
> Armstrong liked the idea and so did the Executive Committee. Lottie had requested two additional women missionaries and prayer. The appeal was made and sent out in time for a Christmas offering to be taken in the churches.
> A total of $3,315.26 was raised at the cost of $72.82 to the Foreign Mission Board. This was the beginning of what was to become the Lottie Moon Offering for Foreign Missions and a token of greater things to come.[28]
> From the time of Lottie Moon's appointment in 1873 until H. A. Tupper's retirement in 1893, they had an exemplary relationship as mission administrator and field missionary. Estep wrote about their relationship.

> (They) were of one mind and heart. Their cultural backgrounds were similar and both were well educated and endowed with unusual linguistic ability.
> They shared a common missionary vision and complete dedication to the cause of Christ. With mutual appreciation they modeled the ideal working relationship of the Foreign Mission Board with its missionaries. Their correspondence was extensive and continued even after Tupper retired from the board. Whatever success the now legendary missionary

may have enjoyed was due in part to the support she received from Tupper and the board.[29]

J.R. Willingham, pastor of the First Baptist Church of Memphis, succeeded Tupper as the Foreign Mission Board's corresponding secretary on September 1, 1893. Lottie Moon continued her missionary service until her death aboard a ship in Kobe, Japan, in 1912. Much has been written about her life and effective Christian service. Perhaps none exemplifies the person she was better than Estep's account of her relationship with the Christians of P'ingtu. "Upon one occasion when she did not return as expected, two men from Shaling walked 120 miles to seek her out. After her death, the P'ingtu church wrote: 'How she loved us.' "[30]

B. 1900–Present
Sunday School Board

The Baptist Sunday School Board (now LifeWay Christian Resources) was established in 1891, to be led by J. M. Frost and located in Nashville, Tennessee. Earlier, the educational materials used in Southern Baptist churches were published by the American Baptist Publication Society or by the Home Mission Board.

> I. T. Tichenor . . . in 1885 . . . called for Southern Baptists to appoint a committee to study the best way to provide Sunday School literature to its constituent churches. . . . (J. M.) Frost's first service as head of the Sunday School Board lasted only eighteen months . . . Frost burned his bridges to the pastorate in 1896 and gave himself fully to the Sunday School Board for the next twenty years.[31]

The twentieth century began with the Convention expanding westward, a new record attendance at the Southern Baptist Convention and a deepening fellowship with other Baptists in the world. There were strong state conventions in Arkansas and Texas. The First Baptist Church of Dallas, Texas, had called George W. Truett, born in western North Carolina, as pastor in 1897, beginning an exemplary pastorate of forty-six years in the same church. The attendance at a Southern Baptist Convention exceeded one thousand the first time in its meeting in Asheville, North Carolina in 1902. State organizations were established in Oklahoma in 1906, in Illinois in 1910 and in New Mexico in 1912. In 1908 Southern Baptists assumed responsibility for Southwestern Baptist Theological Seminary, which earlier had been a Theological Department of Baylor University.

Baptist World Alliance

The internationalization of the Southern Baptist Convention took a giant step forward in 1905. The Baptist World Alliance (BWA) was organized that year in London. "Southern Baptists played a significant part in the Baptist World Alliance, with Southern Seminary's E. Y. Mullins and Dallas's George W. Truett offering statesmanlike leadership in the early years, and Theodore Adams of Richmond, Virginia, and Kentucky's Duke McCall serving as president in later years."[32]

European Baptist work was also expanding geographically and was becoming unified.

> . . . Many hundreds of delegates from sixteen European lands assembled for the first European Baptist Conference in Berlin from 29 August to 3 September 1908. Reports described it as an inspiring occasion. People who had suffered hardship for their faith found new heart through meeting with their brothers and sisters in Christ from other lands. For all who were there it was a living experience of the power of Christ and the Gospel to cross the boundaries of nation, language and culture. Among the decisions made were three requests addressed to the Baptist World Alliance: to recognize Europe as a primary mission field, to assist in the building of new churches, and to work for the establishment of a European theological seminary.[33]

Brotherhood

Capable Baptist laymen exerted leadership in the Southern Baptist Convention. Judge Jonathan Haralson of Alabama; W. J. Northen, a former governor of Georgia; and James P. Eagle, governor of Arkansas; served as convention presidents from 1890 until 1910.

> The Laymen's Missionary Movement of the Southern Baptist Convention was organized in 1907 at the annual meeting in Richmond. Its purpose . . . was to enlist men for inspiration and instruction of the world mission task of the Convention. This gave the men a counterpart of sorts to the Woman's Missionary Union, which was continuing to build its state-by-state structure and garnering dedicated, even sacrificial support for the missionary cause. . . . In 1927 the organization's name was changed to the Baptist Brotherhood of the South.[34]

Woman's Missionary Union continued its strong support of missions. In 1907 it expanded its work by establishing the Woman's Missionary Union Training School on the campus of Southern Baptist Theological Seminary in Louisville.

"The Sunday School Board provided them a building in 1907, and in 1918 the women completed their own building. 'In a chapel of their own, women could plan and women could speak.' "[35]

Baptist Student Movement

Baptists saw the need for a Christian ministry to students in Baptist colleges and in state-supported institutions.

> ... in 1914 the Home Mission Board launched the Baptist Student Missionary Movement in Ft. Worth, Texas. ... By 1921, the Baptist Student movement was conventionwide and received official status from the SBC under an inter-Board Commission. Its work was soon transferred to the Sunday School Board. Under the leadership of Frank H. Leavell, it achieved broad acceptance in Southern Baptist life in every state.[36]

J. B. Gambrell was the first Texas Baptist elected as president of the Southern Baptist Convention.

> (Gambrell) presided over the Convention during the years of 1917-18 while America was enmeshed in World War I. This had the unique effect of healing some of the old scars that dated back to the Civil War. Southern Baptists found themselves wearing the same uniform as Northern Baptists, and their Confederate legacy began to recede, though it reflected itself for years in their culture and their attitude toward the descendants of slavery.[37]

Baptist Bible Institute (BBI), an institute founded for the training of ministers, and forerunner of New Orleans Baptist Theological Seminary (NOBTS), was the third Southern Baptist seminary established.

> The institute was actually birthed in a meeting at Coliseum Place Baptist Church on July 10, 1917 ... and given a president in the person of B. H. DeMent, pastor of the First Baptist Church of Greenville, S. C. DeMent penned a ten article confession of faith for the new institution called the 'Articles of Religious Belief.'
>
> It reflected the New Hampshire Confession with its approach to inspiration, atonement, and the local church ... That fall a campaign was held to secure funds to buy the old campus of Sophie Newcomb College and classes began on October 1, 1918.[38]
>
> The Southern Baptist Convention assumed responsibility for the institute in 1925, re-naming it New Orleans Baptist Theological Seminary.

Annuity Board

The Convention established the Board of Ministerial Relief and Annuities in 1918. Two years later the name was changed to the Relief and Annuity Board, and later to the Annuity Board (now GuideStone Financial Resources). The Convention decided that its location be in Dallas, Texas, with William Lunsford as the board's first secretary. The Annuity Board provides a wide spectrum of financial services to Southern Baptist pastors, missionaries, Convention employees and employees of churches, including retirement, medical insurance and investments.

The convention celebrated its seventy-fifth anniversary in 1920 with its annual meeting in Washington, D. C.

> A great outdoor service on the steps of the capital on Sunday highlighted many's memories of the Jubilee. Dallas's R. H. Coleman led an estimated ten thousand in such hymns as 'My Country 'Tis of Thee,' 'Battle Hymn of the Republic,' 'Rescue the Perishing,' and 'My Faith Looks Up To Thee.' Then George W. Truett, in his finest hour, spoke on the subject 'Baptists and Religious Liberty;' it was Southern Baptists' most exhilarating gathering to that time.[39]

Early Fundamentalist Issues

Strong Southern Baptist leaders and institutions withstood a violent attack by fundamentalists led by J. Frank Norris, who had been editor of the *Baptist Standard* and who was called as pastor of the First Baptist Church of Ft. Worth in 1909. He was a gifted orator with a flair for sensationalism. He ruled his church with authoritarian methods.

> A major concern was Norris's tendency to suppress any internal organization, committee, or member who might challenge his authority. He accomplished this by conferring all church authority to an inner circle of deacons completely committed to him . . . In 1914, the Fort Worth Pastors' Conference expelled Norris for calling a fellow pastor a 'long, lean, lank, yellow suck-egging dog.' That was to be only the beginning.[40]

> Norris . . . charged rampant liberalism and corruption among Southern Baptist teachers and officials. Norris consistently failed to substantiate such charges, but that did not deter him. His actions were the thunder and lightning of the next storm approaching Southern Baptists . . . In 1984, successors to the Norris-led Fundamentalist Movement would say it had six watermarks: fidelity to Biblical and Baptistic doctrines, emphasis on heritage and succession, fervent evangelism, Bible preaching, militant opposition to error, and separation, not inclusivism . . . He was a leader

of the World's Christian Fundamentals Conference . . . Norris later sent deprecating telegrams to (George W.) Truett just as he was preparing to preach . . . Lee Scarborough wrote a pamphlet entitled 'The Fruits of Norrism,' saying, 'It thrives on sensationalism, misrepresentation, and false accusations of good men and true causes. It masquerades under the cloak of anti-evolution, anti-modernism, anti-catholicism in order to ride into public favor and cast poisonous suspicion on the leadership of constructive Christianity. . . . '

In 1922, Norris was expelled from the Tarrant County Baptist Association. The Baptist General Convention of Texas (BGCT) censured him in the same year and refused to seat him the next . . . Energized by both attention and rejection, Norris helped found the Baptist Bible Union of America in 1923 . . . In 1926, Norris, who had earlier been indicted for arson, shot a man to death in his study. He was acquitted in both cases, but his influence among the ranks of Southern Baptists was greatly diminished.[41]

Confession of Faith (1925) Versus a Creed

The conviction of the founding fathers that Baptists need no creed but the Bible carried Southern Baptists eighty years, from 1845 to 1925, when the first Confession of Faith was adopted.

. . . When the committee reported its findings in 1925, they were in the form of a Confession of Faith taken from the 1833 New Hampshire Confession with additions . . . The 1925 Confession was introduced by a number of denials that it was in any form a step toward creedalism. It stated,

'Confessions are only guides in interpretation, having no authority over the conscience.' It went on to explain that it was not 'to be used to hamper freedom of thought or investigation in other realms of life.' . . . In a wrap-up of the Convention in the next *Baptist Standard*, E. C. Routh complained, 'There was a considerable element in the Convention opposed to the adoption of any Confession of Faith whatever, and this group had no opportunity to be heard.'[42]

Baptist historian Leon McBeth offers these distinctives between a confession and a creed.

Throughout their history, Baptists have claimed to be *confessional* but not *creedal*. While the words mean much the same, they can be used and have been used to mean different things. A confession designates what people *do* believe; a creed what they *must* believe. A confession is *voluntary* and serves to inform, educate and inspire; a creed is *required* and serves to discipline and exclude. A confession offers *guidelines* under the authority of Scripture; a creed tends to become *binding authority*, in subtle ways displacing the Bible.[43]

Cooperative Program

The Cooperative Program, a brilliant and new concept of financing Southern Baptist ministries and missions, was adopted in 1925. The genius of the program was that it enabled every member of a Southern Baptist church to offer tithes and offerings in worship of God, knowing that a portion of the offerings would go to support Christian ministries and missions through the Convention.

> The Cooperative Program was basically an agreement between the state conventions cooperating with the Southern Baptist Convention to receive funds from the churches and forward an agreed-upon percentage of those funds to south-wide causes. It eliminated the need for agents and competitive fund-raising efforts in the churches and let the pastors promote the broader view of the denominational program.[44]

To be successful, the program required integrity and accountability at every level at which funds were handled. Those who handled funds at the local church, state convention, Southern Baptist Convention and all convention agencies, boards and institutions which received funds were important links in the chain. The Executive Committee of the Southern Baptist Convention was tasked to promote and administer the funds sent to the convention.

George W. Truett of Dallas was president in 1927 when a spirit of optimism prevailed throughout the Convention.

> In the twenty-seven short years of the twentieth century, the denomination had not only survived, but it had come of age. It had at last begun to define itself in terms of the potential inherent in the convention system that first Richard Furman and then W. B. Johnson had so fervently sought. The four key boards managing missions at home and overseas, developing literature and religious education, and supervising relief and retirements were alive and flourishing. Three seminaries trained a new generation of leadership and a student movement, a laymen's movement, and a vibrant Woman's Missionary Union organized a broad base of support for Southern Baptists' total program.
>
> In addition, the Southern Baptist Convention had survived its second major controversy, further defined its confessionalism, reaffirmed its connectionalism, and discovered a new basis of cooperation. It had developed a financial plan and a coordinating management structure. It had expanded its representative approach to decision making and to the management of its collective endeavors.[45]

Great Depression Impact

The spirit of optimism soon encountered the devastating effects of the early signs of the Great Depression. Both the Foreign Mission Board and the Home Mission Board were deeply in debt.

> To make matters worse, in 1927 the Foreign Mission Board discovered that its treasurer had embezzled a little over $103,000 . . . the next year the Home Mission Board revealed its own case of embezzlement . . . of just under a million dollars . . . The total (debt) approached $2,500,000 . . . The Executive Committee called on Southern Baptists to respond positively to the problem by declaring Sunday, November 11, 1928 as Baptist Honor Day . . . Southern Baptist churches . . . raised just under $400,000 to apply on the Board's debt.
>
> That one offering probably saved the Home Mission Board from bankruptcy and preserved the Southern Baptist Convention's agency record of never defaulting on a debt.[46]
>
> With the exception of the Sunday School Board, which remained solvent, leaders of other agencies struggled through great indebtedness brought on by the Great Depression which followed the stock market crash of October, 1929. Both mission boards were deeply in debt and saw a reduction in the number of missionaries. The implementation and success of a remarkable vision of Frank Edward Tripp, a young pastor from St. Joseph, Missouri, led the convention through the crisis. The plan was called the "Baptist Hundred Thousand Club . . . before the task was accomplished in 1943, had given $2,627,822.36 (to convention debt retirement). . . . The Executive Committee, in 1936, expressed 'undying gratitude' to Tripp and the St. Joseph Church for the service and sacrifice which to a large extent saved our mission causes."[47]

The Convention moved farther westward in 1929 when the Baptist General Convention of Arizona was voted into membership.

> Baptist life in the West had a strong Landmark tinge through the years as evidenced by the famous 'Apostle to the West,' Willis J. Ray. Ray headed the Arizona Convention beginning in 1944. Because Arizona became the initiator and sheltering arms for new work all over the West and Northwest, at one point Ray presided over Convention activities stretching from Mexico to Canada and including ten states . . . In 1944 Golden Gate Baptist Theological Seminary was founded (in California) and began classes with sixty-five students.[48]

In 1950, Southern Baptists accepted ownership and support of the seminary. World War II captured the nation's attention and resources from 1941 to 1945.

Baptists were very much a part of this total experience. Ministers became chaplains, even as college and, despite deferrment, seminary students became soldiers, sailors, marines and airmen. On their mission fields, Southern Baptists coped even as they had learned to do during the Civil War and, with the kind of leadership in place, managed to keep their work going in China and Africa and Latin America, though the work in Europe and the Middle East went on the back burner. War encouraged religious feelings and church attendance grew dramatically. New churches sprang up with the displacement of Southern Baptists around the country . . . By 1943 Charles E. Maddry announced that the Foreign Mission Board was debt free and by 1944 the Convention was debt free.[49]

Another result of the war was that many Southern Baptists who had traveled the world in wartime and had seen the spiritual needs of people everywhere later became foreign missionaries.

The one hundreth year of the Convention's existence coincided with the end of World War II in 1945, although the celebration of the centennial was delayed until 1946. The Convention adopted a Statement of Principles which, as Fletcher wrote, "revealed Southern Baptists' belief, at least among the leadership, that they had come into being for a unique purpose that would unfold in the second century."[50]

The Convention grew rapidly in total members, total gifts and baptisms as its second century began. It expanded its ministries by establishing the Press Service, the Historical Commission, the Southern Baptist Foundation, the Radio and Television Commission and the Stewardship Commission.

Post World War II European Developments

During this period of expansion in the Southern Baptist Convention three important events occurred among Baptists in Europe, all intended to bring Baptists together after the devastation of World War II. In 1948 the Foreign Mission Board purchased property in Rüschlikon, near Zürich, Switzerland, for an international Baptist Theological Seminary. As far back as 1908, European Baptists expressed the need for a theological seminary in Europe where students from many countries could be trained for Christian ministry. The first classes began in September, 1949.

The second event in Europe was the organization of the European Baptist Women's Union.

> In August 1948 the BWA Executive Committee met in London and, as part of its agenda, arranged a conference on post-war planning in Europe. The Women's Missionary Union of Virginia, USA, paid Mrs. Martin's expenses for this conference, and also suggested that funds be made available to

enable women representatives from European Unions in membership with the BWA to be invited to the meeting . . . The determined women found a corner in a spacious hotel lobby and met to hammer out a future plan. Within the providence of God, the world dimension of Baptist women's needs took second place, for a short while, to the overwhelming desire to form a European fellowship. A group of European women's leaders were face-to-face for the first time, and the opportunity was not allowed to slip away . . . Alice Moore, SBC missionary, proposed: That a European Baptist Women's Union be formed for the purpose of stimulating closer fellowship, greater co-operation, deeper sympathy for and understanding of mutual problems . . . this motion was carried unanimously.[51]

The third important event in Europe was the organization of the European Baptist Federation (EBF). European Baptists and BWA leaders had met periodically since 1908.

In the summer of 1937 Dr. G. W. Truett, the Baptist World Alliance President, and Dr. Rushbrooke (J. H., BWA Associate Secretary), held another series of ten regional conferences in Europe, to strengthen Baptist fellowship in face of the mounting tensions and to generate spiritual confidence.[52]

Meetings about the establishment of a Federation of Baptists in Europe took place in 1947 in Copenhagen and in London in 1948. The EBF was established in Paris on 20 October 1950. The representatives approved a constitution, elected officers and an executive committee, planned future meetings and outlined their vision for the next few years. The vision included a remarkable gesture of reconciliation.

. . . to help rebuild the bombed Bohmkenstrasse Church in Hamburg as a memorial to Oncken . . . to open work in key places where no Baptist churches existed . . . European and American Baptists would provide financial support . . . Many saw Rüschlikon as an ideal centre for conferences and courses for women, men, young people, lay leaders, preachers and pastors.[53]

The Southern Baptist Convention continued its expansion in providing theological education. Southeastern Baptist Theological Seminary began its work in Wake Forest, North Carolina in September, 1951. Classes began in 1958 in Midwestern Baptist Theological Seminary in Kansas City, Missouri. The six seminaries owned and operated by Southern Baptists were strategically positioned in the vast area in which churches were located.

Billy Graham, a Southern Baptist evangelist from North Carolina, conducted a crusade in Los Angeles, California, in 1949 that was the beginning of a highly effective, respected and successful emphasis in evangelism for non believers and spiritual renewal for believers. His openness to all Christians who accepted the deity of Jesus Christ drew supporters from many denominations. His acceptance of all races of people broke down walls of separation between people and opened doors for evangelism internationally.

The Civil Rights Movement, led by aggressive and courageous people such as Atlanta Baptist pastor Martin Luther King, Jr., and given a boost by the 1954 Supreme Court ruling concerning segregation in public schools, opened doors of opportunity for many people who earlier had been trapped by discrimination in its various forms.

Many Baptists do not see a necessary conflict between biblical scholarship and responsible and open scientific study. Others see the Bible as containing all the information needed even in matters of science. A major controversy over these varying views in the Convention erupted in 1961 when Broadman Press, owned by the Sunday School Board, published *The Message of Genesis*, written by Ralph Elliott, an Old Testament professor at Midwestern Baptist Theological Seminary.

> The Broadman commentary became a cause around which fundamentalist and other sympathies coalesced. The basic problem in both these battles had to do with the interpretation of Genesis and whether the first eleven chapters were to be taken as literal history. In both cases, the argument had to do with the nature of scripture. Elliott, among other things, had challenged the story of Abraham's sacrifice of Isaac. The book raised the questions, as most such works do, as to whether the Genesis record was to be interpreted literally and whether Moses wrote all of the Pentateuch. Both works were a little strong for most Baptist appetites.[54]

The controversy over the commentary continued for two years.

> The Convention in 1962, held in San Francisco, was all but consumed by the Elliott issue or as others termed it, the Genesis Crisis. State papers fueled the controversy with articles, editorials, and letters to the editor. At San Francisco the Pastor's Conference became a forum for the issue, presaging a growing role for this preconvention meeting in Southern Baptist life. In the Convention meeting itself there were efforts not only to call for Elliott's dismissal, but to recall the book and censure the Sunday School Board and its president, James Sullivan.[55]

The result of the Broadman controversy was that Elliott was dismissed from the seminary, Broadman Press recalled the volume and Clyde Francisco, professor of Old Testament at Southern Seminary in Louisville, rewrote Volume I on Genesis.

On the one hand, many Southern Baptists were leery of creedalism. On the other, they were suspicious of liberalism. K. Owen White, pastor of the First Baptist Church of Houston, and W. A. Criswell, who had been called as pastor of the First Baptist Church of Dallas following George Truett's death in 1944, were outspoken against what they believed was liberalism in Southern Baptist life. The charges and suspicions of liberalism resulted in a decision by Convention leaders to propose "the appointment of a special committee to study the Statement of Faith that had been been developed from the New Hampshire Confession of Faith and adopted by the Southern Baptist Convention in 1925."[56]

Baptist Faith and Message (1963)

As noted, Southern Baptists worked together eighty years with only the Bible as their confession of faith. The 1925 Statement of Faith helped hold the Convention together another thirty-eight years, until the Convention adopted The Baptist Faith and Message in 1963. Herschel Hobbs chaired the committee that proposed the statement.

> The whole exercise, however, was directed to conservative concerns in hopes that it would contain the spreading suspicion of liberalism in SBC seminaries and universities . . . The Committee made a crucial decision from the beginning . . . and opted to present a revised form of the 1925 Statement . . . included the five key concerns of the 1925 preamble and 'safeguards of the individual conscience in the interpretation of Scripture.' To the article on Scripture they added, 'The criterion by which the Bible is to be interpreted is Jesus Christ' . . . After heated debate, the Convention agreed to approve the document as presented.[57]

The ordination of some women as ministers of the gospel and others as deacons or deaconesses drew some protests, but generally such actions were respected as being under the autonomy of the local church. "The BSSB (Baptist Sunday School Board) publication, *The Deacon*, estimated that two or three hundred Southern Baptist churches had women deacons by 1973, and Virginia Baptist churches recorded 520 women deacons in 1976."[58] Serious opposition to and public stands against the ordination of women were expressed in Oklahoma and Arkansas in the 1970s.

Controversy and polarization became intense and threatened the long-standing consensus that had held Southern Baptists together for more than a century.

> At the meeting of the Executive Committee in September 1969, W. A. Criswell, president of the convention, told the members that Baptists

who did not believe the convention-adopted statement of faith should leave and go to another denomination. He asked how long the convention could stay together, saying: 'There are among us liberals, conservatives, fundamentalists; open communionists, closed communionists, alien immersionists; persons who would emphasize the social application of the gospel; those who would emphasize evangelism . . . in my humble judgment, I think we ought to take those articles of faith of 1925 and 1963 and say: 'this is what it is, being a Baptist. If you don't believe that, you are not a Baptist.' The next month he termed 'liberals' 'termites who would destroy the church.'[59]

Two private theological schools were started which were not established or supported by the Southern Baptist Convention. W. A. Criswell and the First Baptist Church of Dallas established the Criswell Institute of Biblical Studies in 1971, and named Paige Patterson as president. The following year Gray Allison established Mid-America Baptist Theological Seminary, which was first located in Arkansas, then moved to Memphis under the auspices of Adrian Rogers and Bellevue Baptist Church, of which Rogers was pastor.

Conservatives versus Moderates in the Modern Era

While the rhetoric of those calling themselves conservatives escalated and called for those who did not agree with them to get out of the convention, other voices called for understanding and tolerance of diversity.

> James Sullivan, president of the Sunday School Board, 'promoted the idea of unity amidst diversity' . . . and Clifton Allen, general editor made a 'plea to give the next generation a heritage of the open mind and open Bible'. . . . The following year (1972) Convention president Carl Bates, of North Carolina, said 'If any member of this convention and its affiliated churches is determined to have theological and ecclesiastical sameness, let him know at the outset that he has one of two choices. He must either join another denomination or deny the basic democratic principles for which our people have been known across the years.'[60]

In 1993, reflecting on the bitter controversy Criswell lamented:

> About 99 percent of the time I cannot understand what is happening. Now that may be a strange thing for me to say, but it is all so different than when I was growing up . . . He thought that most Southern Baptists would stay in the Convention . . . The breach that has been created between so - called moderates and conservatives is largely in the attitudes of the people involved. Many, many of them basically believe the same thing and love

the same programming. It carries with it an overtone of sadness that is almost inexplicable.[61]

In 1978 the Convention approved Bold Mission Thrust, a vision and plan prepared over several years to challenge Southern Baptists to make it possible for every person in the world to hear the Gospel of Jesus Christ before the end of the century.

From the beginning of the Convention in 1845, heads of the Convention's boards, commissions, and seminaries had been fully committed to the historic principles held by Baptists throughout the world. The principles of administration had been established over time and included integrity, vision and accountability. Professors in seminaries and home and foreign missionaries were committed to these principles, were loyal to the Convention that employed them and grateful to the churches that supported them. They looked forward to participating in Bold Mission Thrust.

Patterson's—Pressler's Plot

Adrian Rogers of Memphis was elected Convention president in Houston in 1979. He was supported by a strong conservative presence in Convention life and a well-organized political element headed by Paige Patterson and Paul Pressler, an appeals court judge from Houston. Patterson and Pressler had discovered that the Convention president had the authority to appoint important committees and trustees of boards and seminaries. By choosing who would be president and getting him elected, they could establish their authority over much of the Convention's life and work.

> At this point Judge Pressler and Paige Patterson took control, organizing rallies all over the Southern Baptist Convention as Pressler, independently wealthy, not only spoke everywhere he found opportunity but computerized an effective mailing list. Together they developed an organization of like-minded persons throughout the Convention . . . By the time the Convention convened in Houston the great sky boxes in the Astrodome were under Pressler's control, and floor lieutenants had been organized to be in direct contact with the leaders high in the boxes.[62]

Patterson and Pressler called their movement the *Conservative Resurgence.* In reality, it was perhaps the biggest hoax ever attempted by some Baptists against other Baptists. It was also the most deceptive form of fundamentalism Southern Baptists had ever encountered. With the successful election of Adrian Rogers as president and the subsequent election of other presidents of Patterson's and

Pressler's choice, the Convention had entered an era of spiritual warfare more deadly, deceitful and divisive than any controversy it had ever faced. The theological issue centered on whether Christians, churches, Convention agencies, boards and missionaries do their work under the authority of Jesus Christ. If not under the authority of Jesus Christ, under whose authority?

CHAPTER 2

Impact of Fundamentalist Takeover

There are six things the Lord hates, seven that are detestable to him: haughty eyes, a lying tongue, hands that shed innocent blood, a heart that devises wicked schemes, feet that are quick to rush into evil, a false witness who pours out lies, and a man who stirs up dissension among brothers. (Proverbs 6:16-19)

The Southern Baptist fundamentalist leaders of the 1980s intended to establish their authority over all aspects of the Convention's life and work. The Bible was used as the primary weapon of attack against other Christians over whom this authority was to be established. An important part of their ambition was the exclusion of women in roles of Christian leadership, whether as deacons or pastors. The fundamentalist leaders not only excluded women from these roles, but also excluded other Christians and churches that accepted women in Christian leadership roles.

About The Bible

The controversy in the Southern Baptist Convention that has lasted more than two decades is **not about the Bible. It is about a theory about the Bible.** A careful study of how the fundamentalist leaders used **a theory about the Bible** to establish their authority should be of interest to all Southern Baptists. There are three dominant aspects of the Bible that are important to understand. The first is what the Bible is. The second is how the Bible came to us. The third is its purpose.

The Bible is a *divine* and a *human* book. It is divine in that God revealed himself to people as one who was loving and merciful in his ways, whose will and purpose they could know, whose character they could trust, and whose commandments they should obey. All people to whom God revealed himself were human beings like all other human beings. God revealed himself to different people in different ways. What he revealed to them was so important that they were inspired by the Holy Spirit to write what they had learned about God.

It is a human book in that human beings, not God or angels, wrote the materials in the languages whose words they understood and used. They wrote about their experiences with God and what he had revealed to them. Human beings were involved in every step of the process, including gathering the various writings into a single book which we call the Bible.

> . . . The unity of the Bible attests its inspiration. The Bible has one central theme: God's redemptive purpose. It has one central figure: Christ. It has one central goal: God supreme in a redeemed universe.
>
> The Bible was written over a period of approximately fifteen hundred years in various places stretching all the way from Babylon to Rome. The human authors included a variety of men in many stations of life — kings, peasants, poets, herdsmen, fishermen, scientists, farmers, priests, pastors, tentmakers, and governors. Among its themes are such content matter as philosophy, poetry, prophecy, theology, history, science, and sociology. Not one of the writers knew that he was writing a part of the Holy Bible. Probably many had no knowledge of what others had written.
>
> Yet when under the guidance of the Holy Spirit the various books were gathered together, they told one complete story. Neither Testament is complete without the other . . . All of the Bible is the Word of God. But the Old Testament finds its fulfillment in the New Testament. For this reason Baptists see the note of finality in the New Testament.[1]

Just as those first writers to whom God revealed himself were inspired to write what they had learned, others who read what they had written were inspired to copy what they had read. Original manuscripts no longer exist.

> It is true that we do not have the first written texts of either the Old or the New Testament. But sufficient evidence exists that our English versions are trustworthy translations of reliable Hebrew and Greek texts, which faithfully represent the originals.[2]

Through the centuries people copied and preserved older manuscripts. It is miraculous how many of those ancient copies of manuscripts have been preserved and discovered.

Students of the classics are fortunate to have as many as ten or fifteen manuscripts of any given work. Think how fortunate are those who make a critical study of the Scriptures! In literary criticism it is an axiom that an older manuscript is more accurate than a newer one. Some New Testament manuscripts date as far back as the fourth century. It can be safely said that in a comparative study of these documents, scholars probably have been able to determine the exact text of the originals.

In the caves near the Dead Sea have been found the most ancient copies of the Old Testament possessed by modern man. Prior to that discovery the oldest and most complete Hebrew copies of the Old Testament dated as late as the ninth century. Now portions of the Hebrew text are in hand dating in the first or second centuries B.C. By 1956, about ninety manuscripts of the Old Testament books had been identified. These included thirteen copies of Deuteronomy, twelve of Isaiah, ten of Psalms, seven of part or all of the twelve prophets, and five of books of the Pentateuch (five books of Moses). Every book of Hebrew Old Testament is represented except Esther. These Hebrew texts are closely akin to the Septuagint (the Greek translation of the Old Testament).

The criterion by which the Bible is to be interpreted is Jesus Christ. The Bible is the written Word of God about the living Word. Therefore, any interpretation of a given passage must be made in the light of God's revelation in Jesus Christ and his teachings and redemptive work. Indeed, the Bible is its own best interpreter as one discovers its meaning in any particular in the light of the whole.[3]

God first revealed himself to people who knew, understood and spoke the Hebrew language. The original Old Testament manuscripts were written in Hebrew. People and languages change. Manuscripts written in Hebrew were translated into the Greek language and were called the Septuagint.

Greek was the most widely used language throughout the Roman Empire. Jesus preached and taught in Aramaic, the common language of Palestinian Jews. His teachings about God and the Old Testament were so powerful, revolutionary, true and unique that his followers believed him and what he said. They repeated orally his words in their preaching and teaching.

Until the first Gospels were written, the teachings and the deeds of Jesus were communicated orally. The apostles and those whom they instructed passed on the good news by word of mouth, in sermons, testimonies, and lessons. Eventually, under the inspiration of the Holy Spirit, these oral accounts were collected and written down in the four Gospels. In addition, other inspired writings by men like Paul, Peter, James and John were circulated so that by A.D. 200 all of the major New Testament books

Impact of Fundamentalist Takeover

were in general circulation and acceptance by the members of the early churches. These New Testament writings were given the same stature the Old Testament held as 'Scriptures.'[4]

New Testament writings were in the Greek language. Early Christian leaders under the leadership of the Holy Spirit both followed the church and led the church in recognizing the writings that were accepted as the authentic books that we call the Bible.

> By the year 200 (A.D.) the church of the western portion of the (Roman) empire had, therefore, an authoritative collection of New Testament books, in the main like our own, to which to appeal. The East was not far behind. The formation of the canon was essentially a process of selection from the whole mass of Christian literature, made originally by no council, but by the force of Christian opinion—the criterion being that the books accepted were believed to be either the work of an Apostle or of the immediate disciple of an Apostle, and thus to represent apostolic teaching.[5]

All early writings were not accepted by Christians as authentic Scripture, also referred to as the canon, which is the Bible. Many writings, such as the Apocrypha, though having some historic value, were not accepted as authentic. There were also disputes about which writings should be accepted as divinely inspired and included as Scripture.

> By the fourth century Eusebius, the early church historian, delineated several categories of books: (1) accepted, (2) disputed, (3) rejected, (4) heretical. The accepted books contain most of our present New Testament books. The disputed group contains James, Jude, 2 Peter, and 2 and 3 John. Revelation was accepted by some and rejected by others.

> The first list of canonical books that contains the 27 books currently accepted appears in Bishop Athanasius' festal letter in A.D. 367. The order, however, is different. The first church council to list all 27 books of the New Testament was the Council of Carthage in A.D. 397. The selection of the canonical books stabilized after each book proved its worth by passing the tests of canonicity.

> . . . It is important to recognize that most New Testament books were considered canonical prior to the application of any kind of tests. The tests only helped the church recognize what was already true: that these books are inspired and authoritative. Neither the church councils nor the application of these tests made any book authoritative or authentic. The book was inspired, authoritative, and therefore genuine when it was written. The councils recognized and verified certain books as the written

Word of God, and eventually those so recognized were collected in what we call the Bible.

The tests involved the following issues.

1. Was the book authored or sanctioned by an apostle or a prophet?
2. Was the book widely circulated?
3. Was the book Christologically centered?
4. Was the book orthodox, that is, faithful to the teaching of the apostles?
5. Did the book give internal evidence of its unique character as inspired and authoritative?

In reality, the early churches displayed surprising unanimity about which books belonged in the inspired collection. Although it is true that a few books, such as Jude and Revelation, were the subjects of considerable debate, no book whose authenticity was doubted by a large number of churches was later accepted. The persecution of the church helped distinguish the canonical books from other helpful writings as the people were forced to decide what books should be protected during times of oppression.[6]

Just as the people to whom God first revealed himself and his purpose wrote about God's revelation, and as many of the first Christians were led to write about Jesus and his teachings, still others were later led by the same Holy Spirit to translate the Bible into other languages and dialects.

All ancient translations were called forth by practical needs . . . The whole Bible existed in at least seven versions (Latin, Syriac, Coptic, Armenian, Georgian, Gothic, and Ethiopic) by the sixth century A.D.

The movement to translate the Bible into the language of the people had very little support during the Middle Ages. The Latin translation, known as the Vulgate, became the church's standard translation. At the time of the Reformation, through the impetus of Martin Luther, the needs of the people again brought about new translations. These movements occurred not only in Germany but also in France and England. Modern Bible societies have translated the Bible into the vernacular of people around the world, even Third World and tribal languages.[7]

Practical needs and resources available dictated the methods by which the Bible was written. God first wrote the ten commandments on tablets of stone. (Exodus 24:12; 31:18) An example of how the Bible was first written was when Jeremiah, the prophet, dictated the words the Lord had spoken to him to Baruch, the copyist, who wrote the words in ink on a scroll. (Jeremiah 36:4,18) Manuscripts were first carefully written by hand by copyists who dedicated themselves to reproducing as accurately as possible works just like the manuscript they were copying. Copyists were concerned not only with the accuracy of their work but also made works of art of the manuscripts. Beautiful manuscripts embellished with rich colors and gold trim were common.

Copying took a giant step forward when Johannes Gutenberg, a German goldsmith who lived in Mainz, Germany, invented a printing press with movable type. About the year 1455 A.D., he printed a 3-volume set of Bibles in Latin called the Gutenberg Bible. In a few years copies of the Bible as well as printing presses were available throughout and beyond Europe. The inventions of typewriters and later computers have revolutionized the reproduction and distribution of the Bible.

The Bible was translated into English by the English reformer John Wycliffe and his associates between 1382 and 1384. William Tyndale completed an important English translation in 1534. One of the most popular and enduring English translations, the *King James Version* (KJV), was commissioned by King James I shortly after his coronation in 1603 and was completed in 1611. As the English language has changed, the Bible has been translated into other English versions many times since the 1800s, usually by numerous scholars. One hundred fifteen scholars completed the *New International Version* (NIV) between 1973 and 1978. The *New King James Version* (NKJV) was completed by one hundred thirty scholars between 1979 and 1982.

The Bible is composed of thirty nine books of the Old Testament and twenty seven books of the New Testament. It is the textbook of faith to Baptists and other evangelical Christians. Most Baptists accept, believe and study the Bible as their ultimate written source of their knowledge of God and for the principles which guide their lives.

It should be noted that many Christians, including Roman Catholics, accept the Apocrypha, a collection of fifteen books written between 200 B.C. and 100 A.D., as authoritative. Protestants have omitted the Apocrypha as part of the Bible since the Reformation.

Purpose of the Bible

No human being is perfect, including prophets, apostles, writers, copyists, typesetters and computer operators. Serious students of the Bible do not deny that copyists made errors. Nor do serious students of the Bible deny that parts of original manuscripts might be lost. The ending of the Gospel of Mark is an example. Notes in some Bibles indicate that Mark 16:9-20 is not found in the oldest available manuscripts.

The fact that some copyists made errors and some fragments of original manuscripts might be lost does not change the essential message of the Bible concerning God's purpose to redeem his creation through Jesus Christ and to recreate the redeemed into his image. The early Christians saw themselves as copies of Christ. *"You show that you are a letter from Christ, the result of our ministry, written not with ink but with the Spirit of the living God, not on tablets of stone but on tablets of human hearts."* (2 Cor. 3:3)

When God revealed himself to people and inspired them to write what later became the Bible, he intended something much more significant than people simply reading and studying the Scriptures. He intended that people believe him, love him, obey him and live by the principles he revealed to them. *"I will put my law in their minds and write it on their hearts. I will be their God and they will be my people."* (Jeremiah 31:33)

For Jesus, the Scriptures were the Old Testament. He studied them, believed them, asked questions about them, understood them, interpreted them and quoted many of them. He understood the Father's intention when he inspired people to write the Scriptures. He said *"All authority in heaven and on earth has been given to me. . . "* (Matt. 28:18) Just as he was master over the waves, the winds and the sea, he was master also over the Scriptures. After understanding the Scriptures, he simplified, clarified, summarized, personalized and prioritized them. He took the commandment, *"Love your neighbor as yourself,"* (Lev. 19:18b) and elevated its priority by placing it alongside the greatest commandment God gave Moses, *"Love the Lord your God with all your heart and with all your soul and with all your strength,"* (Deut. 6:5) and combined them into one great commandment with two parts. (Mark 12:29-31)

Jesus not only exercised his authority over the Scriptures that were already written, he had authority also to make a new commandment that was not in the Old Testament. *"A new command I give you: Love one another. As I have loved you, so must you love one another. By this all men will know that you are my disciples, if you love one another."* (John 13:34-35)

Because his authority was complete, he commanded his disciples and all who heard him to **believe him and obey him.** He said he did not come to abolish the Law or the Prophets, but to fulfill them. (Matt. 5:17) he viewed the Scriptures primarily as testimony to himself. *"You diligently study the Scriptures because you think that by them you possess eternal life. These are the Scriptures that testify about me, yet you refuse to come to me to have life."* (John 5:39-40)

The main purpose of the Bible is to guide and lead people to experience life, which is described in the Bible as being *abundant* and *eternal*. The Bible, rightly preached and taught, leads people to faith in Jesus Christ and to a life of obedience to him, who is *"the bread of life"* (John 6:35), the *"resurrection and the life,"* (John 11:25) and *"the way, the truth and the life."* (John 14:6)

The apostle John explained that he wrote the gospel of John in order to help people know Jesus Christ and find life in him. *"Jesus did many other miraculous signs in the presence of his disciples, which are not recorded in this book. But these are written that you may believe that Jesus is the Christ, the Son of God, and that by believing you may have life in his name."* (John 20:30-31)

The Spirit led John to select some of the most important teachings and events about Jesus. He could not and did not write everything Jesus did and said. He intended to write enough that everyone who reads what he wrote would believe in Jesus Christ and have eternal life in him.

Inerrancy

The Bible is what it is, although some people describe it differently. How people describe the Bible does not change the Bible. It might be impossible to adequately describe the Bible with a single word, although some people try to do just that. There are numerous terms used by people to describe the Bible: *infallible, sufficient, authoritative, inspired, inerrant,* etc., are common.

Of all the terms used to describe the Bible, *inerrant* is the most complex and potentially the most confusing. Inerrant means without error. It is complex because it deals both with a theory about original manuscripts, called *autographs*, which no longer exist, and with the Bible, which is available today in many languages and versions. Inerrancy theory holds to the belief that the *autographs* were without error. David Dockery defined inerrancy:

> *Inerrancy* means that when all the facts are known, the Bible (in its autographs, that is, the original documents), properly interpreted in light of the culture and the means of communication that had developed by the time of its composition, is completely true in all that it affirms, to the degree of precision intended by the author's purpose, in all matters relating to God and his creation.[8]

A close examination of the theory about the autographs is appropriate. Dockery explains the theory.

> Inerrancy applies to all aspects of the Bible as originally written. A claim to complete inerrancy is limited to the original words of the biblical text, not applying to the text itself. In other words, a reference to the autographs

is not restricted to some lost codex but affirms the original words that were written by the prophetic-apostolic messengers. Our confession of inerrancy and inspiration applies also to translations to the degree that they represent accurately the original words. We believe that we can express great confidence in our present translations. Therefore, the appeal to autographs is not intended as an apologetic sidestep but as a theological appeal to the providence and veracity of God in his superintending work of inspiration. The appeal to the autographs is never intended to remove trust in our present-day translations but to ensure and confirm faith in these translations, emphasizing that they rest on a sure foundation.[9]

While it must be recognized that the Bible originated from early manuscripts, it must also be recognized that those manuscripts no longer exist. The appeal to a theory about those manuscripts loses much of its meaning because people actually live by practical application of principles. It should be understood that the theory is not the Bible nor is it about the Bible. It is about manuscripts that no person living has ever seen or will ever see. It should be understood also that, since the manuscripts under discussion are not available, the theory cannot be either proved or disproved. The *autographs* were divine/human writings just as are translations.

One can legitimately question the value of paying much attention to a theory that can be neither proved nor disproved. It adds little to the practical application of our faith, to our understanding of the Bible, to our growth and maturity in Christ, to evangelism and missions, to unity among Christians, or to the fulfillment of the Great Commission. In fact, focusing too much on such a theory might have the opposite effects of all of the above. To hold too tightly to a theory about manuscripts that do not exist could lead to a rejection of the Bible, which exists.

After the theory concerning the *autographs*, the second emphasis in inerrancy thought is on the inerrancy of the Bible. Highly capable biblical scholars who call themselves *inerrantists* recognize that numerous qualifications are necessary if the Bible is to be truthfully described as inerrant. The qualifications deal with *what an error is **not**.* Some qualifications exempt such minor problems as grammatical error and misspellings, precision in relationships, approximations in numbers and distances, and varying accounts by different writers of the same events. Russell Dilday described inerrancy in terms of intent. "Inerrancy refers primarily to error in the sense of an intentionally misleading statement, not error in the sense of technical inaccuracy. The Bible is inerrant, therefore, in that it does not mislead us or intentionally teach us a falsehood."[10] Some of these qualifications would have to be applied also to the *autographs* if such were available.

Conference on Biblical Inerrancy

The six Southern Baptist seminaries sponsored a Conference on Biblical Inerrancy at Ridgecrest May 4-7, 1987. Thirty-six Christian leaders, including seminary presidents, professors, and pastors were responsible for either presenting a major paper or responding to a paper that someone else had presented. Scholars from within and outside the Convention participated. Those from outside the Convention included Baptists and other evangelicals. More than 1,000 persons gathered to hear the papers read, participate in seminars, and engage in dialogue on the subject of biblical inerrancy. Afterwards, the presentations were compiled and distributed under the title: *The Proceedings of the Conference on Biblical Inerrancy 1987*.

The thirty-six Christian leaders came from two very different church traditions. For the most part, those from outside the Southern Baptist Convention and some from within came from traditions which for several decades have described the Bible as being *inerrant*. Many of those from within the Convention came from a church tradition which describes the Bible by the Bible's own term, *inspired*, (2 Tim. 3:16) which means *God breathed*. There seems to have been complete agreement among the leaders that the Bible is God's written word. There was a lack of agreement on whether the Bible should be described as inerrant since several leaders had strong convictions that the Bible is and should be described as inerrant. These leaders call themselves and are called by others "inerrantists."

There are two important meanings of inerrancy. On the one hand, reference is to the *autographs*, the original documents on which Scripture was first written. None of those is in existence. In addition, there is reference to the Bible as being inerrant, meaning *without error*. On this point there was serious disagreement. There was disagreement about what *inerrancy* means among inerrantists and between inerrantists and those who do not describe the Bible as *inerrant*. There were good reasons for serious disagreement.

One of those who presented a paper was Millard J. Erickson, a Baptist inerrantist and dean of Bethel Theological Seminary in St. Paul, Minnesota. His paper was entitled, "Problem Areas Related To Biblical Inerrancy."

> I do not believe that this view is taught explicitly in the Bible. It is, however, an inference from the teachings of the biblical writers about the Scripture and the way they treated the sacred writings which they had in their time. It is not merely a deduction from the nature of God, or what we think he must have done. In this respect, inerrancy is like the doctrine of the trinity, which, while not taught explicitly in the Bible, is a valid inference from a number of Bible texts.[11]

His definition of inerrancy as a *valid inference* is important to understanding what he means by *inerrancy*. To infer means "to derive as a conclusion from facts or premises . . . to guess, surmise . . . to lead to as a conclusion or consequence . . . to hint, suggest . . . to deduce, conclude, judge, gather. (Webster)

Erickson did not presume to define inerrancy for other inerrantists. He wrote:

> There are undoubtedly differences of opinion among us here about the exact meaning of inerrancy. We may and should seek to engage in courteous and respectful dialogue, attempting to persuade one another of our own convictions. To short-circuit this process, either by acrimonious debate or by withdrawing from the dialogue and from fellowship entirely, may prematurely and unnecessarily fragment the body of Christ, which surely grieves our Lord, in view of the biblical statement about the value of unity in that body (e.g., Psalm 133:1; Acts 4:32; 1 Corinthians 11:17-22; Ephesians 4:3-4, 13; Philippians 1:27; 4:2).[12]

Erickson divided his paper into two parts.

> The first (part) is the problems which a doctrine of inerrancy must face. These constitute the agenda of unfinished business, the unresolved difficulties, which must be dealt with to maintain a doctrine of inerrancy. The other (part) relates to the dangers which may attach to a view of inerrancy. Here we are talking about the misconceptions or misinterpretations which may erroneously cause problems for the church.[13]

While firmly believing in the doctrine of inerrancy, Erickson dealt with eight "Problems for Inerrancy." One of the problems is the *definition of error*.

> More vexing, however, are the places where two accounts refer to the same matter but in a different fashion. These examples are numerous: did Jesus say 'take a staff' or 'don't take a staff?' . . . While much progress has been made at reconciling these differences, there are still problem passages which require continued attention.[14]

Another problem Erickson dealt with was "Identifying Inerrancy and Interpretation." he saw in this case that the main problem was people and the fact that they might misuse and/or misunderstand the Bible.

> Here we encounter a problem with a largely lay-oriented approach to the Bible. As Baptists, we have stressed the authority of the Bible and the priesthood of the believer. Together these produced an important emphasis upon each person reading and studying the Bible for oneself. This reading was largely devotional in nature, in which the reader sought to make immediate application of the material being read. But in so doing,

the 'obvious meaning' or face value rendering frequently was followed, without asking whether this was what the meaning today would be, or whether it might actually mean the exact opposite.

In this concern, we want to be careful to avoid creating a new priesthood, the exegete who alone is capable of understanding the Bible and upon whose every word of wisdom the lay person must wait. It would seem strange indeed if a God who removed the human intermediary from the reception of grace, would require a human intermediary for people to understand just how that grace is to be received.[15]

He wrote further, "If we have the truth objectively present, we still have the problem of understanding it. Otherwise, the message of the inerrant Bible may become corrupted by a fallible and erring interpreter."[16]

J. I. Packer, another inerrantist, wrote:

I would like to begin with the question of whether inerrancy is an inference as distinct from some unexplicit teaching of Scripture. I am not happy simply to say it is an inference. I want to use the philosophical word *entailment*. An entailment is a necessary inference and biblical inerrancy is a necessary inference. I believe that the inerrancy of Scripture is an entailment from all that is said about Scripture having God as its origin and all that is said about the character of God as a teller of truth.[17]

Paige Patterson, a Southern Baptist inerrantist, wrote:

If theists in general are not persuaded by such positivistic arguments about God, then it will not do for them to marshal the same arguments against the idea of inerrancy. Of course, we must qualify what we mean by 'inerrancy' and what we mean by 'God.' That does not eliminate either idea. Neither does it unduly complicate the perspicuity of the idea.[18]

Such language is complex, complicated, and confusing. Erickson believes the word *inference* best describes inerrancy. Packer believes the word *entailment* best describes inerrancy. Patterson writes about the *perspicuity of the idea* of inerrancy. One has good reason to doubt whether they have improved on the biblical word *inspired* to describe Scripture.

Other scholars and pastors who participated in the conference believed the biblical word *inspired* is a more appropriate and less divisive word to describe the Bible than the word *inerrant*. They, too, believe the Bible is the written word of God. Peter Rhea Jones, a Southern Baptist scholar, responding to Erickson's presentation, expressed much appreciation for it, while pointing out that numerous groups claim to believe in the inerrancy of Scripture but have departed from purely Christian thought. Among those named were Jehovah's Witnesses,

Mormons, Unitarian Pentecostals and Seventh-Day Adventists. Expressing his complete faith in the Bible, Jones said, "Believing the Bible is in my bones. I thank Dr. Erickson for a resourceful presentation."[19]

Another presentation was "The Baptist Faith and Message and the Chicago Statement on Biblical Inerrancy" by Fisher Humpheys, professor of theology at New Orleans Baptist Theological Seminary. The Baptist Faith and Message he dealt with was that of 1963. He compared the two statements of faith from several points of view and listed seven "generous" qualifications for inerrancy made in the Chicago Statement on Biblical Inerrancy.

He conceded that the differences in the two statements of faith are very small, with some important distinctions between the two. The first was that the Baptist Faith and Message affirms the inspiration of the Bible, while the Chicago Statement on Biblical Inerrancy attaches inspiration only to the original documents, which don't exist.

> I believe that, probably unintentionally, the authors of The Chicago Statement have forfeited something valuable about Scripture. They have eroded our confidence that the Bible which we now have is itself the very Word of God. All modern texts and all responsible translations of the Bible are, I believe, completely and fully inspired, authoritative, normative and revelatory.[20]

Another distinction Humphreys made was that the The Baptist Faith and Message is a consensus document for all Bible-believing Christians, while the The Chicago Statement is a more divisive document. Christian leaders should strive for clarity, not confusion over what it means to believe the Bible. When Herschel Hobbs wrote *What Baptists Believe* in 1964, he treated the theories of inspiration of the Bible on one page. When Russell Dilday wrote *The Doctrine of Biblical Authority* in 1982, he wrote of three views of inspiration.

When David Dockery wrote *The Doctrine of the Bible* in 1991, he listed six views of inerrancy alone. They are: 1) Naive inerrancy; 2) Absolute inerrancy; 3) Balanced inerrancy; 4) Limited inerrancy; 5) Functional inerrancy; and 6) Errant but authoritative. He states: "Views 2, 3, 4, and 5 all attempt to affirm the Bible as God's Word, inspired by the Holy Spirit and written by human authors."[21]

Complex language should not detract Christians from using common sense in applying to life the principles of life and salvation taught in the Bible. Dilday quoted W. A. Criswell:

> The Bible is a book of redemption. It is that or nothing at all. It is not a book of history, science, anthropology, or cosmogony. It is a book of salvation and deliverance for lost mankind.[22]

As Christians grow and mature in the likeness of Jesus Christ, their understanding of the Bible matures also. Dilday quoted B. H. Carroll, the first president of Southwestern Baptist Theological Seminary (SWBTS):

> When I was a boy, I thought I had found a thousand contradictions in the Bible. In the old Bible of my young manhood I marked them. Well, I had then nearly a thousand more contradictions than I have now. I do not see them now; they are not there. There are perhaps a half dozen in the Bible that I cannot explain satisfactorily to myself . . . Since I have seen nine hundred and ninety-four out of the thousand coalesce and harmonize like two streams mingling, I am disposed to think that if I had more sense I could harmonize those other six.[23]

The terms inerrantists use to define inerrancy are, to a great degree, subjective terms. They are full of meaning to those who call themselves inerrantists. To them, it might be unthinkable for someone to say that the Bible is not inerrant.

Those who prefer not to call the Bible inerrant have good reasons for their preference. Inerrantists have great difficulty in giving a clear, concise definition of what an error is. It seems that multi-page documents are required to define what an error is *not*. When so many possible dangers can be attached to the term inerrant, when so many qualifications are required to comprehend its meaning, when it cannot be defined without complex language, it should be understood why many people prefer not to use *inerrant* as the best term to describe the Bible.

It is important for Christians who do not use the term *inerrant* to understand to the best of their ability what Christian inerrantists mean when they use the term. Likewise, it is important for Christian inerrantists to understand what those who do not use the term mean when they do not use the term. Christians should not divide over terminology about the Bible. Christian love is the bridge that can and should unite people who describe the Bible differently.

Language in the Marketplaces

From the pews of churches and from the classrooms of universities and theological schools, people go to the marketplaces of the world. They mingle with scientists and refugees, with philosophers and factory workers, with Christians and non Christians. Most people do not understand the language of church cultures or complex language some people use to describe the Bible. Ideally, Christians make the language of faith as practical as possible to those interested in eternal life. The language of eternal life need not be too difficult for people to understand.

One aspect of the genius of Jesus was his ability to communicate. He spoke the language of the people in terms they could easily associate with their lives and experiences. Jesus combined eternal truths with language the people clearly understood. He spoke to them about fields, flowers, food, freedom, love, hate, money, wheat, vineyards, houses, kings and servants. *". . . And the common people heard him gladly."* (Mark 12:37b NKJV)

One of the tasks Jesus entrusted to his disciples was to communicate their witness of him by their lives and by their words. The first disciples he chose were ordinary, unschooled men. Filled with the Holy Spirit, they preached with boldness, conviction and power. *"Now when they (the religious leaders) saw the boldness of Peter and John, and perceived that they were uneducated and untrained men, they marvelled. And they realized that they had been with Jesus."* (Acts 4:13 NKJV)

The official language of Roman government was Latin. The language throughout the vast Roman Empire was Greek. The apostle Paul was highly educated and trained in philosophy and religion. For the sake of the gospel, he used language people could easily understand. He wrote, *"When I came to you, brothers, I did not come with eloquence or superior wisdom as I proclaimed to you the testimony about God."* (1 Cor. 2:1)

Christian leaders should equip people to go into the world's marketplaces and be witnesses for Christ. Language that is easily understood can best serve this purpose.

Accusations Against Others for Not Believing the Bible

In Southern Baptist history, when people talked about the Bible they talked about the Bible in the various versions and translations now available. Although many people realized that in ancient history there had been original manuscripts, they also had confidence that the same God who inspired authors to write those manuscripts, watched over the translation of those documents so that the essential facts and substance of meaning were preserved in the Bible.

When Southern Baptist fundamentalist leaders accused other Baptists of not believing the Bible, they accused them of *not believing the original manuscripts.* Although it was a deceitful scheme and the accusations were false, many people actually believed that some Southern Baptists, especially Southern Baptist seminary professors and other leaders, did not believe the Bible.

Paul Pressler, one of the principal architects of the Southern Baptist fundamentalist movement, wrote about what believing the Bible means to him and how he labels others.

Terms are often confusing. Therefore, let me explain how I am using certain words. I use the word *liberal* to describe a belief that the original text of the Bible can or does contain errors or mistakes. I use the word *conservative* to describe a belief that the original text of the Bible was written by God in such a way that it is free from error or mistakes. A liberal is a person who holds to a liberal belief as it regards the Bible. Frequently I refer to an individual member of the liberal group as a 'moderate,' believing that a *moderate* is a person who protects the teaching of liberal theology regardless of his or her personal theology. A *conservative* is a person who holds to a conservative belief as it regards the Bible.[24]

Pressler's statements omit some important factors in Christian teachings and practices. In reality, the original texts of the Bible were not written by God, but by people who were inspired by God to write as they did. He does not mention that men wrote the original manuscripts. He does not mention the Bible, which Christians through the centuries have believed is the inspired, written word of God. He does not mention Jesus Christ, who is God, or the Holy Spirit, who is God. He does not mention the church, which is the body of Christ and is guided by the teachings of Jesus Christ and is led by the Holy Spirit. He does not mention Christians, whose faith is in Jesus Christ, whose lives are built on obedience to him, who relate to other Christians as their brothers and sisters in Christ and who do not practice labeling other Christians by derogatory terms that might divide the body of Christ. His entire focus is on manuscripts which do not exist.

The fundamentalist leaders used terminology which centered on the *autographs*, manuscripts which do not exist. Accusations against other Christians as *not believing the Bible*, as being *liberal, moderate,* or *having a low view of Scripture* were based on their belief in the *inerrancy of the autographs*. In contrast, the fundamentalist leaders presented themselves as *believing the Bible,* as being *conservative* and as *having a high view of Scripture.* The people who believed them and followed them thought the fundamentalist leaders were telling the truth and that by electing them as leaders they were actually helping to save the Convention from liberalism and ruin.

The unspoken objective was to exercise authority over the Convention by getting presidents and trustees of various Convention boards and agencies elected who submitted to their authority. The inerrancy issue served as a smokescreen to divert attention from the real issue. The tactic worked.

The Bind: A Crisis of Conscience

Southern Baptists had never experienced such an efficient and well organized political organization with the focused objective of controlling all aspects of the

Convention's life and work. They had never experienced such open and hostile language used by Christians against other Christians; neither had they known such exclusion and rejection by some Christians against other Christians. They had never experienced such blatant and deliberate exercise of some Christian leaders' authority over other Christian leaders.

The initiative of the fundamentalist leaders brought a crisis of conscience upon many people who loved the Convention, believed in and practiced historic Baptist principles, respected its leaders, cherished the inclusive fellowship and liked the principle of agreement by consensus that had nurtured the Convention's unity for more than a century. The crisis of conscience was the conviction on the part of many that Southern Baptists throughout their history had committed themselves to be obedient to Christ and his great commission. The initiative of the fundamentalist leaders was believed to be in conflict with and a repudiation of the Christian teachings and principles that had nurtured their unity. The fundamentalist leaders were purposefully and rapidly gaining control of all aspects of the Convention's life and work.

Those who opposed them were in a bind. They knew it is wrong to falsely accuse and deceive others, whom Christ has commanded his followers to love and encourage. They did not have an efficient organization through which to oppose the fundamentalist leaders. Their own consciences would not allow them to use deceit in their work. Appeals to reason, fairness and reconciliation were not heard by the fundamentalist leaders. Their relentless aggression and accusations prevailed as they consolidated and extended their authority over all aspects of the Convention's life and work.

Previous leaders had been supporters of a rich fellowship, comprehensive educational and theological programs, and effective home and foreign mission work, all of which were being violently taken from them. In addition, control of valuable properties throughout the United States and overseas was being grasped by deceitful people.

The administration of Cooperative Program funds and the training of young ministers were falling under the authority of leaders whose primary motivation was not love, who practiced deception in their work, and who did not practice reconciliation.

One of the most tragic changes was the loss of respect and the good reputation of Southern Baptists as people of peace and reconciliation at home and overseas. To abandon all that they had experienced and all that the Convention's founding fathers had built for more than a century because the fundamentalist leaders excluded them was painful and even unthinkable to most Southern Baptists.

Early Efforts Toward Reconciliation

Many Southern Baptist leaders were alarmed over the political maneuverings and spoke and wrote against such activities. Some meetings were called to try to change some policies in order to bring peace to the troubled Convention.

> In September (1982), moderates led by Cecil Sherman of Asheville, North Carolina, offered a proposal to depoliticize the denominational presidency. They suggested that instead of the president having the sole power to appoint the committee on committees, the source of presidential power, that these nominations be made by state leadership. The suggestions included having the executive secretary, state convention president, and the chairman of the state executive board nominate four names for each state's positions on the committee on committees. From this list the SBC president in consultation with the two vice presidents would choose one layman and one ordained person to be appointed to the two positions. Similar provisions would be made for the committee on resolutions.
>
> Draper (James, SBC president) was asked 'voluntarily' to follow the procedure in his appointments and to support changes in the SBC Constitution and bylaws. President Draper rejected the idea. He added that he did not believe Southern Baptists would accept such a change and added he had contacted a 'variety of leaders' in the denomination, 'none of whom could support this.'
>
> Sherman was disappointed and frustrated by the response. The North Carolina pastor said the meeting was 'congenial and harmonious,' but the bottom line is that Draper, in essence said 'no' and 'trust me.' Sherman commented, 'Well, I have been there before. Two years ago, I went to breakfast with Bailey Smith (then president of the SBC) and he said, 'Trust me.' I had a hard time believing it then, and my misgivings were generously confirmed.'[25]

Call for Parity

Although most Southern Baptists considered themselves to be conservative in their theological beliefs and considered professors in the Convention's theological seminaries to be conservative also, some fundamentalist leaders said they wanted "parity" on the faculties of the seminaries. In 1982, SBC president Draper told the faculty of Southwestern Seminary that he wanted "fair representation of all theological views in the classrooms of the colleges and seminaries . . . Most conservatives would be happy with parity in our classrooms. We would be happy with a fair presentation of all views, but we should make a concrete attempt to bring known conservatives to our faculties."[26]

In reality, a fair presentation of various views was not the objective of the fundamentalist leaders. Nothing short of their complete authority would be satisfactory.

> These views would be popular for a time. 'Parity' became the code word of the fundamentalists until the power base was completed. Then, the demand would be for faculties of the 'conservative' position—all this in spite of the fact that the vast majority of the seminary faculty members would be classified as conservative by any impartial judge.[27]

Integrity and false accusations were openly addressed by Frank Pollard, president of Golden Gate Baptist Theological Seminary, speaking in New Orleans in 1983.

> (Pollard) implied the integrity problem involved the spread of innuendo and false accusations. Tracing accusations of heresy, Pollard scheduled conferences with two of his former professors who were named as teaching heresies. He said he learned the charges were untrue, and that no one accusing them had ever talked to them about these matters . . .

> When I told that New Testament professor someone had said he didn't believe in the virgin birth, he shook his head and cried . . . I fear there has been too much of this kind of slander. Broad general statements may sometimes contain a half-truth, but if they are half true they are also half false . . .

> If you really believe the Bible to be God's word you need to know it forbids you to slander anyone . . . Calling a Southern Baptist seminary professor 'liberal' is akin to calling a U. S. senator a 'communist.' His life's calling and ministry is at stake . . . Liberalism can kill a church or a denomination, but, an even greater warning for us is that a judgmental, negative spirit can kill a church or denomination also.[28]

Peace Committee

The danger of further division in the Convention was so obvious that some moderate leaders proposed that a Peace Committee be formed in the Convention meeting in Dallas in 1985. The record for the highest number of messengers in the history of the Convention was set that year when 45,531 registered. Incumbent president Charles Stanley of Atlanta defeated the challenge of Winfred Moore of Amarillo by about 55 percent of the vote. Moore was elected first vice-president.

A Peace Committee of twenty-two persons, chaired by Charles Fuller of Roanoke, Virginia, with Stanley and Moore as voting, *ex-officio members,* was named for the following purpose:

> That this committee seek to determine the sources of the controversies in our Convention, and make findings and recommendations regarding these controversies, so that Southern Baptists might effect reconciliation and effectively discharge their responsibilities to God by cooperating together to accomplish evangelism, missions, Christian education, and other causes authorized by our Constitution, all to the glory of God.[29]

The committee was composed of representatives from a wide spectrum of Southern Baptist leadership. Fuller reported on the composition of the committee.

> There was a distinct representation on the moderate side, distinct representation on the conservative side . . . I think there was an effort to give representation left, representation right, and representation center, and positions in between.[30]

Although the sources of the controversies, evangelism, missions and Christian education were named as the specific areas of concern, theological conformity was the *actual* goal of the fundamentalists. All six seminaries were visited by members of the committee for the purpose of interviewing the presidents, deans, and some others.

> Visits were made not only to the seminaries, but to the Foreign Mission Board, the Home Mission Board, the Sunday School Board, the Historical Commission, and the Christian Life Commission. All agencies were asked to reply to the concerns of the committee.[31]

The seminary presidents did all they could to answer the concerns of the committee saying, "We commit ourselves . . . to the resolution of the problems which beset our beloved denomination. We are ready and eager to be partners in the peace process."[32] Some even thought they went too far in efforts to accommodate the fundamentalists. Cecil Sherman resigned in protest, stating:

> The statement made by the six seminary presidents sets a course for theological education in the Southern Baptist Convention for years to come . . . Fundamentalists began with the premise theological education was 'drifting into/toward liberalism.' The Peace Committee bought this premise . . . The seminaries have taken a long step toward their critics . . . What they have done will satisfy for a season, but Fundamentalism will ask for more concessions from our educators. In the end, serious theological education will wither.[33]

Albert McClellan said that the inerrancy issue would have made a difference if it had ever been publicly debated by the Peace Committee.

> If debated by competent debaters, new understanding would have emerged, giving the traditional side enough votes at least to launch a minority report. But it was never debated . . . The committee spent two years dealing with symptoms . . . The talk did not deal with the broader, deeper, and wider subject of biblical authority but always with alleged infractions of limited detailed inerrancy.
>
> Some of the (fundamentalist) members of the subcommittees were unhappy that the visits had not been a witch hunt. As late as the last meeting of the committee, some were still complaining that 'we have not done our job, we have not talked to the professors.'
>
> Meetings and talks did little except relieve general accusations accusing all agency employees and professors of being liberal. Unfortunately, it did intensify attacks on individuals. The interviews did not move the denomination closer toward reconciliation.
>
> The (diversity) statement recognized diversity as a fact of life in Southern Baptist life. The traditional side (moderate) was committed to it because they assumed diversity is good. The (fundamentalist) side was for the statement, because it recognized SBC diversity as a fact, which in their estimation is bad.[34]

The committee issued statements concerning political activity within the Convention.

> After its investigation, the committee found that . . . These groups have developed organized coalitions centered on theological perceptions and individual leaders committed to a defined viewpoint. The coalitions have adopted political strategies for electing officers of the convention, appointing committees, and changing or preserving the character of accepted institutions. These strategies have included extensive travel, numerous mailouts, (a) network of representatives who share in this common strategy, and sustained efforts to recruit messengers to attend the convention . . . The extent of political activity within . . . at the present time promotes a party spirit; creates discord, division, and distrust . . . is detrimental to our influence; and impedes our ability to serve our Lord . . .
>
> The committee requested writers and individual Baptists (to) refrain from characterizing fellow Southern Baptists in terms such as 'fundamentalists,' 'liberal,' 'fundamental-conservative,' 'moderate-conservative'. The convention approval of this request had little if any effect on either side.[35]

The report of the Peace Committee did not alter in the least the relentless work of the fundamentalist leaders to elect not only Convention presidents who would submit to their authority, but to elect trustees of all agencies, boards and theological seminaries who would do likewise. Year by year gains were made toward the objective of exercising complete authority over all of the Convention's life and work.

Responses to Fundamentalism

Many leaders were not deceived by the fundamentalists and would not submit to their authority. In 1983 Nancy Sehested, an ordained Southern Baptist minister, led in the organization of Women in Ministry in Louisville.

> . . . They wanted to encourage women in ministry in Southern Baptist churches and in denominational ministries . . . They determined to provide the support system needed for encouragement and contact . . . They sought to 'explore new paradigms of leadership' in Southern Baptist churches.[36]

The Southern Baptist Alliance, later renamed the Alliance of Baptists, was organized to preserve historic Baptist principles and to embrace diversity in Baptist life and work.

> In 1986 a group of moderates formed an organization they hoped could move beyond politics on the Southern Baptist scene. Meeting in Charlotte, North Carolina, in November, they formed the Southern Baptist Alliance and elected North Carolina pastor Henry Crouch as chairman. According to Crouch, 'The SBA would be the voice of conscience in the Convention.' The SBA was a societal type of organization open to both individuals and congregations and advocating seven principles which reflected reaction to much of the conservative agenda.

> The seven principles developed in a 'covenant' cited the individual's freedom to read and interpret Scriptures; the freedom of a local church to shape its own life and mission, including the ordaining of males or females for ministry; cooperation with believers everywhere; the servant role of leadership; theological education characterized by reverence for biblical authority, inquiry, and responsible scholarship; a gospel that calls people to repentance and faith as well as to social and economic justice; and the principle of a free church in a free state.

> Moderates did not flock to the ranks of the Southern Baptist Alliance, however. Some explained that they did not want to do anything that would undermine their efforts to assert themselves as the real Southern Baptists or to regain their role in Southern Baptist life.[37]

Another response to authoritarian fundamentalism developed in December, 1988, when "Baptists Committed to the SBC" was organized in Dallas.

> Winfred Moore was named chairman of this group, which hired a former Christian Life Commission staff member, David Currie, as a salaried coordinator. The group, citing declines in baptisms and contributions and shattered unity, said they wanted to 'lead us out of this despair' and proceeded to organize chapters in a number of states.[38]

Authority Over Information

As early as 1981 leaders of Baptist Press and state Baptist papers came under criticism by fundamentalists for not being fair in the presentation of news.

> In February 1982, the Southern Baptist Press Association (SBPA), made up of Baptist Press editors and state convention paper editors, agreed with their liaison study committee that the Baptist Press should remain a part of the SBC Executive Committee. The committee said in part, the present arrangement will be 'satisfactory as long as we have Baptist Press staff members with the integrity of those now serving. But we need to remember that every establishment is always tempted to control the news and if this happens editors will have to resist.'

> In a resolution, the SBPA members noted that the 'purpose of the news service is to provide accurate and adequate reporting, whereas SBC history indicates resistance to information that is threatening or embarrassing and the result is often attacks on the news service . . . The news service is vital to the democratic processes of the convention . . . and (SBPA) is opposed to attempts to stifle or hinder it in its duties.'[39]

After several years of intense criticisms and pressures from fundamentalist leaders, highly competent and respected Baptist Press journalists Al Shackleford and Dan Martin were fired by the Executive Committee in 1990. They were asked to resign and were promised generous benefits if they resigned, but they refused the benefits and refused to resign their posts because of their integrity.

Shackleford told of a call from a member of the Executive Committee just before midnight on a Saturday night urging him to resign so the dismissal would not be necessary . . . "He even said in the conversation that he just felt like the brethren would be so grateful that not only would they give us six month's salary but they might choose to divide the $50,000 that it (the meeting) would cost between Dan and me. . .

"No charges were brought against the journalists either in private or in the committee meeting and action. No official reason has ever been given for their termination... The Southern Baptist Press Association immediately endorsed the concept of a new press service to ensure the free flow of Baptist news and information".[40]

Exclusion of Women

During the Convention in 1984 the fundamentalist leaders proposed a resolution, based on 1 Timothy 2:12ff and which passed by 58 percent, that excluded women from pastoral leadership "to preserve a submission God requires because the man was first in creation and a woman was first in the Edenic fall."[41]

This was not balanced with the fact that after Adam and Eve had sinned in the Garden of Eden, God went looking for the man and held both Adam and Eve responsible for their sin. (Genesis 3:8ff) Adam is held responsible for the fall also in Hosea 6:7 and in Romans 5:12-17. The broad view throughout the New Testament is that all people, men and women, have sinned; but by faith in Jesus Christ all believers experience forgiveness and life in him and are given the gift of the Holy Spirit. (John 1:12; 3:18; Romans 8:1)

Exclusion of Lay Leadership

Having established their authority over women, the fundamentalist leaders moved in 1988 to establish their authority over men. W. A. Criswell said in a session of 'The School of the Prophets' at the then Criswell Bible College that 'the pastor is the ruler of the church.' he continued:

> Lay leadership of the church is unbiblical when it weakens the pastor's authority as ruler of the church... A laity-led, deacon-led church will be a weak church anywhere on God's earth. The pastor is the ruler of the church. There is no other thing than that in the Bible.[42]

The view of Criswell was a contradiction of the biblical and historic Baptist view that all people who accept Jesus as Lord are members of *"the chosen people, a royal priesthood, a holy nation, a people belonging to God."* (1 Peter 2:9) Paul viewed the church as being composed of its entire body. *"To all the saints in Christ Jesus at Philippi, together with the overseers and deacons..."* (Philippians 1:1) The work of the pastor (overseer) is under the Holy Spirit (Acts 20:28), who produces in them love, gentleness, and self-control. The Spirit does not allow them to be conceited, greedy, quarrelsome or violent. (1 Timothy 3:1-7)

At the Convention meeting in San Antonio in June 1988, the messengers voted for Criswell's point of view in a resolution which gave lip service to the priesthood of all believers while emphasizing the submission of the church to the pastor and his authority. The resolution stated:

> ... Be it further resolved, that the doctrine of the priesthood of the believer in no way contradicts the biblical understanding of the role, responsibility, and authority of the pastor which is seen in the command to the local church in Hebrews 13:17, *'obey your leaders and submit to them; for they keep watch over your souls, as those who will give an account'*; and be it finally resolved, that we affirm the truth that elders, or pastors, are called of God to lead the local church (Acts 20:28).
>
> Efforts to change some of the strong language in the resolution failed. No amendments were accepted.
>
> About a hundred messengers in protest of the resolution turned in their ballots. Led by Randall Lolley, past president of Southeastern Seminary, about 200 gathered at the Alamo. Standing in front of the site where Americans died for the cause of freedom more than 150 years ago, Lolley declared that the resolution on priesthood was 'the most non-Baptistic, most heretical from the Baptist free-church point of view, statement ever made.' he wrote the word 'heresy' across the resolution and tore it up.
>
> The issue of pastoral authority would torment many churches for years to come. As the incidence of pastoral terminations rose, the evidence mounted that many Baptists did not care for 'pastoral authority.' Priesthood would be defended and debated many times.[43]

Of the two passages cited in the resolution above, the point should not be lost that in the passage in Hebrews, leaders are accountable. It would be only a matter of time before the fundamentalist leaders would be held accountable to Southern Baptists for using deceit in their work. Concerning the passage in Acts which pictures the pastor as the shepherd who watches over the flock, throughout Scripture good shepherds feed and protect their flocks, rather than fleece and flog their flocks. They love and gather their flocks, rather than despise and scatter them. (Ezekiel 34; John 10:1-16)

The view that the pastor is the ruler of the church contradicts the command of Jesus to his disciples that they be servants, just as he was a servant, and that the greatest of all would be servant of all. (Matthew 20:25-27) The most compelling appeal to leadership is love.

Ignoring these contradictions, the fundamentalist leaders with the blind loyalty of trustees and numerous other followers who were submissive to them and voted for their nominees and proposals, effectively excluded from meaningful participation in Convention leadership all who were not submissive to them.

Further Baptist Developments in Europe

The year 1989 brought two significant developments in Europe. In May, Southern Baptists gave a great gift to European Baptists. The trustees of the Foreign Mission Board (FMB), later called the International Mission Board (IMB), gave the Baptist Theological Seminary (BTS or IBTS) in Rüschlikon, Switzerland, including the property on which it sat, to the European Baptist Federation (EBF).

> The 'Key of Ownership' of the property of the Baptist Theological Seminary in Rüschlikon was given by FMB president Keith Parks to EBF General Secretary Knud Wumpelmann on May 28. The gift of the property represented a further step in the rich 40-year partnership in theological education between European Baptists and Southern Baptists.
>
> The history of the European Baptist Theological Seminary spans much of this century. As far back as 1908, European Baptists expressed the need for such an institution. The fulfillment of the dream, however, was realized only in 1948 when the FMB voted to establish a theological seminary in Europe where students from many countries could be trained for the Christian ministry. The present site was chosen that same year, and the first classes began in September, 1949. At a conference in Rüschlikon one month later, the European Baptist Federation itself was organized. In the Chapel service, European Baptist leaders emphasized their gratitude for this immense gift. They also recognized the strategic role which Rüschlikon has played in the life of European Baptists during these four decades while speaking of the new possibilities which the transfer of ownership affords. . . . At the ceremony Dr. Parks emphasized that the partnership between the Foreign Mission Board and European Baptists would not end with the passing of the key. He assured his hearers that the contributions will continue at the present level until 1992 when, by prior agreement, a gradual curtailment of funds will begin. Nevertheless, Rüschlikon Seminary needs increased giving from European Baptists at once to maintain and develop its work. Gradually after 1992 European Baptists must find ways of meeting an increasing share of the Seminary's budget.[44]

The second development was the fall of the wall that had divided Europe between free nations and those ruled by Communism. On November 9, 1989, the people of the world were both shocked and thrilled as they watched on television the fall of the wall in Berlin. A gate was opened through which people poured from East Berlin to West Berlin and vice versa, with no effort made by guards to prevent free movement. With hammers and other tools people attacked the wall, chipping away large and small pieces and opening holes in it.

The fall of the wall was only symbolic of a much greater fall of tyranny and tyrants. It was the fall of an elaborate system of oppression of people and a denial of their freedoms. As the spirit of freedom continued its sweep throughout the countries that had been dominated by Communism, the people in leadership positions fell with the system they could no longer hold over the people. In all countries except Romania, transitions were made without loss of life. It was miraculous that in a vast area encompassing nine time zones, with warplanes loaded with bombs, tanks and other armored vehicles ready for war, soldiers trained to obey orders from superiors, and nuclear missiles of mass destruction stored underground and aimed at much of the free world, the people of the world escaped a nuclear holocaust. Only in Romania were shots fired and people killed in violent clashes between soldiers and people.

Changes in SBC Leadership

The expansion of the authority of the fundamentalist leaders in the Southern Baptist Convention had been so successful that their trustees could make radical changes in the leadership of Convention agencies and institutions.

The late years of the controversy had seen a radical shift in the leadership of the agencies and institutions. One source of stability and continuity in the denomination was seriously disrupted.

- Lloyd Elder, president of the Sunday School Board was forced out of office.
- William Tanner, president of the Home Mission Board, moved to Oklahoma.
- Larry Baker, executive director of the Christian Life Commission, feeling harassed, took a pastorate.
- Randall Lolley, president of Southeastern Seminary, resigned in protest to the actions of the board of trustees.
- Frank Pollard had left the presidency of Golden Gate Seminary to return to the pastorate.
- Jimmy Allen, president of the Radio and Television Commission, left the job in frustration.
- Carolyn Weatherford left Woman's Missionary Union to become Mrs. Joe Crumpler.
- Harold Bennett, president of the SBC Executive Committee, announced his forthcoming retirement at the 1991 convention meeting.
- James Smith, president of the Brotherhood Commission, announced his retirement.

Almost none have been challenged because of 'liberalism,' but they have been severely criticized for differing with members of their trustees.[45] The trustees filled those positions with people who could not or would not openly challenge the authority of the fundamentalist leaders.

Further Responses to Fundamentalism

Many highly capable Christian leaders were neither asleep nor deceived by the purges conducted by the fundamentalists. Even though they were unable at that time to effectively halt the aggression of fundamentalism, they used their creativity and resourcefulness to initiate new and diverse ways to do education, evangelism and missions.

> Reaction began in July of 1990, when Dan Vestal and other leaders of Baptists Committed called for a national consultation in Atlanta to discuss alternate ways of dealing with their sense of disenfranchisement . . .

> Surprising even the most optimistic moderates, more than three thousand registered for a meeting expecting five hundred. Leadership from Baptists Committed, the Forum, *SBC Today*, and Women in Ministry all took part. When the meeting was over they had approved a newly chartered Baptist Cooperative Missions Program, Inc. as an alternate funding program to bypass the SBC Executive Committee.[46]

Associated Baptist Press was organized with a self-perpetuating board by state Baptist paper editors as an alternative to Baptist Press, from which Al Shackleford and Dan Martin had been fired by fundamentalist trustees. The new press service "was designed to be free from the control of any denominational agency or faction. Its goal was to provide news about Baptists and of interest to Baptists to secular newspapers, Baptist newspapers and other Christian publications."[47]

In 1991, after extensive preparation, the Cooperative Baptist Fellowship was organized.

> . . . before six thousand Baptists meeting in Atlanta's Omni Coliseum . . . Initially designed not to be an alternative to the Southern Baptist Convention but an alternative within the Southern Baptist Convention, the Cooperative Baptist Fellowship was a call for churches to use state conventions to bypass traditional Cooperative Program lines and still support Southern Baptist mission work and institutions . . . One participant, Bill Bruster, pastor of the First Baptist Church of Abilene, reported in his church bulletin, 'It had the kind of enthusiasm and the kind of fellowship we haven't seen since the fundamentalist takeover began.'[48]

Baptist pastors and other leaders who would not submit to the authority of fundamentalist leaders initiated in their state conventions various plans by which churches could designate contributions for Christian education and missions without any or all of those funds being administered by the Southern Baptist Executive Committee, which had fallen under the control of fundamentalist trustees. Such plans were implemented first in Kentucky, North Carolina, Texas and Virginia, with some other states making such provisions later.

Numerous state conventions had established Baptist colleges and universities for Christian education. Trustees of some of these institutions saw the threat of political forces trying to control those institutions, just as they had gained control of the Convention through political strategies. Trustees of Baylor University, the largest of the Baptist colleges, changed its charter "to replace the current 48-member board of trustees with a 24-member board of regents who will have 'sole governance' of the institution."[49] Baylor trustees assured Texas Baptists that they intended to continue a close relationship between them and the university, but reasoned that the threat of a takeover of the university by fundamentalists motivated their action. Furman University in South Carolina, Stetson University in Florida and Meredith College in North Carolina took similar actions.

It took Southern Baptists about one hundred years to establish six theological seminaries, all strategically located across the nation. Baptist leaders in various areas, concerned that young seminary students in the six seminaries were unable to study freely in institutions controlled by fundamentalist trustees, established twelve theological seminaries and/or theological departments in universities and Baptist houses of study in non Baptist institutions. (See Appendix A)

The fundamentalist leaders were unable to comprehend that the Convention was in serious fragmentation, or that the fragmentation would only get worse under their leadership. By establishing authority over Convention officers and trustees, they thought they had, in effect, established authority over the entire Convention. They thought their scheme had worked and that they had achieved their objectives. They had excluded from leadership the voices of those who opposed them. They had carefully selected Scriptures to be used to support their arguments, had ignored Scriptures that present different points of view, had eliminated from consideration the teachings of Jesus on servant leadership, and most importantly, had omitted entirely the greatest commandment to love God and others as we love ourselves. Instead, the argument of the inerrancy of Scripture was used to their advantage. They emphasized that the Scriptures they quoted were without error while ignoring the fact that the Scriptures they omitted were also inspired by God.

The practical and theological dilemma for the fundamentalist leaders was that they could not coerce free churches and free people to follow them. Their authority was in conflict with the authority of Jesus Christ, whose kingdom is administered by the Holy Spirit. *"Now the Lord is the Spirit, and where the Spirit of the Lord is, there is freedom."* (2 Cor. 3:17)

CHAPTER 3

Changes In Foreign And Home Missions

Then we will no longer be infants, tossed back and forth by the waves, and blown here and there by every wind of teaching and by the cunning and craftiness of men in their deceitful scheming. Instead, speaking the truth in love, we will in all things grow up into him who is the Head, that is, Christ. From him the whole body, joined and held together by every supporting ligament, grows and builds itself up in love, as each part does its work. (Ephesians 4:14-16)

As more trustees and heads of agencies and boards were elected who were submissive to the authority of the Convention's fundamentalist leaders, profound changes were made in foreign and home missions. The Home Mission Board had reflected the diversity that had existed in Southern Baptist churches in commissioning chaplains, including some ordained women chaplains. Larry Lewis, who was elected President of the Home Mission Board in 1987, was against women serving as deacons or pastors. When elected, Lewis said:

> The convention has very emphatically and very explicitly expressed their feeling that they do not favor women serving in the role of pastors. So I do not feel that the Home Mission Board should implement a policy that would be contrary to the expressed will of the convention.
>
> I personally never have been able to discover from scripture justification for the ordination of women, either as pastors or deacons. The biblical guidelines are very explicit that those who are ordained to lead the church in a pastoral role should be men.[1]

Lewis and the new Home Mission Board trustees reversed the policies of previous Home Mission Board leaders regarding the service of women as chaplains.

Keith Parks, President of the Foreign Mission Board (FMB), later renamed International Mission Board (IMB), had a different view. He was a consensus leader who accepted not only the diversity of beliefs and practices in churches in the Southern Baptist Convention, but who also led a staff, a mission program and missionaries who worked with conventions and churches overseas that had diverse beliefs and practices regarding the roles of men and women in church leadership. As the number of IMB trustees who were submissive to the authority of the fundamentalist leaders increased, so did the probability of a collision of authority in the work of the FMB.

FMB Trustees Pressure Rüschlikon Seminary

Some FMB trustees wanted the Baptist seminary in Rüschlikon, Switzerland, to conform to their particular view of what a theological seminary should be. On September 25-26, 1990, the EBF Council met for its annual meeting in DeBron, Holland. During the Council meetings, the EBF Executive Committee dealt with a request from Isam Ballenger, FMB Vice President for Europe. Some FMB trustees, who were dissatisfied with the seminary, had requested a reply from the trustees of Rüschlikon regarding the document agreement which led to the passage of the Rüschlikon property to the EBF. Seminary trustees referred the request to the EBF Executive Committee, since the EBF owned and operated the seminary.

The EBF Executive Committee agreed on a reply to Ballenger and the FMB which affirmed the following:

1. The question of European Baptist identity should be determined by Baptists in Europe.
2. We welcome the diversity which exists and has existed among European Baptists.
3. At this stage in our history we would affirm that the "Statement of Purpose" in the seminary brochure is acceptable to us. However, we recognize the need for some work to be done in light of the new situations in Europe. We have begun this process.
4. We have invited the Board of Trustees to look at the core of Baptist identity with us.
5. It is not common in Europe for theological schools to require professors to sign a creedal statement. However, it was noted that the Baptist unions meet with prospective teachers, discussing their theological views, etc., before they are hired.

Peter Barber, EBF President; Karl Heinz Walter, General Secretary; and Wiard Popkes, chairman of the trustees of the Rüschlikon seminary, signed the letter.

In the spring of 1991, some FMB trustees contended that the seminary in Rüschlikon was "liberal," and questioned whether European professors at the seminary believed in the virgin birth of Christ. Isam Ballenger informed John D. Hopper, Rüschlikon president and a Southern Baptist missionary, that accusations had surfaced again among FMB trustees that European professors at Rüschlikon denied the virgin birth of Christ. Hopper called the professors together to discuss the accusations. They decided that a letter clarifying their beliefs should be written to Ballenger. On June 21, 1991, they wrote:

> Dear Isam,
>
> Thank you very much for informing us that our statement from 1985 in defense of Dr. Eduard Schuetz has caused further discussion among members of the Foreign Mission Board relating to the future support of the Baptist Theological Seminary in Rüschlikon.
>
> We had thought that the matter had been put to rest in 1988 at our conversations with the 'visiting team' of the FMB. The statement of Baptist Principles requested at that time is now in your hands.
>
> Our statement relating to Dr. Schuetz was formulated in response to the false charges that Dr. Schuetz had denied the truth of the doctrine of the Virgin Birth.
>
> If further clarification is needed, we would like to emphasize that the Virgin Birth belongs to the doctrines in the New Testament which affirm that Jesus Christ is truly God and truly human. Neither in our statement written in 1985, nor in our teaching activities have we ever denied the truth of the infancy narratives in the Gospels of Matthew and Luke.
>
> Hoping that this clarifies the matter somewhat, we remain,
>
> Yours sincerely,

The letter was signed by the three full time European professors, Thorwald Lorenzen, Hans Harald Mallau and Guenter Wagner.

FMB Trustees Defund Rüschlikon Seminary

On October 9, 1991, the trustees of the FMB voted to completely defund the International Baptist Theological Seminary (IBTS, also called BTS) in Rüschlikon, effective January 1, 1992. The action came as a complete shock to European Baptist leaders, to the administrators and trustees of the seminary and to the entire seminary family of faculty, students and staff. None of the above had any idea that such an action was being contemplated, or that it would actually be taken without any consultation with European Baptist leaders. In reality, the action was also against the FMB staff, against Southern Baptist missionaries, and against many Southern Baptists who were not submissive to the Convention's fundamentalist leaders.

The conditions of the defunding were that the FMB would continue their financial support to Rüschlikon through the calendar year 1991, after which all financial support would end. The amount of annual support from the FMB for Rüschlikon was $365,000, which was almost 40% of the seminary's budget. Practically, it was impossible for European Baptist unions to make up such an enormous financial loss with less than three month's notice. Many Baptist unions were operating under serious budgetary limitations and were operating their own Bible schools or seminaries. The number of these institutions was increasing, especially in former Communist countries. These schools needed as much of the financial resources from their unions as they could possibly get.

The news of the decision by the FMB trustees spread quickly throughout Europe. Reactions to the decision were immediate. On October 10, Rüschlikon seminary trustee chairman Wiard Popkes, from Germany, wrote:

> The decision of the FMB to cut off all funds for the Baptist Theological Seminary (BTS) Rüschlikon as of December 31, 1991, is a veritable shock for the Board of Trustees. It is difficult to find appropriate words of response. The decision was made altogether unexpectedly, without any consultation with the Board of Trustees or the BTS . . . The sudden change of mind of the FMB cannot be regarded by us other than an unfriendly action and a break of trust . . . The cooperation between the SBC and Baptists in Europe has been long, fruitful, and trustful. The attitude of the FMB and its many representatives—as also in the BTS—has been extremely benevolent, generous, and helpful in many aspects.
>
> The EBF would not be what it is without this aid . . . We do not really know the underlying motivations of the FMB's decision. It seems, though, that they were not aware of the repercussions of such a step for the credibility of future activities of the FMB/SBC in Europe. We do hope that the Lord will prevent even greater damage and that the trustful, fraternal cooperation with FMB missionaries, as we know and appreciate them in Europe, will be maintained.

On October 11, 1991, European Baptist Press Service (EBPS) printed a special "FLASH" bulletin in which the following letters and comments on the defunding by several European Baptist leaders were quoted. EBF General Secretary Karl Heinz Walter wrote to FMB President Keith Parks:

> This is not a breach of trust primarily with the Seminary in Rüschlikon, but with the EBF and the 32 Baptist unions affiliated with it. The European unions immediately registered their view that the Board's action is unfair. Furthermore, European Baptists question the trustworthiness of the Foreign Mission Board, especially in view of pending partnership agreements between the Board and European unions. We do not find the loss of the money to be the major issue. Rather, the decision destroys confidence in future partnership with Southern Baptists.

Peter Barber, from Scotland and immediate past EBF President, wrote:

> I was party to the agreement made in 1988 between the EBF and the Foreign Mission Board. The agreement specified that the grant would be sustained at its present level until 1992. On the strength of that pledge we continued to plan the future of Rüschlikon. To have 40% of your income cut off at less than two months' notice is a cruel blow, whatever the reason. It makes it all the harder to know it is the result of a decision by the leaders of a mission board whose support had been guaranteed in a carefully framed agreement.

David Coffey, General Secretary of British Baptists, said his union had been considering a large-scale partnership with the FMB. He wrote, "These plans have not been changed so far, but they are now being questioned as a result of this action."

Birgit Karlsson, General Secretary of the Baptist Union of Sweden, wrote, "This action is bound to have an effect on Southern Baptist relationships throughout the entire Baptist World Alliance."

Walter Zeschky, President of the German Baptist Union, wrote that he was "very upset. We as Europeans should not accept this kind of thing. We must inform our people that this is not the basis for cooperation."

Per Midteide, General Secretary of the Baptist Union of Norway, wrote, "We feel this is breaking an agreement we thought we could trust, if not legally, certainly morally."

The EBF Executive Committee wrote to the FMB:

> Our plea would be that the Foreign Mission Board Trustees think again and reinstate the grant to the close of the agreed period. Otherwise we fear irreparable damage will be done to the honor in which the Foreign Mission Board is held in Europe and confidence eroded in any future dealings European Baptist leaders may have with the Board.

The European Baptist Convention, meeting in Hoensbroek, Holland, October 23-24, 1991, passed a resolution unanimously that dealt with the issue and read:

> WHEREAS, the Foreign Mission Board, SBC has provided a most constant and generous support for the EBC for many years through prayer, financial assistance and provision of personnel;
>
> BE IT RESOLVED, that the messengers of the 28th Annual Meeting express their gratitude for that support and care;
>
> WHEREAS, the recent action taken by the FMB to withdraw its financial support of the International Baptist Theological Seminary of Rüschlikon, Switzerland, before its agreed upon plan; and
>
> WHEREAS, this is perceived and reported among the 32 Baptist unions of Western and Eastern Europe as a potentially divisive and destructive action;
>
> BE IT RESOLVED, that we humbly, but strongly request that this action be reconsidered and that future decisions affecting agreed upon joint plans with other Baptist entities be made after prior consultation;
>
> BE IT FURTHER RESOLVED, that the 28th Annual Meeting of the European Baptist Convention conclude its final session with a period of prayer to invoke the changeless, powerful Spirit of God upon us as his vessels depart to meet the needs found in these changing times.[2]

Another resolution approved in the same meeting called for EBC churches and committees to "provide extraordinary cooperation with our General Secretary, staff and officers in this time of great opportunity when our General Secretary, Dr. John Merritt, serves as President of the European Baptist Federation."[3]

Reactions to the defunding continued. Many were negative among Southern Baptists, just as they were among European Baptists. In response to the financial crisis of the seminary, the Cooperative Baptist Fellowship (CBF) appealed to Southern Baptists to continue to fund the Rüschlikon seminary. "We'll send every cent of every offering straight from Atlanta to Zürich," said John Hewett, CBF moderator.[4] On November 2, 1991, Wiard Popkes sent a letter from the trustees of Rüschlikon to William Hancock, chairman of the FMB trustees, saying:

> After 42 years of partnership and co-operation between Southern Baptists and European Baptists in the mission and ministry of the IBTS Rüschlikon, this came as an unexpected shock; a unilateral break in a long friendship. For us this is not primarily a decision regarding finances. It raises profound *moral, missiological and theological issues*. It has consequences for future partnership between the FMB and Baptists in Europe. It is our sincere hope and trust that there are friends of Rüschlikon who will not condone such disrespect and unilateral use of power.

Concerning the *moral* aspect . . . in 1983 (confirmed in 1988) the FMB committed itself to continued support for the IBTS Rüschlikon for a ten year period ending December 31, 1992. Then in a written statement, the FMB agreed in October 1988 to continue the support for the IBTS Rüschlikon for a period not to exceed 15 years beyond 1992 on a decreasing scale to provide for an appropriate transition. The seminary has based its plans for the future upon these formal actions of the FMB and has made commitments to students, faculty and staff accordingly.

These commitments and agreements have been deliberately broken. We consider the decision to cut immediately almost 40% of our seminary budget without consultation and without consideration of the lives of students, staff and faculty to be highly irresponsible and morally indefensible.

Regarding the *missiological* aspect . . . For the past 42 years at Rüschlikon, the FMB has operated under a missiological principle of partnership. Southern Baptist missionaries and volunteers have worked hand in hand with Europeans to facilitate the mission and ministry of the IBTS Rüschlikon. It seems to us that the Trustees of the FMB now abandon the principle of partnership in mission which we consider to be vitally important for continued and effective mission in Europe. Partnership is built on fidelity and trust. This action damages the credibility and integrity of the FMB in Europe and around the world.

Furthermore, the decision of the Trustees of the FMB displays a blatant disregard and disrespect for the sacrificial work that Southern Baptist missionaries have invested in the ministry of the IBTS . . . The FMB founded and funded this Seminary. Missionaries of the FMB have been presidents, faculty members and staff members through the years . . . They have shared in educating Baptist ministers, missionaries, teachers and leaders who have served the cause of Christ around the world . . .

Regarding the theological aspect . . . Freedom of conscience and courage to express one's conviction are at the very heart of our Baptist heritage. The Board of Trustees of the IBTS Rüschlikon accepts full responsibility for inviting Dr. E. Glenn Hinson to teach at Rüschlikon. He is the David T. Porter Professor of Church History at the Southern Baptist Theological Seminary, Louisville (Kentucky), a Christian scholar of integrity, a man of faith, and of deep commitment to the Word of God and to the church. We regret that the reason for withdrawal of funds is reportedly his presence as guest professor on our campus for four months. It is ironic that this should happen to professor Hinson at Rüschlikon, less than ten miles from where our spiritual forefather Felix Mantz in 1528 was drowned for his baptistic convictions.

The letter expressed appreciation and support for FMB administrators Isam Ballenger, Keith Parker, Keith Parks and John David Hopper. It concluded, "We urge the Trustees of the FMB to reconsider their decision which has damaged their relationships with the IBTS Rüschlikon and the many Baptist unions in Europe."

Fundamentalist Communication

Also in November 1991, a letter from Ron Wilson, an FMB trustee from California, to FMB board chairman William L. Hancock, reached and was circulated throughout Europe. The letter, dated May 3, 1991, was written on the stationery of the First Baptist Church of Thousand Oaks, California, of which Wilson was pastor. Although whoever leaked the letter remained anonymous, it was invaluable to people who were not in the inner circle of the fundamentalist movement to gain some insight into the kind of information that was being circulated among fundamentalists. Even though the letter is lengthy, Southern Baptists are entitled to know the content of the letters their elected trustees write.

> Dear Bill:
>
> I thought I would drop you a line expressing some of my concerns about the Foreign Mission Board.
>
> It was great to get our slate elected at the last meeting and in the overall scheme of things it was absolutely crucial. We finally are in a position to begin to make the changes that need to be made. However, I am concerned that we are running out of people who came on the board when the liberals were in firm control of the situation. If we are going to make changes we are going to have to do it in the next 24 months for after that the trustees will primarily be made up of people who are not clued in to the former regime. The result of that would be the tendency to go along with the status quo and assume that all is well at the FMB. Depending upon the person that we elect as chairman next year, it is possible that you are the last chairman with such knowledge.
>
> (a) I am still of the opinion that our greatest problem centers around the Word of God and what kind of missionaries we have sent out and are sending out. In a recent meeting of the FMB it was requested by some of the staff that we do not export the denominational controversy overseas, that to do so would greatly harm missions. In one of the meetings I pointed out that the denominational controversy has already been transplanted overseas and it was done so over the last 25 years by members of this board that allowed missionaries to be sent who were neo-orthodox in their theology. Thus, for over a generation now we have exported our own

heresy all over the world through some of our missionary force. The crime has already been conducted: the question is what are we going to do about it. Sooner or later we must address the theological difficulties on the field in the same way that we addressed it here in the states. Ultimately, we have got to ask people what is it that you believe and what is it that you are going to be teaching or, in some cases, already teaching.

In my way of thinking, the obvious place to start is Europe and in particular, Rüschlikon Seminary. I laid the ground work to approach the problem at the last meeting when I questioned the teaching on the virgin birth. Now you and I know that there are many other questions to be raised to that teaching faculty but I felt that the virgin birth is so fundamental and would be a safe controversy in the SBC because even among liberal circles of Southern Baptists, there are few who openly question or deny the virgin birth. That's one controversy that we could welcome because it would expose our problem to the denomination at large.

(b) A second area that we need to zero in on is the appointment process. On Tuesday night at the last meeting, it became apparent that the same battles you and I fought on Mission Personnel are still being fought. Obviously what is occurring is that staff simply deals with a problem as it comes up, but policy is never changed or if it is changed, it is ignored until a new group of board members figures it out and wants to do something about it.

I would remind you of Mark Corts remembering a policy passed by the board that the staff had ignored and indeed, had acted like it did not exist. In fact, the subcommittee studying the problem had wrestled with the question for almost two years before Corts' revelation.

We must change the appointment process. The copy of Jack Harwell's editorial from the January 25, 1991 SBC Today confirms our suspicions. Non-Bible believing people are slipping through the process. There are a number of ways that we could change the process.

(1) We could increase board involvement by Sub A and B interviewing the candidates at Richmond. Remember, the board used to meet eleven times a year so we could go back to a time of greater commitment of board members. Or we could have Sub A, B, C, D and have everyone on the board be in the personnel section plus all the other things. This would require no more travel than is currently done and everyone on the board would have direct involvement with the missionaries.

(2) We could again make the regional committees a time of questioning and the giving of final approval. Under the current policy, they may have already sold their home and have their family and representatives

from their churches there and we are faced with the possibility of turning them down the day before they are supposed to be appointed. The simple solution to that is to have them there before the regional committee two months before their appointment. In other words, you would simply just delay the process by two months. I know that many objections will be made to the idea and statements made that it would just almost be impossible to change, but I am sure that in a few hours we could figure out a smooth running system that would allow for this kind of involvement. In fact, Bill Sutton was not aware that board members did not interview candidates until this was revealed to him at the last board meeting. To say that that revelation provoked him to anger would be an understatement.

(3) Some have suggested that we get rid of the current field reps and that would solve our problem. I certainly am in agreement that that's the location of the heart of the problem. However, that may not be the controversy that we want in the denomination. The policy change would not be controversial because most Southern Baptist people have the understanding that we currently interview these candidates.

(4) We can change the policy that allows staff to choose the reps. We could make a policy that requires board approval for the field rep slots.

(c) About two meetings back the light finally went on in my head on how things really work at the board. Basically, it is what any staff person wants to do and then they justify their actions by policy. We need to zero in on policy. Phyllis Randall's committee is currently studying policy. I have talked at length with Phyllis about her findings and basically, she is finding out that not much of what we call policy has ever been voted on by the board. Hunter Riggins has exposed the fact that Baker James Cauthen ran the board most of the time without any policies being written down.

(d) Eastern European and in fact, the whole European debacle must be addressed and soon. The opportunities before us will not remain for long. We have done missions differently in Europe and we must change. I do not claim to have the answers on how we could change, but I do know that change is absolutely required. I finally have found the nerve on which to approach Rüschlikon and that is alluded to earlier about the virgin birth. I talked to Phil Roberts on the 11th of April and he reminded me of a copy of a letter signed by three of the teachers at Rüschlikon which gives insight to their belief concerning the virgin birth. Paige Patterson has a translation of that letter and as soon as he can find it, he will send me a copy.

Beyond the theological, we also have the personalities. Who are we going to deal with? I realize that we have dealt with people and developed relationships over 40 years of time and that we would be taking a chance if we changed horses at this point in time. However, the positive possibilities should far outweigh any fear we might have of making a mistake in this matter. The worst thing that can happen if we make a mistake is that we end up with the same kind of results that we currently have in our present approach. Therefore, to change can only help. It will not hurt for the worst that can happen is failure and we already are experiencing much of that.

In order to do something with the European situation, I hate to say the following but it must be said. We will not accomplish much if Steve Hardy continues as chairman of that committee. Pesonally, I like Steve. I have no difficulty with him as a brother in Christ or as a fellow conservative. But something happens to Steve when he is placed into a position of authority. I don't know how to describe it, but he seems to try to impress the staff too much. If Steve is left chairman of the committee, my guess is that I will end up having to take many of the issues to the full board where we will certainly find a much greater climate for change.

Several good men are on that committee but few are willing to speak out. I have challenged Bob Claytor on his move to South Carolina because I told him that it could be the devil getting him to move down there just so he couldn't see the changes in Europe through. Isam probably danced a jig when he heard of Bob's new call.

Much is at stake here. I would hope that you would consider putting Bill Sutton, Bill Blanchard, John Jackson, Phyllis Randall, and Pat Bullock on the Europe and Middle East Committee. I would also hope that you would give consideration to Skip Smith as chairman of the committee and making Steve vice-chairman. Another person who would be good to come on that committee even as chairman would be Bill Pace, but you probably have him scheduled to be chairman of his own committee, which is CSI. If you move Paige Patterson over to be chairman of the Administrative Committee (John Sims has served in that capacity for his two year term), then you would probably want to keep Pace as chairman of CSI. We desperately need at least two more talkers on that committee and a chairman who will direct until the problems are solved. There is not that much happening in the rest of the world and we need to stack this committee with people who will see it through. If we cannot address liberalism and the mistakes of Europe, we will never be able to address liberalism and other problems in other parts of the world.

We need to deal with different people in all of Europe and we desperately need to show the staff that that is our desire. The giving of money to Oradea is our finest opportunity to move in that direction. Bob Claytor and Phil Roberts both say that if we do not end up moving quickly and decisively in this matter that we will be sending a message to the real leadership of eastern Europe that the Southern Baptist Foreign Mission Board is going to be status quo. If we initiate from the board the financial request and carry that through we will be (1) expressing our authority as trustees (2) symbolically making a statement for the whole board (3) symbolically making a statement to the conservative leadership of western Europe (4) symbolically making a statement to the new evangelical and non-compromised leadership of eastern Europe.

(e) We need to have a time when the FMB meets. The other boards and agencies have a time when the trustees meet as a group and not after everything has been settled and everything is to be simply a rubber stamp. I know this idea will bring consternation to the staff, but I would propose that we meet as a board from 9:00 until 12:00 noon on Monday morning at every board meeting. That board meeting would consist of board members and when requested, Dr. Parks. Dr. Parks could be asked to come almost all the time, but I think that it is important that he is there at our request. No press should be allowed at such a meeting and at the meeting we can go over things, concerns, reports, etc. like we now have to do in small groups in the halls and on Monday or Tuesday nights. There is nothing wrong with the board meeting. Press will get very little mileage out of that. If need be, we could then have the full board meeting moved to Wednesday afternoon from 1:00 until 4:00. I realize that that would mean most of you Southern boys would not get back for Wednesday night. However, since current organization makes it impossible for westerners to make their Wednesday night services, I feel little sympathy for you southerners. It costs us all to be on the board and missing six Wednesday night services would not be too great a price to pay.

In fact, we could change the schedule to meet on Tuesday, Wednesday, Thursday and that would allow all of us to be in church on Sunday and would require that all of us miss Wednesday. The laymen would miss the same number of days that they currently miss from their jobs for they could then fly on Monday evenings. Everybody could be in church on Sunday morning and Sunday night and no one would have to travel all night long to get to the meeting. If we would go to a Tuesday, Wednesday, Thursday setup, it would not create hardship on anyone. In fact, we would get better attendance because people would not be leaving early on Wednesday to get back to their church on Wednesday night. We would have greater participation, which is our job as trustees. I have always thought it to be kind of nonsensical to have people spend all that money to come to the board meetings and then walk out at 10:15 on Wednesday morning because they have to catch an 11:30 flight to make it back for Wednesday night service. As you well know, we have lost some critical votes because some of our brethren had to bail out early.

(f) An additional item would be to make a policy change by bringing Zeb Moss and his group under communications. Keith made the appointment by insisting that he had the right because of policy. If that is true, then he certainly had the right. Let's change the policy to the way we want it and in the future it will be done that way.

(g) Bill, we have talked in the past about the importance of moving decisively and quickly. Many of us deferred to your leadership (and I think you were right) to wait until June to begin the changes. In June I would hope we could address some of the changes we have mentioned in this letter.

I have one fear now that we have delayed until June and that is that we will meet in June and people will be saying 'Let's not be controversial because it will hurt Lottie Moon' because it's getting close to the time of Lottie Moon. Frankly, it is my opinion that our indecision at the FMB and the activities by Dr. Parks, Bill O'Brien, and other staff people is what has hurt Lottie Moon. The Home Mission Board took their stand, made their changes, including changes in personnel, and took their lumps. Their result has been increased giving to Annie Armstrong. We, on the other hand, have been cautious making few changes and the perception throughout the denomination is that things are the same at FMB. The real Bible believing Southern Baptist people will again sacrificially give to Lottie Moon after we make the stand for biblical truth.

Sooner or later we must make the changes. Let's make them while we still have the opportunity.

In Christ,
Ron Wilson

Fundamentalist World Vision

While much in the letter might be of interest to Southern Baptists, some of it should be carefully examined in light of the teachings and Great Commission of Jesus Christ, historic Baptist principles, and the fact that Ron Wilson was an elected trustee of the FMB, in whom Southern Baptists had entrusted our mission work throughout the world. He stated his vision: *"If we cannot address liberalism and the mistakes of Europe, we will never be able to address liberalism and other problems in other parts of the world."* This is an entirely different vision than the one Jesus gave in the Great Commission: *"Therefore go and make disciples of all nations, baptizing them in the name of the Father and of the Son and of the Holy Spirit, and teaching them to obey everything I have commanded you . . ."* (Matt. 28:19-20a)

Wilson made the point that the action to defund the seminary in Rüschlikon would show the authority of the trustees over the president of the board and the staff, even though the president had been elected by the board to lead the entire world mission program. For any group of Christians to demand total authority over other Christians is a denial of the partnership principle expressed by Paul, *"For we are God's fellow workers . . ."* (1 Cor. 3:9a)

Oradea, Romania, was the location of an independent, evangelical seminary. The administrators of the school ran the school apart from the Romanian Baptist Union and would not submit its books to be audited with the reports of the audit made known to Romanian Baptist leaders. Some trustees intended for the money that had been used to support the Rüschlikon seminary to be redesignated for the school in Oradea.

Eduard Schuetz had been president of the German Baptist Theological Seminary in Hamburg, Germany. He had been accused of not believing in the virgin birth of Christ and had been fired, although he said the accusations about his beliefs were false. Three European professors at the Rüschlikon seminary wrote a letter of protest about his being fired because of false accusations. Because of their letter of protest, some FMB trustees accused the three European professors at Rüschlikon of not believing in the virgin birth, even though they wrote a letter and signed it that they believed in the virgin birth and had never denied it.

Wilson accused Baptist leaders from both eastern and western Europe of not being real leaders, even though they had been elected as leaders by their own Baptist unions. Although he did not name them, he wrote about "the conservative leadership of western Europe and the non - compromised leadership of eastern Europe." All Baptist leaders in eastern Europe had suffered persecution in various forms under Communism. Many Baptist pastors had been sent to prison, where some died. **For an FMB trustee to accuse them of not being real leaders and of compromising was unconscionable!**

False Accusations Against Missionaries

Wilson also accused Southern Baptist missionaries of not believing the Bible and of spreading heresy throughout the world. The great majority of these same missionaries had come from Southern Baptist churches, had been trained in Southern Baptist colleges and seminaries and had responded affirmatively to God's call to missionary service. They had gained experience in Christian service in Southern Baptist churches. They had undergone extensive spiritual, psychological, emotional, financial and doctrinal scrutiny by the personnel section of the FMB. By faith they had left family, friends and country to be obedient to God's call.

Many had given most of their adult years in missionary service, during which time some had been martyred for Christ, others died by accidental means, while others died of natural causes. Thousands had continued in missionary service after their family members and friends had died. **Any FMB trustee who accuses missionaries of not believing the Bible and of spreading heresy throughout the world without proving his accusations will be held accountable to God and to Southern Baptists for his words!** (Matt. 12:36-37)

FMB Trustees Reconsider Defunding

Such a storm of protests from European and Southern Baptists followed the defunding of the seminary in Rüschlikon that the FMB scheduled a meeting of trustees in December to reconsider their previous action. On November 27, 1991, an unsigned letter on the stationery of the First Southern Baptist Church of Thousand Oaks, California, was written to FMB trustees. Copies of the letter reached Europe in January, 1992. Although this letter also was lengthy, Southern Baptists are entitled to know what their trustees write.

> Dear Fellow Board Members,
>
> Because of the importance of the upcoming Board meeting and my desire not to bore you by repetition in various committees, I am writing this letter so you only have to hear me once. I thank you for your time in reading this lengthy letter.
>
> It is no secret that our denomination has been embroiled in controversy for two decades and openly debating since the conservative resurgence began thirteen years ago. The 'resurgence' has been successful because it has spoken to the heart of Southern Baptists, standing solidly on the inerrancy of Scripture. The response has been a strong show of support for conservative leadership in our denomination. The man in the pew finally stood up and said, 'Enough!' to those who ridiculed the fundamentals of the faith and had a low view of Scripture. Mr. Baptist no longer wanted to support liberal theology which included neo-orthodoxy and its offspring. He correctly understood that liberalism was leading to the death and destruction of the denomination. He voted for trustees to oversee the various agencies in whom he had the confidence that the 'faith once and for all delivered to the saints' would not be compromised. It is in that context that every member of this Board was elected to serve as a trustee.
>
> Now we find ourselves going through the ordeal of orchestrated attack through the media and a letter campaign by a well-organized moderate organization who desires to gain financial and numerical support. As has been their custom, they are attempting to distract from the issue of Scripture by throwing up smoke screens of various kinds, including the constant

accusations of 'politics' and 'secret agendas.' We must remember, when a moderate or liberal cannot stand on an issue, he will say it is 'political' or he will argue Ad Hominen. We would do well to translate the word, 'politics,' when used by a liberal, to mean 'standing on scriptural issues.'

This attack has unfortunately been fueled by some on the staff of the FMB and so the issue has grown to the point that it must be dealt with in some fashion. The simplest and wisest way to respond would be to do nothing. The Board has voted, and according to *Roberts Rules of Order*, cannot discuss the issue unless someone on the prevailing side makes a motion to change his vote and moves to reconsider. At that point, a majority of trustees have to vote for reconsideration in order to discuss the issue. If a majority vote is forthcoming, then the subject can be debated and voted on again. For example, if someone who voted for the giving away of the Rüschlikon property back in 1988 wanted to change his vote and a majority desired to reopen the issue, it could be done. In fact, reconsideration could go on ad infinitum.

Not knowing the desire of fellow trustees in this matter, I feel a need to share these thoughts on why the Oct. decision was correct and warn of the catastrophic effects it will have in the SBC if we were to reverse our decision.

WE GET LETTERS; STACKS AND STACKS OF LETTERS

Not only did that apply to Perry Como, it applies to the FMB following our October decision concerning Rüschlikon Seminary. It is apparent that the great majority of the letters come from folks liberal or at best, moderate bent. Indeed, it would be interesting and revealing to know how many of those writing letters are participants in the new denomination of liberals called the Cooperative Baptist Fellowship. A few letters have arrived from conservative pastors who have protested our action. When contacted, they realize that they have received only partial facts concerning our action, and when informed usually respond with approval. One leading pastor in his state was very upset with our action until he discovered we had given $365,000 for theological education in Eastern Europe. He went from opposition to support for our bold and brave move.

Upon close reading of the letters, you obviously noticed the similarity of wording and phrasing. One wonders if a model letter was used. Just as obvious is the fact that most people did not have the full story. How in the world could any sane person say we are missing the door of opportunity in Eastern Europe when we are giving the $365,000 to train hundreds of students instead of the 38-48 at Rüschlikon? Do they actually believe the handful of students at Rüschlikon will impact Eastern Europe more than the hundreds trained in national seminaries?

Many have reacted negatively because the full truth was hidden from them. Some staff leadership could have helped in getting the complete story out to the denomination, but for some reason they chose to accentuate the negative, play to moderates and their organization, and raise needless fears among Southern Baptists.

Why haven't we received more letters of support? I wondered about that myself. I asked some leading conservatives in California whom I personally know are supportive of our action, why they had not written. They expressed surprise that I would expect a letter. Indeed, they challenged me if I had written letters of support to the HMB trustees or to Southeastern Seminary trustees when they made their brave and bold steps in making the necessary changes at their institutions. *'So likewise you, when you have done all those things which are commanded, say, We are unprofitable servants. We have done what was our duty to do.'* (Luke 17:10)

The simple truth is that conservatives in our denomination expect us to stand on Scripture. They expect nothing more and nothing less! Right action does not require a letter each time it is exhibited.

I also noticed many letters from Virginia. One even came from a lady who has the same name as a trustee of the new liberal seminary starting up in Richmond. We all know how committed that institution is going to be to truth and the SBC! Having observed the accuracy of the primary religious reporters in that state, it is not surprising that Baptists there would over-react. That poor state has not received an accurate report in years! I am enclosing a copy of an article from a few years ago that will serve as example to prove my point. I still have not received from Mr. Briggs or Dr. Parks clarification as to where the misunderstanding of that meeting rests.

The threatening tone of some letters cannot be overlooked or ignored. In some circles of society a few of the letters border on what is commonly referred to as blackmail, especially the letter from the leadership of WMU. Shame on those ladies for writing what is blatantly a political epistle designed to intimidate this Board and fuel the fires for the liberal organization in Atlanta! They have jeopardized support for their once fine organization and have certainly raised many questions as to exactly what their role is in the SBC. I know it made me wonder what they were suggesting their role would be with the FMB if we didn't succumb to their threats. That letter certainly raised my horizons of understanding the role of the WMU! Until I received their letter it was my impression the responsibility of the organization was to support the HMB and FMB. Perhaps there is some truth to the rumors that the WMU desires to become a sending agency.

Then there are the letters from a few in Europe. Again, one must wonder as to how much information they had been given. People who do not know facts usually over-react. I have received information from a person in Richmond that strongly suggests some staff in the home office encouraged our missionaries to help mount a letter campaign from nationals, in order to pressure the Board to change the October decision. I would hope this is not true, because if it is true, it raises a number of issues that would need to be dealt with soon.

Unfortunately, some of the letters from Europe are also threatening in nature. Those who were on the Board in 1988 will remember the similarity of threats received then if we refused to deed over the property at that time. Why is it that if we do not do what they want, they are always going to take the ball and go home? A few of the letters suggest a reexamining of our agreements and working relationships. If they insist, we should accommodate them and have a thorough re-evaluation from all sides. A clearing of the air would not be harmful and certainly might be helpful to all concerned. A number of people have strongly suggested that we have dealt with, and are currently dealing with, the wrong people in some of the countries if we are expecting to see a real harvest of souls. Could our critics be correct? Are we dealing with like-minded people or in some instance are we dealing with the same stagnant neo-orthodox mentality that we have had to deal with here in our US institutions and colleges?

It is easy to discern why we haven't received more letters from conservatives in Europe—especially the conservatives of eastern Europe. Many have not been told about our action. I have been told that the major reason has been to use the tact of waiting, to see how strong our resolve is going to be in this matter. Why should they 'stick their necks out' and risk retaliation by publicly making statements of support when they well-know the power politics being used against this Board? They have been disappointed before, and I certainly do not blame them for their caution. When we stand firmly for the faith and a high view of Scripture and are willing to be ridiculed for doing so, then we will see a strong show of support.

CONTROVERSY AND LIBERALISM

Our action in October is not controversial with mainstream Southern Baptists. The concerns over Rüschlikon by knowledgeable Baptists have always been centered in Scripture and the seeming lack of respect for the Scriptures at that institution. This concern is not of recent vintage but goes back many years. Glen Hinson is not the issue at Rüschlikon. He simply proves the point. His teaching there should not be a surprise to any of us. He is not out of step with the historical mainstream of teaching at that institution. Back in the days of the Ralph Elliot Genesis Commentary controversy, John D. W. Watts was the president of the seminary, and he wrote a letter commending the Commentary.

Then, a few years ago, some of the faculty members wrote a letter of support for a teacher fired at another school because of his heretical views concerning the virgin birth. I have been told the letter raises some serious questions as to their views on the subject.

We could have a thorough investigation on all of this, but we would be wasting mission money. In 1988 John David Hopper and Foreign Mission Board staff leadership admitted to long-term theological problems at the seminary. Indeed, because of their assurance that these problems would not continue, the majority of the Board voted to give the property to the Europeans.

The accusation has been made that this current Board, by its action in October, has exported the controversy to Europe. Nonsense!

If it has been exported, it was exported by staff that has continually refused to acknowlege Southern Baptists' concerns about liberalism. After years of the conservative resurgence, it was 'business as usual' at Rüschlikon.

A college professor described Rüschlikon as 'being the toxic waste dump for liberalism in Europe.' The staff, both in Richmond and on the field, has allowed modern liberalism to continue to be taught at that school. How do I know this to be true? . . . Glen Hinson!

When the FMB staff refused to address the problems or give heed to conservative concerns, it was inevitable that this Board would have to address the problems.

Some serious questions must be asked. Why are people anywhere, whether in America or Europe, upset by our standing strong on the issue of Scripture? How will our Christian witness be hindered by our standing strong on the issue of Scripture? Will not this stand, and our insisting that conservative theology be taught, enhance our witness and ultimately our opportunity? Are our critics suggesting that we are required to fund institutions where they can teach anything? Is that the message we desire to be sent out? Are there limits?

If our critics disagree with the lines drawn, perhaps they can explain where they would draw the lines. So far, they just draw the line some place beyond where any conservative Board has drawn a line. Nothing is acceptable to them unless it is total capitulation.

We are accused of having personal agendas. The opposite is true. We are placing Scripture at its proper place in the discussion.

MISSION STRATEGY FOR EUROPE

The time has come to break out of the mold and dream dreams and plan great things. It is time for a review of our strategy in Europe by a committee of this Board. Expert advice from men such as Dr. Cal Guy and Dr. Phil

Roberts would be beneficial to this Board. The opportunities in Eastern Europe might be of short duration and must be seized post haste.

John Hewitt of the liberal Cooperative Baptist Fellowship denomination (who is using the October event to increase funds and support for his organization) has challenged us by asking, 'What kind of mission strategy is that?' Even though a blind man can see the plain political motives in his letter, his question does deserve a reply.

If he is referring to the spending of the $365,000 in the East instead of at Rüschlikon, we can reply with confidence that it is an excellent mission strategy. Look at it in light of the following observations:

1. The multi millions spent over the years at Rüschlikon have produced startlingly few results in church starts and converts.
2. The continually small enrollment of students shows a lack of commitment on the part of the European community to the seminary.
3. In 43 years we have had only 400 graduates — less than 10 a year.
4. Having a seminary in an extremely expensive location is not wise financial stewardship.
5. Having a seminary that requires most students to leave their homeland and relocate in a strange environment to work, witness and study in a foreign culture, is not the best way to train preachers in reaching their homeland.
6. The Europeans have yet to really fund the seminary in any grand fashion. Their continual lack in this area indicates their true feelings toward the school.
7. By taking the $365,000 out of Rüschlikon and spending it on Eastern European theological education we can increase the students taught tenfold or more.
8. Dr. Phil Roberts, a seminary professor from Southeastern and a knowledgeable man about Europe, strongly agrees with the concept of building Bible Schools and Seminaries in various countries of the east. So much so that he is soon to become the academic dean at a new school in Oradea, Romania.
9. Dr. Roberts has stated, 'A basic education can be provided for 200 students in Romania for what it costs Rüschlikon to pay the head cook. For $50,000 we can educate 190 students, paying their rent and providing three meals a day.'
10. By placing education closer to the home of students it will create:
    - a greater availability,
    - lower costs,
    - more students,
    - more service to the local churches,

- increased ministry opportunity in the local churches,
- a lessening of the language barrier,
- an understanding of localized needs and traditions, and
- less cultural shock which facilitates learning.

Does John Hewitt really have a problem with such a mission strategy? Let's be serious. He just wants the same old liberalism to be taught at Rüschlikon.

WHAT ABOUT RÜSCHLIKON?

There is no need to fear the demise of the institution. Since it is so important to Western Europeans, they will make it a priority and increase funding. But they really may find that unnecessary, for if I discern the threats made in some letters correctly, Rüschlikon is about to receive all kinds of money if we do not revoke our vote. Indeed, could this entire drama be a plot to achieve such a response?

Since liberals can in clear conscience fund almost anything, let those that are threatening to pull Lottie Moon funds do just that. If it is their desire to put all of our missionaries in a hostage situation, that is something for which they will answer to the Lord. It will be totally their responsibility if they carry out their threats of spiritual blackmail.

By now, you are aware of the fund-raising contract signed with an American company which is going to raise all the money that Rüschlikon will ever need. There is a rumor that the fund-raising company was in the works before our October vote - but then who is counting days? Indeed the trustees of that seminary should be thanking us for our action, for we have most certainly filled their coffers. So much so that we probably need to watch closely to ascertain if the school needs 'any' support from us.

I do foresee one problem the liberals might have and one the moderates certainly will have—they might not be able to get away with the funding of the school if their people know the whole truth. If somehow it gets out exactly what they are funding, that will saddle them with having to defend the indefensible.

It is doubtful that any explanation of liberal heresies will fly with the men and women in the pew. Baptists do not want to support institutions where fundamentals of the faith are ridiculed. However, to date, the liberals have not been known to be that open with their congregations.

BREAKING OF TRUST

A few Europeans and some staff have suggested there has been some kind of breach of trust by this Board. Supposedly, we broke our agreement made on October 11, 1978. But if you read the motion you certainly cannot come up with any great moral obligation by the FMB. Read closely! In 1978 we placed the property at their disposal for five years. Then in 1983 we simply reaffirmed the 1978 agreement regarding the administration of the school. Please note that nothing is said about money or even allowing the use of the property in 1983. In 1983 the minutes do not show any discussion, which leads me to question if the Board really knew what they were voting upon. In 1988 we gave them the property, and that gift was based on promises made by staff and John David Hopper that have not been kept.

If there was an implied agreement, that implication must have been a two-way street. What about the responsibility of the leadership in Rüschlikon? Was there no limit in the implied agreement? Also, why weren't the 1978 and 1983 agreements brought to our attention in 1988? Obviously, they would not have supported the argument that it was necessary to immediately give the property away in 1988. Why give it away when you have already agreed to let them use the property, and use it free of charge, in addition to funding the costs of the school? There would have been no need for ownership on their part if those binding agreements existed. What was the great urgency in 1988 if we had a moral obligation until 1992? The tremendous speed of the giveaway and the threats of no longer doing business with us make no sense if we were already obligated until 1992!

There has been a breach of trust. The 1988 agreement has been breached. Breached by some of our staff and Dr. Hopper and the trustees of Rüschlikon Seminary. Their promise was not fulfilled and Dr. Hinson proves that point. Since moral obligation has been dominant in numerous letters and articles, perhaps it should be pursued. Since they broke their promise, would it not be the proper action on their part to give the property back to the FMB? Especially in light of the fact the property was given on the basis of those promises.

INTEGRITY

Fellow Board members, it is important to know that our integrity is intact. Among the Bible-believing Baptists of the world it has never had a higher value. The whole Baptist world understands that we will no longer support neo-orthodoxy and the heresies it produces. Baptists over the world have been encouraged by our action. To bow to political pressure and organizational and spiritual blackmail will create a malaise not only in the SBC but among Baptists all over the world. If we rescind our vote the results will be disastrous. Please remember that the Baptist in the pew in Europe loves the Word just like the Baptist in the pew in America.

Integrity is a word used at this Board with the implication that others do not possess it. How unfortunate.

The question of integrity of the FMB as it pertains to our responsibility to the SBC is real. Do we think that the SBC expects us to support junk theology? If we reinstate the money, could we in good conscience be able to stand before the SBC and say their trust is being fulfilled as it pertains to theological integrity?

There is now the question of Dr. Hopper's integrity as it relates to his involvement in the creating of this controversy both in Europe and the USA. Is it a breach of integrity to receive support from this Board and to actively work against a vote by this Board? Is it a breach of integrity to only share partial facts with both European and American supporters? Is it a breach of integrity to forget to mention the promises made to this Board concerning the addition of conservative scholars at the school? Were promises emphatically given and pled for at Glorietta? Is it a matter of integrity to not present a comparison of the number of students helped by our action? A tenfold increase in students helped cannot be considered a waste of funds! I can easily understand Dr. Hopper's having a difference of opinion with our action. What I cannot understand is his working publicly against what we have voted for while under our employment. Also, in light of the thirteen-year controversy, and especially in view of the meeting in 1988, why didn't he alert the Europeans that the SBC is seriously concerned about theological matters?

To my regret, it is obvious that some of the same questions raised in the preceding paragraph could be raised about members of the staff in Richmond.

The FMB could lose our integrity. If we allow ourselves to be intimidated by threats or to give in to blackmail of any kind, we will cease to be a true Board of Trustees. If we are never going to be able to disagree with staff leadership without having to face attacks that come about because of staff reaction to our decisions, then we have it backwards and the staff controls the FMB. In effect, we would answer to them, and they would answer to no one but themselves. If that is the case, then no one is really answering to the SBC. I seriously doubt the SBC elected us to act in trusteeship for them by mailing in our rubber stamp.

I thought it was our responsibility to vote budget and make policy. We did both. It was then the responsibility of the staff to carry out that vote. They have yet to do so.

Yes, we can lose our integrity. If we were to back up on what is clearly a scriptural issue, we would find the conservative majority of our denomination being very disappointed in us. They are not going to buy the ghost 'ethical commitment' excuse. Instead of worrying about a few liberals and their threats, we would do well to remember that the conservatives could do in mass what a few liberals have already done—refuse to continue to support this Board.

A man had a terrible addiction of chain smoking. Once in a while a friend would warn that the cigarettes would harm him and perhaps even take his life. He ignored those occasional warnings and continued to puff away. His addiction grew as he advanced in years. The warnings came more frequently, but they went unheeded as he thought them to be trivial and useless. Then one day a good doctor examined the patient and informed him that he had lung cancer and that surgery could take care of the cancer. The patient said that he would rather try chemotherapy, and did so in 1988. It didn't cure the cancer. In later examination, the doctor discovered that surgery was needed immediately if the body were to have any chance of survival. The lung had to go or the body was going to die. Some thought the doctor to be mean in his manner. They said his bedside manner could have been better. Some wanted to try some more chemotherapy, but only the doctor had the cure. Unfortunately, throughout his ordeal the man continued to smoke.

Brethren, this Board is not the bad guy. Rüschlikon Seminary has been smoking liberalism for three decades. This Board is the doctor.

The letter was unsigned. On December 5-6, 1991, John D. Hopper, President of the seminary in Rüschlikon; Karl Heinz Walter, EBF General Secretary; and Wiard Popkes, Chairman of the trustees of Rüschlikon went to Richmond, Virginia for discussions with FMB trustees. They met with the FMB Europe, Middle East and North Africa Committee; officers of the FMB; representatives of the CSI Committee; and FMB staff. The officers of the trustees did not allow the representatives of the EBF and Rüschlikon to meet with the full Board, or to address the full Board about their concerns over Rüschlikon and the FMB defunding action, or to face the accusers concerning liberalism at the seminary. The officers of the trustees controlled the entire schedule of meetings. Capable representatives had traveled at considerable expense in time and money from Europe to Richmond to engage in serious discussions concerning partnership in missions and theological education, but no such serious discussions were allowed or conducted.

If they had been allowed to have discussions with the full Board in an atmosphere of Christian courtesy and freedom, they could have told what they believe, what the governing principles of theological education in the seminary in Rüschlikon were, and could have answered questions concerning liberalism before the entire Board. In addition to discussing the "Charter of the Baptist Theological Seminary," they could have given "The Summary of Doctrinal Principles" which governed theological education at Rüschlikon. They were:

1. God
   1.1 The Sovereignty of God
   1.2 God the Father, who created the world and who providentially cares for it.
   1.3 God the Son, who redeemed the sinful world through his life, death and resurrection.
   1.4 God the Holy Spirit, who creates faith, sanctifies the believer, and empowers the church for mission.
2. The Holy Scriptures
   The authority of the Bible, the canonical writings of the Old and New Testaments, inspired and illumined by the Holy Spirit, as the only norm and rule for our Christian faith and practice, pointing us to Jesus Christ our Lord.
3. Salvation
   Salvation by grace through faith as God's answer to human sinfulness.
4. The Church
   4.1 The church as the gathered community of believers, proclaiming the Gospel, and administering believer's baptism and the Lord's supper.
   4.2 Congregational in government, autonomous in determining the will of God, yet cooperating in ministry.
   4.3 The priesthood of all believers through a personal relationship with God, who sets the believer free to bear witness to the Gospel of Jesus Christ and to work for justice and peace.
5. The Christian Hope
   The coming Kingdom of God, the hope for God's future, the consummation of the redemptive work of Jesus Christ, our Lord.

FMB Trustees Refuse to Reverse Defunding

On December 11, 1991, FMB trustees voted 54-27 to take no further action on IBTS Rüschlikon. Although they received many letters of protests from both Europeans and Southern Baptists, and although EBF and Rüschlikon leaders Karl Heinz Walter, Wiard Popkes and John David Hopper were in Richmond to meet with the full board, to plead the case of the seminary, to answer accusations concerning liberalism and to tell what they believed, they were not allowed to meet with the full board of trustees. The defunding of the seminary stood.

Some comments on the letter to FMB trustees are appropriate. The Europeans faced some of the same practical problems that the FMB trustees faced regarding the seminary in Rüschlikon. It was expensive to operate the seminary in Switzerland. It was true that more students could be trained for ministry in other places and that Rüschlikon had a relatively small number of students compared to some other institutions. One of the main purposes of Rüschlikon was to provide a high level of theological education in continental Europe so that Baptist students could earn academic degrees which were recognized in the complex European university educational system. Baptist schools could offer such degrees only through affiliation with a European university. Rüschlikon was unique among all Baptist seminaries in continental Europe through an affiliation with the University of Zürich. The intention of European Baptists was to send some qualified students from their countries to Rüschlikon to get high quality theological education with recognized degrees and return to service in their countries as church or union leaders or as teachers in national seminaries or Bible schools.

The seminary could not afford to pay full time professors to teach every subject that the curriculum required. For many years they had made requests to the FMB for Southern Baptist professors on sabbatical from their seminary to meet curriculum needs in Rüschlikon as adjunct professors. The seminary needed a professor to teach Latin for four months so that students could get the required courses when they needed them in order to graduate on schedule. Otherwise, they would have to extend their time at the seminary, disrupting their plans to enter ministry in their country and incurring additional expenses to the seminary and to themselves. Seminary administrators sent a request to the FMB for a professor to teach Latin for four months. FMB administrators filled the request by enlisting Dr. Glenn Hinson, a highly respected theologian by many Southern Baptists, but unaccepted by Southern Baptist fundmentalist leaders. Dr. Hinson could teach Latin; he would be on sabbatical at the time Rüschlikon needed a professor to teach Latin, and he accepted the assignment. Fundamentalist trustees at the FMB interpreted Hinson's teaching Latin at Rüschlikon for four months as evidence that Rüschlikon was liberal.

The letter to FMB board members mentioned that the agreement to give the property at Rüschlikon to European Baptists was an implied agreement. The actual agreement, negotiated and signed by European and FMB representatives was for the FMB to continue its level of annual support to the seminary of $365,000 through 1992, after which an annual decrease would occur for fifteen years, at which time the terms of the agreement would have been fulfilled. European and FMB leaders knew the terms of the agreement. One of the sins which brought God's wrath on Tyre was for ". . . *disregarding a treaty of brotherhood* . . ." (Amos 1:9b).

The letter to board members emphasized that it would be "a breach of integrity to receive support from this Board and to actively work against a vote by this

Board." Christians are accountable first to God. In Southern Baptist life, churches fund the various Convention activities, agencies and boards. Employees of the Convention receive support *from* the churches, *through* the boards, not *from* the boards. Convention employees hope they can avoid working against the board which supports them. Many Christians have faced the dilemma of whether to obey God or men. Peter and John faced such a dilemma by the demands made by the Sanhedrin. *"Then they called them in again and commanded them not to speak or teach at all in the name of Jesus. They replied, Judge for yourselves whether it is right in God's sight to obey you rather than God."* (Acts 4:18, 19)

The purpose of the seminary from its beginning was that it be an institution of higher education for all the Baptists of Europe. Diversity of Baptist beliefs and practices in the various unions and countries was at the core of the seminary's history, life and purpose. Regardless of how deeply some FMB trustees felt about what Baptists should believe about the Bible and how they viewed liberalism, they could not change the deep convictions of European Baptists about accepting and loving each other in their diversity. They could not impose their authority over European Baptists.

The letter was written about four years after the SBC Peace Committee appealed to Southern Baptists to stop labeling others as "liberal," "moderate," etc. Not only did the writer of the letter use such terms thirty-nine times, he applied them to European Baptists as well as to Southern Baptists.

The practical problem the fundamentalists faced was what to do when European Baptists would not submit to their authority. What they could do and what they did was to use Cooperative Program money as their weapon. They controlled and withheld the money they had promised. In partnership with European Baptists, Southern Baptists had generously purchased the property in Rüschlikon with Cooperative Program money and had been partners in various roles and ways for almost half a century to enable the seminary to fulfill its purpose. Yet, in one vote fundamentalist trustees reversed more than a century of partnership with European Baptists and almost half a century of partnership with them in theological education. The fundamentalist leaders knew and practiced no other way but to have their way.

Throughout Scripture the giving of false witness is a sin against God and man. It is one of the Ten Commandments. *"You shall not give false testimony against your neighbor."* (Deut. 5:20) The seriousness of the sin of falsely accusing another person is treated in Deuteronomy 19:15-21. Jesus said, *". . . So that every matter may be established by two or three witnesses."* (Matthew 18:16b) The apostle Paul wrote to Timothy, *"Do not entertain an accusation against an elder unless it is brought by two or three witnesses."* (1 Tim. 5:19)

These facts remain. During the entire ordeal not a single witness came forward to personally accuse with evidence any professor at Rüschlikon of denying the virgin birth of Christ. No student or former student joined the FMB accusers in charging seminary professors for teaching against the virgin birth of Christ. Not one sentence, paragraph, or page of anything the professors at Rüschlikon had ever written was produced to substantiate the accusation by FMB trustees that they did not believe in the virgin birth. Neither was any evidence produced against European Baptists leaders that they did not believe the Bible. The FMB trustees had built the substance of their crusade against liberalism on accusations they could not prove.

The practical and theological problems for the fundamentalist leaders would continue to mount. How could exclusive Baptists relate to inclusive Baptists throughout the world? How could they lead a program of missions throughout the world; claim to be obeying the Great Commission; exert their authority over Baptist people, churches, missionaries and unions who are free in Christ; and distribute credible information to intelligent Southern Baptist people in the information age?

CHAPTER 4

The (non) Apology

If we claim to be without sin, we deceive ourselves and the truth is not in us. If we confess our sins, he is faithful and just and will forgive us our sins and purify us from all unrighteousness. (1 John 1:8-9)

After the FMB trustees confirmed their earlier decision to completely defund the seminary in Rüschlikon, European Baptist leaders faced two new dilemmas. The first concerned how to relate to the FMB, which had been a reliable and trusted partner in missions for more than a century, but which had now unilaterally broken a signed agreement without consultation. Not only had the seminary been defunded, serious accusations against European Baptist leaders had been made. They had been accused of not believing the Bible, of being liberal, of having compromised their faith and of not being real leaders. In addition, Southern Baptist missionaries, with whom European Baptists had worked in full partnership, had been accused of not believing the Bible and of spreading heresy all over the world. The source of the accusations was FMB trustees.

The second dilemma European Baptist leaders faced was how to operate the seminary in Rüschlikon without FMB partnership in money and personnel.

Birth of the Cooperative Baptist Fellowship in Europe

It was in the context of these accusations and events that the Cooperative Baptist Fellowship (CBF) was born in Europe. The CBF acted quickly by taking an active, appropriate and needed role in Southern Baptist mission work in Europe. The CBF promised to raise all the support for Rüschlikon that the FMB had decided to withhold. In addition, the CBF reached out to Southern Baptist missionaries by promising to appoint and support any missionaries who were fired by the FMB or found it impossible to continue missionary service with the FMB while its trustees were accusing, judging and threatening to purge them.

In an effort to deal with the new relationship problems with the FMB, European Baptist leaders announced plans for a Consultation on Baptist Mission in Europe, to be held January 26-29, 1992 in Dorfweil, a German Baptist retreat center near Frankfurt.

The turmoil in Richmond over the defunding of Rüschlikon and the relationship between FMB staff and trustees worsened with the beginning of 1992. On January 3, 1992, Keith Parker, FMB Area Director for Europe, announced plans to take early retirement and to terminate his work with the FMB effective July 1, 1992.

Also on January 3, 1992, FMB chairman William Hancock wrote a letter to about 40,000 Southern Baptist pastors, state convention leaders, editors and foreign missionaries in which he explained from the FMB trustees' point of view the actions that had been taken concerning Rüschlikon. His letter dealt with: 1) The historical background, 2) The financial feasibility, 3) The theological concerns, 4) The questions of trust, and 5) The actions and conclusions.

On January 7, Isam Ballenger, FMB Vice President for Europe, announced his plans to terminate his work with the FMB effective May 31, 1992. With the announcements of Ballenger and Parker of their intentions to terminate their work with the FMB later in the year, FMB trustees terminated their active employment immediately, with salaries to continue a few months. They were unable to participate in the Consultation on Baptist Mission in Europe January 26-29, 1992. Winston Crawley was named FMB Interim Vice President for Europe.

During the turmoil European Baptist leaders tried in various ways to intervene in the worsening relationship with the FMB while at the same time they remained firm regarding the provisions in the agreement. On January 14, Rüschlikon trustee chairman Wiard Popkes wrote a letter in response to Hancock's letter. He dealt with the same five areas Hancock had addressed. In his letter Popkes quoted the agreement between European Baptists and the FMB when the property was transferred in 1988 and at which time the following financial promise was made. It stated: "that the Foreign Mission Board continue financial support until 1992 according to our current agreement (1988) at which time a gradual subsidy reduction be made up to a 15 year period to provide for appropriate transition."

People of integrity keep their agreements. The Psalmist described a person of genuine character and integrity. *"Lord, who may dwell in your sanctuary? Who may live on your holy hill? he whose walk is blameless and who does what is righteous, who speaks the truth from his heart and has no slander on his tongue, who does his neighbor no wrong and casts no slur on his fellowman, who despises a vile man but honors those who fear the Lord,* **who keeps his oath even when it hurts**." (emphasis added . . . Psalm 15:1-4)

Dorfweil Statement

European Baptist leaders invited representatives of all member unions to meet in Dorfweil. Thirty seven leaders from twenty three Baptist unions participated in the Consultation on Baptist Mission in Europe. The main objectives of the meeting were to discuss the action of the FMB concerning the defunding of Rüschlikon and to discuss the basis on which Baptists can work together in Europe. These issues were discussed with frankness and openness.

By the time of the meeting in Dorfweil the letter by FMB trustee Ron Wilson, written May 3, 1991, had been widely circulated among European Baptist leaders. At their initiative European Baptist leaders addressed the attacks by Wilson against Southern Baptist missionaries. They wrote a response to Wilson's letter, which stated: "We thank God for the effective work Southern Baptist missionaries have done among us. In our experience they have proved themselves to be committed servants of God, faithful to his Word and true partners with us in the work of the gospel. In particular we thank God for the outstanding contribution Dr. Isam Ballenger and Dr. Keith Parker have made to our mission in Europe."

The Statement also addressed the offensive language against European Baptists in Wilson's letter: "We have felt keenly the derogatory remarks made by some members of the Board of Trustees about European Baptists. We dare to believe such remarks would not have been made had there been more personal contact between the trustees and our churches."

Another decision the group made in Dorfweil was to request the EBF Division of Theology and Education to prepare a study paper on "What Are Baptists? On the Way to Expressing Baptist Identity in a Changing Europe."

Toward the end of the meeting a statement was prepared and agreed on by all participants except two, who abstained. A summary of the discussions was made in what was called "The Dorfweil Statement." The essence of the statement was five principles of Baptist partnership in Europe, with Scripture references given with each principle. They are:

1. Mutual respect in which the partners deal with each other with candour but with Christian courtesy. (Eph. 4:1-3.)
2. Spiritual freedom in which the partners, working within a common commitment, recognize and welcome differences of outlook and diversity of practice. (Rom. 15:7; Mark 9:38-41.)

3. Moral integrity in which the partners honour and maintain solemnly made agreements. (2 Cor. 1:12,17.)
4. Genuine consultation in which the partners confer together and aim for mutual consent. (2 Cor. 8:8-9.)
5. Reciprocal sharing in which the partners learn, work and grow together, each giving and receiving. (Rom. 1:11-12.)[1]

This statement followed the five principles: "We would see the above understanding as basic to any partnership into which we would wish to enter as European Baptists with any overseas Baptist mission agency."[2] The statement concluded with a proposal for a consultation in Europe between EBF leaders and representatives of the FMB, which stated: "We trust that such a Consultation might take place in the near future."[3] Within a short time both the CBF and the FMB adopted the Dorfweil Statement as a basis of cooperation in mission work with European Baptists. The FMB responded positively to the proposal that a consultation between FMB representatives and European Baptists be planned to mend the relationships that had been severely damaged.

International Baptist Church of Brussels Defunds European Baptist Convention

The defunding of Rüschlikon created difficulties in relationships for Baptists in Europe far greater than FMB trustees probably knew or intended. On January 26, 1992, the International Baptist Church (IBC) of Brussels, Belgium, voted to defund the European Baptist Convention (EBC). At that time the EBC was a convention of fifty-four international, English speaking Baptist churches and missions located in fourteen countries in western Europe. The total number of resident members was 4,065.

The roots of the EBC in the Southern Baptist Convention were close and deep. For the most part, Southern Baptists had established the churches. Many of the members of the churches were Americans living in Europe for a limited time and supported by the U. S. government as members of the Armed Forces or by U. S. businesses. The EBC had a long standing partnership with the FMB, with some Southern Baptist missionaries serving as pastors of EBC churches and others serving on the Convention's staff. It was a loyal supporter of the SBC Cooperative Program and of the Lottie Moon offering for missions. It was also a member and a supporter of the Baptist World Alliance and the European Baptist Federation. As a member of the EBF, it was one of the Baptist conventions/unions of Europe that Rüschlikon depended on for support.

The Brussels church had been a member of the EBC from its beginning in 1968. Both the EBC and the Brussels church accepted the SBC Baptist Faith and Message (1963) as their statement of faith. Although its contributions to the EBC had been decreasing for several years, the decisive action of the church and the stated reasons for it were shocking to EBC leaders and churches. The decision to defund the EBC meant that the church's annual contribution to the EBC would be slashed from 120,000 Belgian Francs to 12,000 Belgian Francs (from $3,636 to $363: One U.S. dollar equalled about 33 BF).[4]

Deacon chairman Nick Hine, from England, explained to the church in the business meeting on January 26, 1992 that the purpose of the action was not to withdraw membership from the EBC since it was an EBC member by its own constitution. The issues were that since the EBC supported Rüschlikon in its budget, the church was convinced the EBC was liberal. If the church supported the EBC, and a part of its budget was going to Rüschlikon, the church was supporting a liberal seminary. The motivation of the leadership of the church was to use their action to: 1) State our protest against what we believe was happening with our money; 2) Try and encourage the European Baptist Convention to review its policy on the seminary; and 3) To promote changes that need to be made throughout that organization (EBC).[5]

It is worth noting that Paige Patterson had considerable influence with some members of the church. About the time when the entire ordeal was occurring, Patterson tried unsuccessfully to raise the funds to purchase the facilities of the Belgian Bible Institute, located near Brussels, for a seminary that would have been established according to his vision.

Apparently the church leaders had intended to completely defund the EBC. When news of this was known by interested people in the USA, Hine said:

> We got blasted from all directions. And we then had some discussions with the Southern Baptist Convention leaders themselves. Phil Roberts was onto us, Paige Patterson was onto us . . . following our discussion with the Southern Baptist Convention we revised our proposal because they did in fact, explain to us . . . that our membership in that organization, if it were to continue, it actually costs them something to administer. And therefore we didn't want other churches paying for us . . . And when we go to the Southern Baptist Convention and explained to them what it was we were proposing, they were in fact very encouraging. And they said, if that is what you feel, that you don't want to be seen as supporting liberal activities, no problem. We support you in it. In fact, we would encourage you in it.[6]

Mr. Hine was asked by the minister of music: "Could you let us know with whom you've spoken, when you say you've spoken with the Southern Baptist Convention and the Foreign Mission Board?" Mr. Hine replied, "We've spoken with Paige Patterson and Bill Hancock, chairman of the Foreign Mission Board."[7]

The church voted to defund the EBC, with four votes against the proposal. Mr. Hine expressed an understandable and sincere complaint to the church. He said:

> This issue was made incredibly complicated for us as deacons because before we even had a chance to discuss it as deacons we were getting phone calls from outside this church. That is not the way to conduct business with this church. The congregation of this church needs to have the opportunity to discuss the issues which affect the life of this church before we start taking phone calls from outside.[8]

The support of the EBC for Rüschlikon should be seen in light of its overall support of missions. The total operating budget of the EBC for 1992 was $441,645, of which $83,870 had been voted for missions. Of the missions part of the budget, missions in Europe received four percent; the Cooperative Program of the SBC two percent; the Baptist World Alliance, the European Baptist Federation and Rüschlikon each one and one-half percent (each $6,419); planting new EBC churches five percent; the Missions Endowment Fund two percent, and the loan fund one and one half percent. Through budgeted giving, special offerings to numerous causes and designated giving, the churches had given $281,902 to missions in 1991, including $93,953 to the SBC's Lottie Moon foreign missions offering. The EBC's support of the Lottie Moon offering represented per capita giving of $23.11. In its vote to defund the EBC, the Brussels church voted to defund also all of the broad range of mission activities supported by the EBC, all of which needed financial support.

On February 11, the FMB Europe, Middle East and North Africa Committee, in light of the defunding of Rüschlikon and the growing unrest among missionaries, sent a letter to all SBC missionaries serving in those areas in which they affirmed the seven historic principles of missionary strategy.

1. A biblical basis for all we do.
2. Our primary purpose is evangelism that results in churches.
3. The incarnational approach, emphasizing the career missionary.
4. The priesthood of the believer—every Baptist is a witness and through volunteer opportunities can be involved personally in mission.
5. The indigenous principle, calling for churches established to be "natural" in their environment.
6. A comprehensive approach, not focusing on a single issue or using only one method, but trying to express the total scope of ministry.
7. Responsibility for communicating to Southern Baptists what is happening on mission fields.[9]

The letter further stated:

> Emphatically, there is no hidden or cryptic global agenda being projected by this Board . . . More than that, we affirm you and your work . . . Globally SBC missions witnessed more baptisms and church starts than any year in history.
>
> We attribute this to God's faithfulness and your witness. You have no cause for anxiety or concern that your ministry, approach, strategies, goals, plans or principles will in any way be modified, challenged, questioned or jeopardized by this Board.
>
> Under the leadership of Dr. Parks and the open door of our generation, we urge you to push on with the task. The past must not distract us, the present must not unnerve us, and the future shall only challenge us.[10]

FMB trustees met in Richmond February 10-12, 1992. The trustees agreed to meet with European Baptist leaders to try to rebuild the damaged relationships and named six persons to represent the FMB in the meeting. They issued this statement:

> We affirm our desire to continue in partnership with European Baptists, as suggested in the European Baptist Federation statement from Dorfweil. We shall appreciate an opportunity for a group of Foreign Mission Board trustees and staff to engage in consultation with appropriate European Baptist leaders, in the spirit of the five biblical principles cited in the Dorfweil statement, to review ways in which we can work together in Christ's global mission in accord with such principles.[11]

The FMB trustees voted how the money which had been budgeted for Rüschlikon would be reallocated among eight European seminaries. Two of those were seminaries in Bucharest and Oradea, Romania.

During the same meeting FMB president Keith Parks read a six-page statement concerning his future service as president of the FMB. He acknowledged: " . . . regrettably, sadly that the 12-year SBC controversy has brought change and crisis to our world mission program. For one thing," he said, "It now requires theological conformity from those who receive Southern Baptist money." he stated that European Baptists are active in evangelism, deeply involved in mission, and committed to spreading the Word of God. He cited statistics that the ratio of baptisms to membership is greater in Europe (1 baptism per 28 members) than it is in the SBC (1 baptism per 38 members.) "I am simply asking if I have the option of exerting positive leadership until 1995 and trying to fulfil the vision I believe God gave me."[12]

Winston Crawley, interim Vice President of the FMB for Europe, the Middle East and North Africa, arrived in Wiesbaden, Germany on February 19. He and John Merritt discussed the FMB's relationship with European Baptists in the aftermath of the defunding of Rüschlikon. On February 20, 1992, Crawley and Merritt met with German Baptist Union (GBU) leaders in their offices at Bad Homburg. Gerd Rudzio, General Secretary of the GBU, expressed his shock over the FMB action and raised numerous questions about the SBC and FMB. Several SBC missionaries were working in cooperation with the GBU and he expressed his appreciation of them and their work, as well as his concern about their welfare under the leadership of the current FMB trustees. On May 28, 1992, Winston Crawley, John Jackson, and Don Kammerdiener of the FMB wrote to Gerd Rudzio summarizing the concerns of German Baptist leaders and affirming Southern Baptist missionaries: "We believe they represent the best of Southern Baptist life and pledge to support them in their calling and ministry." They also "gave assurance that the Board has no global agenda (as has been reported) other than the following principles which have been reaffirmed twice in the last six months."[13]

CBF Supports Rüschlikon

On February 20, 1992, fifty Southern Baptists spent the day on the Rüschlikon campus. The group was led by John Hewett, moderator of the CBF. Speaking in chapel, he said:

> We have come to say 'yes' to you at Rüschlikon and to you Baptists in Europe. We have not come here to investigate you, or to try to find out what points of the Chrstian faith you may have missed, or to make you American Christians. We have come to sing God's praises with you and to affirm you. We are convinced beyond all shadow of doubt that you are God's people. You have had a whole year of Baptists in American saying 'no' to you, giving with one hand, taking away with the other . . . there are brothers and sisters who, when they think of you, thank God for you.[14]

At the end of his message Hewitt presented seminary president John D. Hopper a check for more than $219,000, making the total contribution from the CBF to Rüschlikon since December $240,000.[15]

On March 3, Romanian Baptist leaders Vasile Talos and Nic Gheorghita, acting for the Romanian Baptist Union, faxed a letter to the FMB's East European office in Vienna rejecting the $20,000 the FMB had voted for theological education in Romania. The letter stated: "Because of the misunderstanding raised around this subject and supported by Baptist Press concerning our stand, we cannot accept this money."[16]

Unrest throughout Southern Baptist mission work was intensified with the announcement of the resignation of FMB president Keith Parks. Following a closed "spiritual retreat" with FMB trustees March 19-20, Parks announced his resignation as FMB president, to be effective in October, 1992. A summary of his reasons for resigning were: 1) He had no clear trustee support for his request to remain until 1995; 2) There were differences in understanding of the president's role; and 3) There were basic philosophical differences regarding missions.[17]

On May 1, *EBPS* reported the resignations of John David and Jo Ann Hopper from their service as missionaries of the FMB. In a letter to Hal Lee, FMB Acting Area Director for Europe, Hopper stated that they "take this step with regret and sadness of heart, having served happily and willingly nearly 27 years with our Foreign Mission Board."[18] Effective with their resignation from the FMB, the Hoppers became missionaries supported by the CBF.

The EBF Executive Committee met in Stabbek (Oslo), Norway, May 1-3, 1992. Discussions within the EC included the future of Rüschlikon with the possibility of a complete relocation of the seminary and the Hoppers' new affiliation with the CBF. Regarding a possible relocation of the seminary, trustee chairman Popkes explained that since an earlier decision by the trustees not to re-open discussion about a possible new location for the seminary, the situation had changed in several significant respects. 1) The difficulties about obtaining visas for students' families had not been resolved, as had been hoped; 2) A sale of the property could be more easily achieved than had been previously thought to be the case; and 3) It was questionable whether the present site had potential for development in the light of new thinking about the seminary as a central institute for the EBF. The two cities under consideration as possible relocation sites were Berlin, Germany; and Prague, the Czech Republic.

Paul Fiddes, president of Regent's Park College of Oxford University and convenor of the EBF Division of Theology and Education, presented a paper on "Baptists in Europe," a work which had been requested in Dorfweil.

General secretary Karl Heinz Walter told of plans developing for EBF and FMB leaders to meet later in the year to try to mend the relationships that had been damaged by the defunding of Rüschlikon. The committee affirmed the decision of the Cooperative Baptist Fellowship (CBF) to commission John David and Jo Ann Hopper as CBF missionaries.

In a development which directly affected the mission work in Europe, the Middle East and North Africa, FMB trustees, meeting June 22-24, 1992, in El Paso, Texas, elected Samuel M. James as the FMB's Vice President for those areas.

EBF—FMB Consultation

Representatives from the EBF and the FMB arrived in the Fuchsbau Hotel in the suburbs of Hamburg, Germany, on Thursday, September 10, for meetings on September 11-12, 1992.

FMB Representatives were:

John Jackson, Chairman of Trustees, FMB.
Skip Smith, Chairman of the Europe, Middle East and North Africa Committee.
William Blanchard, Vice Chairman of the Europe, Middle East and Africa Committee.
Don Kammerdiener, FMB Executive Vice President.
Sam James, FMB Vice President for Europe, the Middle East and North Africa.
Also representing the FMB were Hal Lee, Acting Area Director for Europe; and Mike Creswell, FMB Staff Writer for Europe.

EBF Representatives were:

Theo Angelov, President of the Baptist Union of Bulgaria.
Peter Barber, General Secretary of the Baptist Union of Scotland and immediate past President of the EBF.
David Coffey, General Secretary of the Baptist Union of Great Britain.
Hans Guderian, Director of the Home Mission Board, German Baptist Union.
Wiard Popkes, Chairman of Trustees, IBTS Rüschlikon.
Karl Heinz Walter, General Secretary of the EBF.
John Merritt, President of the EBF and General Secretary, European Baptist Convention.
Also representing the EBF was Stanley Crabb, Director of European Baptist Press Service (EBPS).
Stanley Crabb, Mike Creswell, Hal Lee and John Merritt were Southern Baptist missionaries.

The representatives of the two groups had dinner together in the hotel restaurant. After dinner each group met separately to discuss the important consultation to follow. The EBF had initiated the meeting, would host the meeting and would bring important issues for discussion. Regarding the spirit they would take into the meeting, they decided to be positive in attitude and spiritual in tone with a view to reaching a clear understanding of each other's position and arriving at a mutually agreed on statement.

The Dorfweil Statement would be the primary basis for discussions. It was agreed that Merritt would serve as Chairman of the meetings and as host for the consultation. Wiard Popkes would serve as Vice Chairman. Merritt would welcome the participants and lead the devotional in the first session. David Coffey would lead the devotional on the second day. There would be times of prayer. Minutes of the discussions for the EBF would be kept alternately by Peter Barber and David Coffey on the EBF side. FMB representatives would be requested also to choose two secretaries to keep minutes. The four secretaries would write a statement at the end to be agreed on by all representatives. Tape recorders would not be used. Stanley Crabb and Mike Creswell would record sessions on their computers.

Among the issues the EBF proposed for discussion were:

1. **FMB policy.** What is the policy of the FMB to be in relation to unions and churches (to cooperate or by-pass?)
2. **Authority.** What authority do the representatives of the FMB have to speak on behalf of the FMB Board of Trustees? What will the outcome of the discussions be?
3. **Partnership.** What does it mean to say the Board of Trustees has affirmed the Dorfweil principles? How do they see the Dorfweil principles being worked out in practice? (could a Rüschlikon-type decision happen again?)
4. **CSI.** What is the role of the Cooperative Services International to be in relation to Baptist unions and local churches? What is Ron Wilson's role to be as chairman of the CSI Committee?
5. **CBF.** How does the FMB look on the EBF's cooperation with the CBF?
6. **Personnel.** What is the future to be on Stanley Crabb and Errol Simmons in terms of FMB support?
7. **Leadership.** What kind of person is to be appointed as Area Director and President?
8. **Theology.** What are the conditions on which the FMB will work with a National Union (in terms of the theology of the missionary and of the Union? Do they accept theological diversity?)
9. **East/West Europe.** How does the FMB look on Mission in western Europe as well as eastern Europe, and what is the policy of the FMB to keep and reinforce the unity among Baptists in Europe?
10. **Missionaries.** On what basis are FMB missionaries to be appointed in the future?

The FMB representatives were invited to bring any issues they chose for discussion, and the EBF could add other issues as the discussions required. EBF leaders did not know what issues the FMB might put on the agenda. Since the entire controversy had been initiated by the accusations of FMB trustees on "believing the Bible," a "high view of Scripture," and "liberalism," EBF leaders did not know what to expect from FMB representatives regarding these issues. In advance of the consultation Merritt sent to each EBF representative a copy of David Dockery's book, *The Doctrine of the Bible*.

The offenses the FMB trustees had committed against European Baptists were so broad, deep and severe that the sentiment among European Baptist leaders was that without a genuine and sincere apology on the part of the FMB representatives, there could be no agreement and no basis for cooperation in the future.

The consultation began as scheduled. After the morning devotional and prayer, Merritt welcomed all representatives and gave an overview of the schedule. Karl Heinz Walter presented a broad explanation of the EBF and its work. Sam James made comments about the FMB, its work generally and its desire to work cooperatively in Europe with European Baptists.

After difficult and intense discussions, an agreement was reached. Representatives from both sides were asked to convene and draft a statement of agreement, which they would bring back to the entire group for approval. This was done. John Jackson and Sam James signed the agreement on behalf of the FMB. Karl Heinz Walter and Merritt signed it on behalf of European Baptists.

The next steps called for the EBF representatives to present the agreement to the EBF General Council, scheduled to meet eighteen days later in High Leigh, Hoddeston, England, September 29-October 1, 1992. FMB representatives would present it to FMB trustees, scheduled to meet in Richmond, Virginia, October 12-14, 1992.

As scheduled, the EBF General Council met in England. The most important item of business was the presentation of the Hamburg Agreement for approval by the Council. The EBF Executive Committee asked Peter Barber to summarize the proceedings of the Consultation and to present the proceedings and the agreement to the Council. His entire statement, which was both accurate and comprehensive, follows.

Peter Barber's Statement

> I realize that not everyone here will be familiar with the background to this Agreement. Let me therefore begin by briefly sketching in the events that made the Hamburg consultation necessary and that lie behind much that was discussed in Hamburg.
>
> Last October, to everyone's surprise, the Trustees of the Foreign Mission Board decided to suspend their annual grant to the Rüschlikon Seminary. This meant a reduction in the seminary's income of almost 40% and at only 3 months' notice. What made it worse was that the

Seminary had been promised a full year's further support, to be followed by 15 years' continued support on a diminishing scale. The reason given was certain theological trends in Rüschlikon. In particular the temporary appointment of a certain Southern Seminary Professor whose theology was suspected by some of the Trustees was instanced.

Shocked reaction to the decision was widespread throughout Europe and also the United States. Many, many letters of protest were written. Yet, despite this protest and despite direct representations to the Foreign Mission Board in Richmond by Wiard Popkes and Karl Heinz Walter, the decision was ratified by a two-thirds majority at a meeting of the Foreign Mission Board Trustees in December.

After December events took a turn for the worse. Many saw in the decision a clear takeover of the Foreign Mission Board by the Conservative (Fundamentalist) wing of the Southern Baptist Convention. They were also shocked at the departure it marked from Christian integrity and the Foreign Mission Board's usual policy. A solemnly-made agreement had been breached without consultation and a decision made in a unilateral manner that was a denial of mission partnership.

As a result respected members of the Foreign Mission Board, who had held leading posts in Europe, resigned their positions by taking early retirement.

The President of the Board decided not to continue in office after 65 years of age, as he could have done. Other missionaries—some in key positions—also resigned, including John David Hopper, the President of Rüschlikon.

He and others like him were pledged support by an alternative mission group which was gaining in support among moderate Southern Baptists—the Cooperative Baptist Fellowship.

Among European Baptists there was grave disquiet. We could see the anxiety and uncertainty created among Southern Baptist missionaries serving among us and decided to hold in suspense any further requests for missionary personnel. In January, at a meeting of European Baptist leaders in Dorfweil, the situation was fully discussed and a Statement drawn up which was presented to the Foreign Mission Board.

In the Statement we expressed our shock at the defunding of Rüschlikon, our appreciation of the mission staff who had worked with us, our understanding of mission partnership and our desire to have a Consultation to air the whole matter. The Foreign Mission Board responded by saying they were willing to have such a Consultation. It was, however, delayed until the appointment of a new Vice President for Europe, the Middle East and North Africa, which only took place in August.

It was against the background of these eleven months of hurt, misunderstanding, strain and damaged relationships that 13 of us met on 11th September in the Fuchsbau Hotel in the outskirts of Hamburg. We knew the Consultation would only be meaningful if we challenged wrong decisions, exposed hurts, shared suspicions, asked difficult questions—and tried to move toward a basis of cooperation. All of these things took place.

At the Consultation the European Baptist Federation was represented by John Merritt, Kark Heinz Walter, Wiard Popkes, David Coffey, Theo Angelov, Hans Guderian and myself. On their part the Foreign Mission Board could not have sent a more influential delegation. They were represented by the Vice President of the Board (who will stand in for the President when he retires); also by the Chairman of the Board of Trustees and two other Trustees, the Chairman and the Vice Chairman of the Europe Committee. Hal Lee was also there as Associate to the Area Director, who is yet to be appointed. And—significantly—Sam James was present, the Vice President for Europe, the Middle East and North Africa, successor to Isam Ballenger.

As we met we were very conscious of being upheld by prayer, and it was in a spirit of prayer that the conversations proceeded with our President, John Merritt, in the Chair. The consultation began with John Jackson, the Chairman of the Board of Trustees, saying four things on the Board's behalf:

1. He offered an apology for the embarrassment caused by the Rüschlikon decision and for the hindrance it had brought to the work in Europe. It had not been the Trustees' intention to cast aspersions on European Baptists.

2. He affirmed that the Trustees did not have a global agenda in terms of spreading a certain brand of Southern Baptist theology; their one agenda was evangelism that plants churches.

3. He indicated that, at their June meeting, the Board of Trustees had wholeheartedly accepted the partnership principles in the Dorfweil Statement.

4. He stated on behalf of the Trustees that the cooperation of European Baptists with the Cooperative Baptist Fellowship would in no way jeopardize their relationship with the Board.

While our representatives were happy to hear these four statements, it was obvious, as the Consultation proceeded, that there were still many unanswered questions and the feeling persisted that the apology had not gone far enough. It was felt to be an expression of regret over the effects of a decision more than repentance over the decision itself. As the Consultation proceeded, time was given to briefing the Board's representatives on the up-to-date situation in Europe, but most time was given to probing certain areas of concern.

We asked—did the Board see Europe as one Europe or were they focusing on the East at the expense of the West? We were assured again and again that the whole of Europe was their agenda, though they were under pressure to give some outlet to the hundreds of Southern Baptist volunteers who wanted to come and evangelize in Eastern Europe. They felt there was the need to appoint someone to help coordinate this—but it was not their intention to treat East Europe as a separate mission field (as had been suggested in a private letter of one Trustee which had been publicly circulated).

Talking of letters, we probed at depth the Board's attitude to the letter of another Trustee in which it was suggested that the Foreign Mission Board should export a particular brand of theology and only cooperate with those who shared it. By way of response the delegation all affirmed that the contents of that letter (as of any individual letter of any individual trustee) was a matter of private opinion and not Board policy. The letter had been a source of acute embarrassment. The only person entitled to speak on behalf of the Board was its Chairman and even then it had to be on the basis of agreed policy, not private opinion.

They all affirmed that, contrary to the contents of that letter, the Board did not have a global strategy involving the exporting of the Southern Baptist controversy; their only global strategy (as already mentioned) was the planting of indigenous Baptist churches through evangelism.

We asked, if this is the case, why some of their senior staff had read the signs of such a development into the Board's policy—to the degree they had felt obliged to resign. By way of reply, they claimed that the situation had been made worse and confused by staff members reading Board policy into private letters; also by a change of stance on the part of the Board of Trustees who are becoming much more pro-active than in the past, in pressing for the implementation of Board policies.

The fact remained, we contended, the staff and ourselves had cause for deep concern over the Rüschlikon defunding decision. It had been morally wrong to breach a clear agreement in a one-sided way and without notice. This was a departure from past Foreign Mission Board policy and from expected Christian standards.

It was as we focused on this point that the breakthrough in the consultation occurred. Skip Smith, the chairman of the European Committee, who had been present in all the Rüschlikon decisions and had cast his vote along with the others, did confess to real regret over the decision. It had been hasty, he confessed, and taken in a spirit of stubbornness. 'I am sorry,' he said on his behalf and on the behalf of the others. 'We were wrong. The only thing we can do is to ask forgiveness.'

The (non) Apology

The forgiveness that was asked for was offered—in the presence of the Cross—and I believe all of us in that room experienced the Grace of God in a fresh way. We really felt we could bury the whole thing and make a new beginning. This is what we have done, I believe, in the 10 points spelled out in the Hamburg Agreement (as we have called it). Please take note of what it affirms:

We have affirmed the principle of freedom. There will be no attempt to bind each other into a creedal orthodoxy. The Federation will be free to develop its relationships with the Cooperative Baptist Fellowship. Unions will be free to decide when and how and whether they will extend their partnership with the Foreign Mission Board.

We have called for the preservation of unity among the Baptists of Europe—and for the avoidance of anything that might threaten that unity.

We have pledged ourselves to give fresh priority to mission in Europe, along with the Foreign Mission Board, on the understanding that the Board will confer with those of us in Europe in pursuing any initiatives. We have also promised to share on a global basis insights gained as we engage in such mission.

I believe the ten points, taken together, point to the possibility of a very positive partnership between the Foreign Mission Board and European Baptists—despite, and beyond, what has happened in the past eleven months.

Some of you may be asking, But what guarantees are there that the agreement will be honored in the longterm future? After all, the members of the Trustees Board change and the Southern Baptist controversy is not a thing of the past.

This was a point we raised—and pressed—during the Consultation. In reply the FMB representatives honestly admitted that they could not give a watertight guarantee that the Board would not change—any more than the German Union could guarantee that it would not change in the next 25 years. What they did guarantee was that as far as they were concerned, the agreement would be honored, and if difficulties did emerge at any time in the future, there would be a process of consultation. To that they were firmly committed.

Others might say—if the Foreign Mission Board representatives were truly sorry over the Rüschlikon decision, why did they not make amends direct with Rüschlikon, and as a sign of that, should they not reinstate the grant they canceled?

I suppose we took the view that the expression of their regret to us was the parent-body responsible for Rüschlikon and therefore sufficed.

No doubt another view can be taken, but any such direct expression to the Rüschlikon Seminary would need to be a matter of the Foreign Mission Board's free choice and could never be coerced if it were to be of grace.

As far as the question of reinstating the grant to Rüschlikon is concerned, this would seem hardly appropriate now that so much has changed. It is now a known fact that the Cooperative Baptist Fellowship has taken on responsibility for the grant and for the President's salary. For the Foreign Mission Board to insist on reinstating the grant would seem to be rather provocative and unnecessary.

All of us in the Consultation, as the discussions proceeded, felt that there was much about the past that would have to remain in the past. Mistakes were made, relationships damaged, people hurt and the cause of missions greatly hindered. The question was whether we lived in the past or moved from it to a new beginning.

Insofar as the past has been squarely faced, confession made and forgiveness offered, we feel we must, by the grace of God, seek to leave the past behind and make a fresh start in faith. It has strengthened our confidence that a person of the calibre of Sam James has been appointed as Vice President for Europe. In the light of his spiritual sensitivity and vision for mission, we feel we can work closely with him.

What the Hamburg Agreement offers us is an opportunity to start again within a partnership in which, by the grace of God and with a spirit of goodwill, we can avoid the mistakes of the past and build a stronger future. It is with this hope that I present the Hamburg Agreement to you on behalf of the Executive of the Federation and ask that you wholeheartedly endorse it.[19]

Peter Barber then presented the text of the Hamburg Agreement.

The Hamburg Agreement

PREAMBLE

Seven representatives of the European Baptist Federation (EBF) and six representatives of the Foreign Mission Board (FMB) of the Southern Baptist Convention met at Hamburg, Germany, September 11 and 12, 1992, to discuss the basis of future cooperation between the two bodies.

Discussions on many key issues were frank and open and carried out in an atmosphere of Christian love and included times of prayer and devotions.

1. REVIEW AND RECONCILIATION

The Consultation began with a review of the events relating to the decision to defund the Baptist Theological Seminary, Rüschlikon, Switzerland, which had led to the breakdown in relationships between the FMB and the EBF.

As the discussion proceeded, both parties increasingly recognized the extent of the damage caused by the decision, but they experienced by the grace of God forgiveness in Christ and reconciliation.

The EBF representatives were greatly encouraged to learn that the FMB trustees at their meeting on June 24, 1992, had unanimously endorsed the five partnership principles embodied in the Dorfweil Statement, written and adopted by EBF leaders on January 29, 1992. These principles are:

1.1 Mutual respect in which partners deal with each other with candour but with Christian courtesy. (Eph. 4:1-3)
1.2 Spiritual freedom in which partners, working within a common commitment, recognize and welcome differences of outlook and diversity of practice. (Rom. 15:7; Mark 9:38-41)
1.3 Moral integrity in which the partners honour and maintain solemnly made agreements. (2 Cor. 1:12,17)
1.4 Genuine consultation in which the partners confer together and aim for mutual consent. (2 Cor. 8:8-9)
1.5 Reciprocal sharing in which the partners learn, work, and grow together, each giving and receiving. (Rom. 1:11-12)

All participants in the Consultation agreed freely, unreservedly and unequivocally that these principles should form the basis of future partnership between the FMB and European Baptists.

2. FMB VICE PRESIDENT

The representative members of the EBF heartily endorsed the election by the Foreign Mission Board of Samuel M. James as Vice President for Europe, Middle East and North Africa. They recognized in him the kind of attitude to mission and Christian spirit which should lead to fruitful cooperation between the FMB and European Baptists. They look forward to working closely with him in the future.

3. PARTNERSHIP IN MISSION

It was the unanimous conviction of the group that they should continue joint ministry in Europe. They affirmed the basis of such cooperation, both in their spiritual unity and in the magnitude of the spiritual needs of Europe. With this conviction in view, they resolved to encourage European Baptist Unions to proceed with partnership relations with the Foreign Mission Board. They further urged the Foreign Mission Board to accept the on-going challenge of the whole of Europe as a mission field and to strengthen partnership with European Baptists.

4. COOPERATION WITH OTHERS

The EBF representatives indicated their intention of working with both the Foreign Mission Board and the Cooperative Baptist Fellowship (CBF). The FMB representatives reported that, by official action, their Board had given the assurance that this would not adversely affect relationships with EBF.

At the same time, the EBF representatives indicated their intention of discouraging any element of competition in developing relationships with both bodies.

5. MAINTAINING RELATIONSHIPS

Since true partnership requires continuous communication, on-going dialogue, and regular review regarding work and common concerns, the participants agreed to make these the basis of their future partnership.

Periodic visits of Foreign Mission Board administrators to European Baptist Federation leaders will be a primary feature of this interchange. This should be complemented by visits of European Baptist Federation delegations to Richmond.

6. PRESERVING CHRISTIAN UNITY

During the meeting it became clear that unity in Christ among Baptist churches and unions in Europe was particularly important in the light of the divisions the continent had experienced in recent years. Members of the Consultation agreed to urge those they were representing to do everything in their power to avoid disrupting this unity; rather, "*to keep the unity of the Spirit in the bond of peace.*" (Eph. 4:3)

7. BELIEF AND STRATEGY

The members of the Consultation jointly affirmed their belief that Baptists are a people who believe in the complete trustworthiness of the Bible and are committed to Jesus Christ as Lord. Likewise, they are a people of a confessional faith rather than a creedal faith. The FMB representatives also stated that the principal objective of their Board continues to be evangelism which results in indigenous Baptist churches. This, however, does not exclude the expression of Christian mission through other forms of ministry.

8. PERSONNEL AND PROJECTS

The Consultation agreed that wherever possible requests for career personnel and projects involving personnel should be arranged in consultation with SBC missionaries, Unions, and/or the European Baptist Federation.

9. URGENT ISSUES

The Consultation heightened the group's awareness of urgent issues in Europe today such as secularism, nominalism, religious bigotry, mass migration, the growth of non-Christian religions and ethnic conflicts. The participants recognized the need to tackle these issues and to share the insights gained on a global basis.

10. FUTURE ACTION

The members of the EBF delegation recognized that, while this agreement is made on behalf of the EBF, it is not binding on individual Unions. It is hoped, however, that it will encourage Unions to proceed with confidence in developing further cooperation with the FMB.

FINAL AGREEMENT

It was agreed that this document will be submitted for ratification to the EBF Council, September 28-October 1, 1992, and to the next FMB Trustee meeting, October 12–14, 1992. End of Hamburg Agreement.[20]

The motion for the General Council to endorse the Hamburg Agreement was approved with the two representatives from the Romanian Baptist Union voting against it. The Council voted also to approve the introductory statement by Peter Barber and to make it an accompanying document to the Hamburg Agreement.

The approval of the Hamburg Agreement by the General Council was an answer to the prayers of many people and the result of diligent perseverance on the part of Christian leaders. Considerable expense and hard work had gone into the preparation for the meeting and many hours of intense discussions had resulted in an excellent agreement.

EBF representatives were confident they had faced a monumental task and that God had led European and Southern Baptists into a new era of cooperation in missions and unity in Christ. They believed they had been faithful to their Christian responsibility to be peacemakers. The foundation of the agreement was the apology offered by FMB representatives, without which the agreement could not have been made. Skip Smith voiced the apology for the FMB. In the EBF's minutes of the consultation, the fifteenth section is entitled, *Apology*.

Full Text of the Apology

Karl Heinz Walter then gave voice to a concern that had remained with him even after the whole of the previous day's discussions. Were we in danger of dismissing too lightly the differences that had emerged over the Rüschlikon decision? What of all the trauma of the visit to Richmond in December when he felt some members of the Board of Trustees were sitting in judgment on his faith? What about the resignation of people like Keith Parker and Isam Ballenger? Were they completely misled in interpreting the situation as they did? Were we not in danger of downplaying the seriousness of the past twelve months and failing to recognize the damage that had been done?

Peter Barber went on to urge that there would have to be some kind of catharsis if relationships were to be fully restored. We could not ignore the past. The way in which the Rüschlikon decision was reached was wrong.

Until that was clearly recognized and confessed then the word of forgiveness and healing could not be spoken. Given that confession and apology we could go together to the cross and experience its cleansing and liberating power.

Skip Smith, in response, thanked Karl Heinz for showing where his heart was. As far as the Rüschlikon decision was concerned he, as a voting member of the Board, had done what he felt he had to do, though he admitted that if he had fully appreciated the ramifications he would have urged that they should not move so fast. He admitted that a certain measure of stubbornness and pride had emerged over the issue. He then referred to the kind of counselling he would offer couples where there had been a breakdown in their relationship.

If the man had been unfaithful and he asked his wife to forgive, she would not say, 'Before proceeding to forgive, what guarantees can you give me?' All she can ask is his confession and all he can seek is her forgiveness. So it was with the Rüschlikon matter. They could not offer absolute guarantees; the only thing they could do was to ask forgiveness. 'I'm sorry,' he said. 'We were wrong. Please forgive us and let us go on together. All five of us can sign a statement to this effect.'

John Jackson reminded all present that he had started off the consultation on a note of apology.

Peter Barber urged that in light of the place we had now reached we ought to go the way of the cross and put the past under the blood of Christ.

Bill Blanchard added that as far as he was concerned he thought it important that the trustees should have expressed their apology. The time had come to stop rehashing the past. As far as he was concerned he was ready to move forward.

The (non) Apology

Karl Heinz Walter thanked him and expressed his own desire to bury the past. We had now touched on the thing that, up till then, had been missing in the consultation. He was ready for a new beginning.

John Merritt led the consultation in prayer.[21]

Denial of the Apology

Apparently the FMB representatives faced serious difficulties in deciding how and what to report about the Hamburg Agreement to the full FMB Board of Trustees. They reported the text of the agreement but denied they had apologized to the European leaders for the defunding of Rüschlikon.

Two important histories of Southern Baptists were published by Broadman and Holman Publishers in 1994. One was *Whole Gospel—Whole World*, written by the late Baptist historian William R. Estep. It is a history of the FMB of the Southern Baptist Convention from 1845 to 1995. The other was *The Southern Baptist Convention—A Sesquicentennial History*, written by historian Jesse C. Fletcher. Although it was not until 1997 that this writer read these books, their revelance to the reporting of the meeting in Hamburg deserves serious scrutiny into the way the FMB leaders treated truth.

Concerning the meeting in Hamburg, Estep wrote: "Although, as (Sam) James reported to the trustees in the October meeting, 'never once did the trustees apologize for defunding Rüschlikon, but what they did say led to fruitful dialogue and the Hamburg Agreement.' "[22] About the meeting in Hamburg, Fletcher wrote:

> In October, just prior to Park's exit from the post he had held for thirteen years, the Board announced a ten-point agreement with European Baptists, worked out between European leaders and a group of FMB staff and trustees.
>
> The Hamburg Agreement, as it was called, allowed the European Baptist Federation to work with other Baptist groups, including Southern Baptist dissidents at work in the Cooperative Baptist Fellowship. An October 1, 1992, Associated Baptist Press release said the Europeans understood it as an apology for the Rüschlikon defunding decision. New FMB member Paul Pressler immediately denied that the agreement was an apology, though he said all concerned regretted the misunderstandings on both sides.[23]

To deny that there had been an apology was to give a false report. ***It was a lie****!* ***Anybody who says there was no apology is lying****!* The apology was essential to reconciliation and future cooperation. European leaders had believed the apology was genuine, had received it with trust that it had been sincere and had confirmed their resolve to resume good relationships by engaging in a prayer of gratitude to God for healing the breach of trust that had developed.

The Meaning of An Apology

An apology from one person to another person, or from a group of persons to another group of persons, is much like repentance to God. It involves acknowledgment of wrong, confession of wrong, and a request for forgiveness. People who cannot recognize and acknowledge personal wrong cannot apologize or repent. If they cannot repent there is no hope of change. They are like the *"righteous persons who do not need to repent."* (Luke 15:7b.)

If what the FMB representatives in Hamburg said was not an apology, what was it? Was it a prank? Did they fake a genuine apology? Did they say they had done wrong when they really didn't believe it and mean it? Did they treat as trivial what was in reality a deeply sacred and spiritual moment? Did some of us pray, believing we had actually reached a point of reconciliation while others were not sincere about it at all? Did we prepare a document of agreement and sign it, while the FMB delegation had no intention to carry out its principles? Did they say what the Europeans wanted to hear knowing they had no intention to change?

The FMB representatives were right in making the apology, because the trustees had committed a serious wrong. They were right in confessing the wrong that had been done and apologized for it. The information Estep and Fletcher got from FMB personnel was deceitful. Quoting the statements by Sam James and Paul Pressler, what they wrote was a serious distortion of what actually happened in Hamburg, which was a critical moment in the Convention's overseas missions work. The FMB representatives did not truthfully report to the full FMB Board of Trustees what they had said and how what they said led to a period of sincere prayer and provided the basis for the important agreement. They did not report that they had said to the Europeans that they were sorry, that they had done wrong and that they had asked for forgiveness.

Authority Over Truth

The FMB representatives deceived the FMB trustees and staff who were not in Hamburg by giving a false report. **A false report is a lie!** Their report betrayed the European Baptists who met, worked out the agreement and prayed the prayer of reconciliation in Hamburg. Broadman and Holman Publishers, the principle publishing agency of Southern Baptists, published the false report, **which was a lie!** Southern Baptists who read those two important histories of the Southern Baptist Convention were deceived by the false report. Most readers of books published by Christians have no reason to doubt the truthfulness of what Christians report, believing they can trust Christian leaders. **Many Southern Baptists read and believed the lie!**

Perhaps one day soon the representatives of the FMB who gave the false report will tell why they reported as they did. It is important for Southern Baptists to know why leaders who held such high positions of trust in the Convention's worldwide missions program deceived each other, lied to each other and gave a false report to their own Board of Trustees.

The theological and practical problems for the fundamentalist leaders were continuing to mount. The theological problem centered in who Jesus is and the kind of people his followers should be. Jesus gave much importance to truth, saying, *"I am the way and the truth and the life."* (John 14:6) He said often *"I tell you the truth."* (John 8:34, 45; 14:12; 16:7) The Holy Spirit, who lives in all believers, is *"the Spirit of truth . . . He will guide you into all truth."* (John 16:13) Followers of Jesus recognize the importance of telling the truth to each other. *" . . . Speaking the truth in love, we will in all things grow up into him who is the Head, that is, Christ."* (Ephesians 4:15) Telling the truth to each other is essential to healthy relationships between Christians and to their unity in Christ.

The practical problems for the fundamentalist leaders centered on the origin of the false reports and the practice of giving false information. **Somebody was lying and spreading lies!** The fundamentalist leaders had carefully selected Convention officers and trustees of all agencies, boards and institutions, all of whom were submissive to their authority. However, the leaders of the movement were not telling the truth to each other. If they were not telling the truth to each other, what had happened to truth in their movement? Where were the sources of false information in their movement? If their reports to each other were not truthful, how could the people in the churches throughout the Convention believe the reports the leaders were making to them? How long could they continue as leaders in the Convention without the integrity of being truthful? How long would it be before the people in the churches who had elected, supported and trusted them would hold them accountable for lying and giving false reports?

CHAPTER 5

One Missionary's Journey

I have been reminded of your sincere faith, which first lived in your grandmother Lois and in your mother Eunice and, I am persuaded, now lives in you also. For this reason I remind you to fan into flame the gift of God . . . For God did not give us a spirit of timidity, but a spirit of power, of love and of self-discipline. (2 Timothy 1:5-7)

My missionary journey probably began long before I was aware of being anything other than what I was at that time—a child growing up in a family of six in the small community of Macedonia, which is located about ten miles northeast of Hattiesburg, Mississippi. It was there that Inman and Lucy Walters Merritt, my parents, met, married and lived most of their lives.

We lived on a small farm, but Daddy always had another job to earn money to supplement what we grew or sold from the farm. My sisters, Mary Katherine and Cora Joyce, my brother J. P. (James Polk) and I were expected to help with farm chores. I did not realize that I was born during the Great Depression and how difficult the times were for my parents. I did, however, realize that I was a part of a larger extended family who loved getting together.

Both of my grandfathers were farmers and Baptist preachers who got to their preaching engagements by horses and buggies. Grandpa James Polk Merritt's ministry was in Forrest and Perry counties, Mississippi. Grandpa John Wesley Walters' ministry was in Jones County, Mississippi.

My parents were active members of Macedonia Baptist Church. Daddy was a deacon and Mama played the piano, taught Sunday School classes, and was the Royal Ambassador (RA: a missions education program for boys) leader. All members of our family attended church regularly.

Education, Evangelism and Missions in Church

Our church took seriously its mission to educate its young people in Christian principles and to plant the importance of Christian missions in their minds. The children of our church were taught that God loves everybody, and we sang often:

> *Jesus loves the little children,*
> *All the children of the world,*
> *Red or yellow black or white,*
> *They are precious in his sight,*
> *Jesus loves the little children of the world.*

A good number of RA boys met regularly in our home, where we sat and studied around our dining table. We had fun at those meetings and learned about missions. Mama taught us from the Scriptures that an indispensable dimension of being reconciled to God is to be reconciled to other people. In RAs, I caught a concept of Christianity, which is at the very root of the church's mission: *"We are therefore Christ's ambassadors, as though God were making his appeal through us . . ."* (2 Cor. 5:20a)

One of my first personal Bibles was a red-letter edition. I believed that all of the Bible was the Holy Bible. I believed also that all the passages marked in red were special because they were Jesus' words—the final words of authority and wisdom from God. *"In the past God spoke to our forefathers through the prophets at many times and in various ways, but in these last days he has spoken to us by his Son, whom he appointed heir of all things, and through whom he made the universe."* (Hebrews 1:1-2)

At a young age I made a personal confession of faith in Christ and was baptized. Some time later, two Scriptures confirmed the validity of my faith and assured me of my salvation. (John 1:12 and 2 Cor. 5:17-18) As a young boy I had a deep impression that God was calling me to be a preacher.

Our church helped to shape a generation of Christian leaders. Six from our generation were appointed by the FMB as foreign missionaries: Ralph and Cora Joyce Davis to Nigeria and Ghana, West Africa; Dewey Merritt to Nigeria; Jimmy and Susie Hartfield to Mexico; and I to Italy and Germany.

In addition, there were Dan Holcomb to theological education (professor at NOBTS); Newell Massey to the preaching and teaching ministry; Rayford and Lorinne (Massey) Moore to the pastoral ministry; C. O. Herchenhahn to the pastoral ministry; Harold Walters to the pastoral ministry, and Joe Walters, Jr. to the church music ministry. Others became Christian educators, business people and church leaders as lay persons. I am grateful for my rich, Baptist heritage.

Education

After graduating from Petal High School, I enrolled in Clark Memorial College, a Baptist junior college in Newton, Mississippi. While attending Clark, I was licensed to the gospel ministry by the First Baptist Church of Newton. I enrolled as a junior in Mississippi College where I majored in Bible and minored in English and Sociology. During college, I served on weekends as director of the youth choir of the Second Baptist Church of Kosciusko. In the summer of 1952 I served as youth director of Highland Baptist Church in Meridian, Mississippi.

I enrolled in New Orleans Baptist Theological Seminary (NOBTS) in the fall of 1952. While at seminary I was part of the team that conducted evangelistic and worship services every week in the Rescue Mission. This was an activity sponsored by the Home Mission Board, later renamed the North American Mission Board (NAMB).

In seminary I learned that every professor does not have to agree with every other professor about every detail of biblical interpretation. It was generally understood that Old Testament professors Dr. J. Wash Watts and Dr. J. Hardee Kennedy did not agree with each other about every detail of Old Testament interpretation. I was free to learn from both of them. I knew, however, that Jesus is the lifelong and ultimate teacher. (Matt. 10:24;11:29)

Dr. Leavell, President, taught the course in evangelism. He required all students to memorize one hundred Scripture verses for use in personal evangelism and witnessing. As demanding as the curriculum was, it was a valuable and meaningful experience. Another important experience while attending seminary was the periodical "Missionary Day," when the entire focus of the seminary was on missions.

It was during a Missionary Day that I heard Dr. Baker James Cauthen, President of the FMB, present a compelling and challenging message on missions. It touched me profoundly and probed the depths of my heart and mind. I knew then that eventually I would have to deal with the issue of whether God was calling me to missionary service.

My First Pastorate

In January 1954, a mission church in Chicora, Mississippi, called me to be pastor. It was a small church, but I was thrilled that I had been called as pastor and gladly accepted the call. I went to Chicora two weekends a month. I was ordained by the Macedonia Baptist Church. Daddy participated in the ordaining council, which was especially meaningful to me.

After a year of service in Chicora, a neighbor church, Big Creek Baptist Church, called me as pastor. I served this church also two weekends a month. Both churches were located in Wayne County, Mississippi.

I continued to serve the two churches as pastor after graduating with a Bachelor of Divinity degree from NOBTS in 1955. While serving the two churches I did a year of graduate school work at the University of Southern Mississippi in Hattiesburg. During the pastorate in Chicora, I met Elizabeth Pope, who later became my wife.

Sneads, Florida

Soon after marriage we moved to Sneads, Florida where I had been called as pastor of the First Baptist Church. Sneads was a small town in Jackson County, in the panhandle of Florida. The church people were wonderful to us and the opportunities for service for the church were many.

We saw Sunday School as one of the ways to develop a strong church. Together with the active involvement of the leadership of the church we experienced the growth we had expected. The Sunday School Department of the Florida Baptist Convention enlisted me to do Sunday School leadership training in several associations in western Florida. Our church was an active member of the Chipola Baptist Association. It was a wonderful time in our lives.

During the seven years we served in Sneads our three sons, Michael Paul; John Mark; and James Philip were born in Marianna. Being the father of three healthy and wonderful sons was a gift of immeasurable love and grace from God.

Beginning a Missionary Career

During the pastorate in Sneads, Elizabeth and I continued to deal with our call to foreign mission service. One day while I was in the pastor's study preparing a sermon, I decided that it was time to seriously consider a personal, specific missionary call. It had been several years since I had heard Dr. Cauthen's message that day at seminary.

I turned to Isaiah 6 and read the verses which tell of Isaiah's call to be a prophet. I read of his conviction of being unclean and unworthy, of his mouth and lips being touched, and of the voice of the Lord asking, *"Whom shall I send? And who will go for us?"* Then I read Isaiah's response, *"Here am I. Send me!"* (vss.5-8) The renewed call to me was clear, and my response was a wholehearted response to God: "Here am I. Send me!"

As we progressed toward appointment, we were surprised to learn that a detour from our original plans was required by the FMB. We had applied to serve in Nigeria. However, leaders in the personnel section of the FMB advised that it was not FMB policy to appoint too many close relatives to the same country. Cora Joyce, my sister and her family were serving in Nigeria. So were Dewey Merritt, my first cousin and his family. We were advised to explore other areas.

One day while I was in my study and reading the *Baptist Witness*, the news journal of Florida Baptists, I read an article about the urgent need for a missionary pastor to serve an English language Baptist church in Vicenza, Italy. My heart and mind became fixed on the need described in the article. Elizabeth and I read the article together, prayed and sought information on Vicenza. We became excited about what we were learning and asked, "Is this God's way of calling us to another place of service?" We believed it was. We requested the FMB to appoint us to Vicenza, Italy.

We were appointed in 1964 to serve in Vicenza. We learned during orientation that we would go immediately to the assignment, bypassing the language study that normally preceded a work assignment for missionaries. In September 1964, our family of Mike, 6; Mark, 3; Phil, 1; Elizabeth and I left New York bound for Italy aboard the steamship *Independence.*

Vicenza, Italy

Vicenza was a beautiful city in northern Italy, about thirty miles west of Venice, with a population of about 100,000 people, almost all of whom were Roman Catholic. There were two other small, non-Catholic churches in Vicenza: a Church of Christ and an independent, interdenominational English language group that met in connection with a Christian book store.

The First Baptist Church of Vicenza, an English speaking church, was composed primarily of US soldiers and their families and other support personnel for the US military base there. Southern Baptists had organized the church in order to worship, evangelize, train, support missions and have Christian fellowship in a community of Baptists and other Christians. Aided and encouraged by Southern Baptist missionaries in Italy, the church had joined the Italian Baptist Union and the European Baptist Convention (EBC).

Our church had invited the Executive Committee of the EBC to Vicenza for its spring meeting in 1965. I met many EBC pastors and renewed acquaintances with some I had known in college and seminary. I was impressed by the great fellowship that was evident in the EBC Executive Committee and was happy that our church was a participating member.

Our family greatly enjoyed the fellowship and work of the Italian Baptist Mission, which was the organization of Southern Baptist missionaries serving in Italy. Rome Baptist Church, served by Helen and the late Dub Ruchti, and the First Baptist Church of Vicenza were the only English speaking churches in Italy affiliated with the EBC.

All other Southern Baptist missionaries were assigned to various activities in cooperation with the Italian Baptist Union. These included an orphanage and home for the elderly, a training school for Christian women, a theological school, radio work and work with churches.

Language Study

Since we were career appointees of the FMB, we had to attend language school and pass a language proficiency exam. Dr. J. D. Hughey, FMB Area Director for Europe, the Middle East and North Africa, advised us to make plans to go to Perugia, Italy, to attend the University for Foreigners and engage in full time language study. I resigned as pastor of the church in Vicenza and in January, 1966, we moved to Perugia. After passing the language proficiency exams, we moved to our next assignment.

Milan, Italy

In the summer of 1967, we moved to Milan, Italy, a beautiful and fascinating city of about two million people. Milan was located in northern Italy, about thirty miles south of the Swiss border. Milan and its suburbs were highly industrialized.

My primary assignment was to serve as pastor of Milan Baptist Church, an English speaking group which met in a two-room chapel on *Via Paolo Lomazzo*. A few Southern Baptist families working with American companies and missionaries Jim and Gene Hester had founded the church.

There was one strong Italian Baptist church in Milan, located on *Via Pinamonte da Vimercati*. In addition, this church sponsored a preaching station across town on *Via Ponchielli*, where services were conducted on Tuesday nights. As soon as we were settled, I started attending the services on *Via Ponchielli*.

The pastor of the Italian Baptist church of Milan was Carmelo Inguanti. Pastor Inguanti and I developed a deep respect and love for each other that would last a lifetime. He was one of the best educated pastors in the Italian Baptist Union, completely committed to the Gospel of Jesus Christ and an outstanding preacher. He never owned an automobile, but used public transportation and the assistance of those who owned automobiles as the means to get to his preaching engagements.

Pastor Inguanti told me of two new missions he was helping to develop near Milan. One was in the small town of Casorate Primo, about a forty-minute drive from Milan. The other was in the suburb of Bollate. He asked me to help him develop these missions by sharing preaching responsibilities with him. One Sunday a month after Sunday School and worship in the English speaking church, our entire family would go to Casorate for worship. Elizabeth started a Sunday School for the Italian children and I preached to the adults. Once a month on Saturday afternoon I went to Bollate, where I first taught Sunday School for the children then preached to the entire congregation. Since neither group owned a building, all activities were in the homes of members.

Some time later the pastor of the Baptist church in Varese, Italy, Luigi Masino asked me to help him develop a mission of the Varese church in Gallarate, a suburb of Varese. I accepted his invitation, and began alternating preaching appointments with him on Sunday afternoons.

The mission elected me to serve on its Executive Committee. The mission was committed to maintaining and promoting good Christian relationships with Italian Baptist leaders and churches. This was not always easy and required hard work, time and genuine efforts for reconciliation. In the early 1970s relationship problems between the mission and leaders of the Italian Baptist Union were so difficult that Dr. Baker James Cauthen, Dr. J. D. Hughey and Dr. John A. Moore, the leading administrators of the FMB and its work in Europe, were called to Italy to intervene and give guidance to the work of the missionaries.

Some difficult issues were discussed and positions were clarified, which helped make continuing partnership possible. The alternative to serious efforts toward reconciliation is division in the body of Christ, which should be the last resort for Christians.

Although I deeply appreciated the opportunity to work in the new Italian Baptist mission churches in the Milan area and enjoyed serving with other missionaries in work that involved all of us, I believed my primary task was to serve as pastor of the English speaking Milan Baptist Church. There was a wonderful spirit of unity among the diverse members. They appreciated having a place to worship in English every Sunday.

European Baptist Convention

In July, 1971 Milan Baptist Church was accepted into membership in the European Baptist Convention during the annual Summer Assembly in Interlaken, Switzerland. The EBC was in the process of seeking an Executive Secretary. Early in

1972, the chairman of the Search Committee wrote me that the committee was considering presenting me for election to the position and that it would like to interview me.

I felt honored to be considered by the committee for the position with the EBC. Elizabeth and I immediately saw a great challenge in such a work. On the other hand, the very thought of making such a drastic change in the direction of our missionary work at that time presented a multitude of dilemmas for us. We had grown to love Italy and had thought it would be our place of service throughout our missionary career. We loved Milan and the work we were doing. We felt loved and accepted by our missionary colleagues and the people we worked with in our area, both in English and Italian speaking work. At that time I was chairman of our mission, which was continuing to work through some difficulties in its relationship with the Italian Baptist Union.

I wrote to the chairman that we needed time to carefully consider whether to proceed with an interview with the committee. It was agreed for us to take the time we needed. Elizabeth, our sons and I prayed earnestly about the decision. We discussed the many changes accepting the new position would require for our family. It would require us to transfer from Italy to Germany. It would mean leaving a language all of us were feeling comfortable in and beginning again in a new country, culture and language. Our missionary work would be structured in a much different way. For the first time I would not be my family's pastor, nor would I be the pastor of a particular church. We informed our missionary colleagues of the decision we were facing and asked them to pray with us about it.

After some months we believed that God was opening a door for us into a new and challenging ministry and that we should accept. The possibility of serving as Executive Secretary of the European Baptist Convention had a growing appeal to me. I had felt a deep and rich Christian fellowship among the people of the EBC in the meetings I had attended. Although the job description was challenging, I believed God would enable me to give good leadership to the EBC. One part of the job description that appealed to me was this: *"The Executive Secretary's dedication to Christian principles, as well as pastoral experience, should make him a trusted friend and counselor to all persons in church leadership."*

Dr. Hughey and the FMB approved our transfer from Italy to Germany. The EBC elected me as Executive Secretary on July 11, 1972, during the Summer Assembly in Interlaken. (NOTE: Over time the title was changed from Executive Secretary to Executive Director to General Secretary, although the job description remained basically the same. For clarity, the last title is used in this book.)

In October 1972, the EBC was comprised of thirty-nine churches located in eight countries of western Europe: Austria, Belgium, England, France, Germany,

Greece, Italy and Spain. Membership was reported as 3,282. The budget adopted for 1973 was $60,750, an increase of more than $15,000 over the previous year. The baptism ratio was one baptism for eleven members.

Unity in Diversity

Building unity in the EBC was important to me. The churches were scattered far from each other over a vast territory. Each one belonged to a larger fellowship of Baptists through the EBC. Building relationships with pastors and visiting churches were important ways to build unity. The pastors, their families and the people in the churches were the greatest resources we had. There were serious limitations on every hand. The EBC owned no property, and only six churches owned a church building. No church had a parsonage. The EBC office was in the basement of our apartment, where we wrote letters to pastors and churches on a typewriter with an Italian keyboard and duplicated materials on a mimeograph machine. There was no additional EBC office staff.

The pastors were a diverse group. Eight were Southern Baptist missionaries. Five were active duty military personnel. Eighteen had been called and were supported by local churches. Some were college and seminary graduates, others were not. A few churches did not have a pastor. Normally, about three years was the maximum tenure of an EBC pastor. Pastors who stayed longer added experience, stability and vision to the work.

Most members of churches were active less than three years, after which they moved to another business or military assignment. Churches were aggressive in outreach. They needed to replace departing members with new members or face decline or even extinction. In such challenging circumstances many churches had excellent growth.

Membership in European Baptist Federation and Baptist World Alliance

Although the EBC was not a member of the European Baptist Federation, a fellowship of twenty-six national Baptist conventions/unions, the EBC supported the EBF in its budget. As a gesture of fellowship the EBF invited a representative from the EBC to its General Council meetings as a non-voting participant. I attended EBF General Council meetings and began to learn about the EBF, its fellowship and its work.

I was impressed by the highly competent people who had been elected by the various unions to represent them on the Council. I agreed with the three basic purposes of the EBF: 1) To draw together Baptists on the basis of their Christian witness and distinctive conviction; 2) To encourage and inspire them in fellowship and shared responsibility in Europe; and 3) To seek in all its endeavors to fulfill the will of Jesus Christ, Saviour and Lord.

Not least among my early impressions was the deep Christian fellowship that was shared among the Baptist leaders of Europe. The fellowship bridged many gaps and man-made barriers of different systems of government of the various nations. It bridged the barriers of historic linkage with the past such as Nordic, British, Germanic and Latin ancestry.

Of vital importance was the fact that it was bridging the barrier between free Europe and Communist Europe. The Baptist leaders from Communist countries and those from free countries genuinely loved each other. There was no doubt or hesitation in my mind that the EBC rightfully belonged in the fellowship and life of the EBF.

In September 1974, the EBF General Council invited the EBC to become a full member of the EBF. In its annual meeting the following month the EBC voted unanimously to accept the EBF's invitation. In the same annual meeting the EBC voted to request membership in the Baptist World Alliance. The BWA accepted the EBC as a member at the Congress in Stockholm, Sweden, in 1975.

First Visit To A Communist Land

In 1975, the EBF General Council elected me as a member of its Executive Committee. Russian Baptist leaders invited the Executive Committee to meet in Moscow in the spring of 1976. We had our meetings and participated in worship services in the Central (First) Baptist Church of Moscow.

After the Executive Committee meetings, we were invited by Russian Baptist leaders to visit Baptist churches and pastors in various parts of the Soviet Union. I visited pastors and churches in Leningrad (now St. Petersburg) and the Baltic States and their capital cities: Tallinn, Estonia; Riga, Latvia; and Vilnius, Lithuania. Although atheistic propaganda was dispersed and Christian churches were suppressed throughout the Soviet Union, Baptists fought to keep their churches open where the gospel of Jesus Christ was openly preached. Christians were often despised, discriminated against, harassed and spied upon. Many Christians were sent to prison, where some died. They were astute in maximizing limited freedoms, legally and morally challenged the civil authorities and entered every door of opportunity open to them. They were well informed about international agreements the authorities of their government signed and challenged those authorities to keep the agreements. Beneath harsh oppression they bent but did not break.

As I learned about some needs of churches and unions in Communist lands, I informed EBC pastors and churches of those needs and encouraged them to give to support such causes, which they did.

Growth and Expansion

The Foreign Mission Board was an invaluable resource for pastors of EBC churches, especially for churches with great potential for growth in large cities. As the number of churches grew, the need for additional office staff to serve the churches grew also. At the EBC's request, various persons on short-term assignments were sent by the FMB to help the churches.

The first request to the FMB for a full time additional staff person to give leadership to EBC was for a journeyman to serve as the convention's youth director. In 1976 the FMB sent James (Jim) Smith who served effectively for two years. Later he and his wife, Becky, were appointed as career missionaries to Austria.

In response to the EBC's request for missionaries to serve as directors of youth and singles ministries, the FMB appointed Rick and Nancy Dill as career missionaries to the EBC. As the EBC continued to grow, a request was made for staff persons to lead in Christian education training in churches. In 1983 Glen and Nina Pinkston were appointed by the FMB for this work.

A competent and hard working staff enabled the EBC to serve churches in ways it had not been able to do earlier. The Dills developed an international ministry to single adults and helped equip churches to implement this ministry. The Pinkstons led in the development of a broad range of educational ministries, Baptist Brotherhoods, deacon training, WMU work and assisting pastor search committees.

The FMB provided the salary and other benefits for EBC staff personnel, while the EBC provided housing, office space, automobiles and travel expenses.

Partnerships in the Gospel

By 1983 the EBC had grown to forty-six churches in ten countries with a budget exceeding $200,000. As valuable as the partnership with the FMB was, in order to serve the churches better the EBC sought a specific partnership with a state convention of the Southern Baptist Convention. In 1983 the EBC and the Baptist State Convention of North Carolina began a three-year partnership. North Carolina Baptists assisted the EBC in numerous ways, including sending and supporting an office secretary and treasurer; sending *The Biblical Recorder* to every pastor; conducting leadership training in education, evangelism and stewardship; and providing pastors and interim pastors.

The partnership with North Carolina Baptists was followed by a five-year partnership with Texas Baptists, followed by partnerships with Arkansas Baptists and Kentucky Baptists, all of which provided invaluable assistance.

While the EBC had partnerships with Southern Baptists it also had partnerships with European Baptists, including the Baptist Union of Poland and Baptist unions in the Czech Republic, Slovakia and Bulgaria.

A Vision for the Nations

In addition to planting and serving EBC churches, increasing the staff and developing partnerships, EBC leaders and churches were enlarging their vision for the strategic role English language churches could have in reaching people from many nations with the gospel of Christ. People from all continents and many nations were coming to great European cities for work, study, research and as refugees. Many spoke English as a first or second language. Others responded readily as churches provided opportunities for people to learn English. Baptists from many nations sought and found English speaking Baptist churches. Some EBC churches were reaching people from more than twenty nations. Practically all churches had members other than Americans.

As more and more people were challenged to enlarge the vision in their churches, some churches changed their names to *International* Baptist Church. Changing the name to *international* was both an acknowledgement that the churches were indeed diverse in membership and an expression of the intention and objective of churches to become more inclusive of all nationalities. A survey done in the early 1990s revealed that more than one hundred nations were represented in EBC churches.

New EBF Leadership

During the EBF Congress in Budapest, Hungary, July 26-30, 1989, the EBF elected Karl Heinz Walter of West Germany as General Secretary. Peter Barber of Scotland was installed as President for a two-year term. I was elected Vice President.

In the EBF constitution the General Secretary is elected to a five-year term and can be re-elected. The election of a Vice President is regarded as the beginning of four years of service in EBF leadership. After two years as Vice President, the person is installed without further election to a two-year term as President. Being elected as Vice President was truly an honor and a humbling experience for me. Never before had anyone other than a European been elected to the office.

Just over three months after the election of EBF leaders, the wall between eastern and western Europe fell. The collapse of Communism throughout the countries of eastern Europe was rapid. Many people throughout those countries faced shortages of food, heat, medicine and electricity as services became chaotic. Christians and other aid services contributed money and sent food parcels to those in need. EBC churches contributed generously to help.

Building Churches Where Walls Stood

The changes in Europe that followed the fall of the wall had profound effects on the EBC in two ways. On one hand, the new freedom and peace were answers to prayer and brought hope and new opportunities to millions of people. On the other hand, the political changes that followed were devastating to the EBC and many EBC churches. The number of churches and missions had grown to fifty-eight, located in thirteen countries in western Europe. The budget was $382,400.

No longer was the large number of American Armed Forces personnel needed in Europe to defend against a threat that had collapsed. In efforts to cut military spending, the United States government acted quickly by reducing the number of active duty military personnel in Europe from about 300,000 to under 100,000. Many military families returned to the States. Numerous U. S. bases, hospitals, schools and other facilities were closed.

Within six years about 20 EBC churches were forced to close. Some bases remained but were reduced in size. Some churches near those bases were severely weakened with the loss of military members and budget decreases.

The closing of twenty churches and the budget crises in other churches resulted in budget reductions in the EBC. Churches that had generously supported the EBC could no longer contribute as much. Difficult choices had to be made about budget priorities.

The other result of the fall of Communism was the opening of a new field of opportunity for the EBC. Great cities of the former eastern Europe were seen with a new vision as places where international, English language Baptist churches could be started. The theme of the 1990 EBC annual convention was ***Building Churches Where Walls Stood.***

Because of the vision to plant international, English speaking churches in great European cities, the EBC requested the FMB to send a missionary couple to lead the venture to plant churches. The FMB transferred Ray and Helen Reynolds from Belgium to Germany to lead the EBC's church planting venture.

In a cooperative venture between national Baptist leaders, the EBC and the FMB, international Baptist churches were planted in Bucharest, Romania;

Budapest, Hungary; Bratislava, Slovakia; Kiev, Ukraine; Moscow, Russia; Prague, the Czech Republic; and Warsaw, Poland. The EBC and national Baptists planted churches in Sofia, Bulgaria; and St. Petersberg, Russia, without pastoral leadership from the FMB.

The vision to plant new churches gave new life to the EBC at a time when a lesser vision might have demoralized the churches. Although the EBC lost churches following the fall of the wall, the number of churches and missions by 1996 had grown to sixty seven, located in twenty one countries in both eastern and western Europe. Although the challenging budget of $387,900 was not met, churches contributed $318,942 to the budget.

EBF Presidency

During the EBF General Council meeting in Varna, Bulgaria, the Council installed me as President on September 28, 1991, in the Varna Baptist Church. Little did I know at that time that the road ahead of me would be long, winding and often surprising and would lead me into the middle of an unwanted international Baptist controversy.

Less than two weeks after my installation as President of the EBF, on October 9, 1991, the trustees of the Foreign Mission Board voted to defund the Baptist Seminary in Rüschlikon, which provoked a new crisis in relationships between European Baptists and the FMB. This crisis presented a difficult dilemma for me personally because of numerous potential conflicts in the new situation. I was the General Secretary of the EBC, which was a member of the EBF and which supported Rüschlikon in its budget. I had recently been installed as EBF President, which suddenly had a serious relationship problem with the FMB. I was a missionary of the FMB, whose trustees had defunded Rüschlikon, and who also had administrative authority over me. After considering these potential conflicts, I called Karl Heinz Walter, EBF General Secretary, and expressed my willingness to resign as EBF President. Karl Heinz did not accept my offer to resign. He consulted with other European Baptist leaders, and in a conference telephone call they affirmed their confidence in me as their President in that crucial time and asked me to continue serving as President.

The potential conflicts for me could also be possible contributors toward healing the difficulties in relationships. On the positive side, I believed God could use me in my various roles with the EBC, EBF and FMB to work with others to make genuine efforts to bring peace, understanding and reconciliation between European Baptists and the FMB. Although I had responsibilities to the EBC, EBF and FMB, ultimately I belonged to Christ. I saw this as a time to help "*settle disputes for many peoples*," (Isa. 2:4b); to exercise "*the ministry of reconciliation*," (2 Cor. 5:18b); and to be a peacemaker, which is a characteristic of Christians that entitles them to be called "*sons of God*." (Matt. 5:9)

The action the FMB trustees had taken regarding Rüschlikon was not only a dilemma for me, but also for the EBC, which had a partnership relationship with the FMB for three decades. If such a sudden and shocking decision could be taken concerning Rüschlikon, might a similar decision be taken regarding the EBC? Might some of our pastors, laypersons and churches approve the action of the FMB and bring division to the EBC, which we had tried to lead in unity? I knew that many uncertainties lay ahead.

FMB's New Policy in Europe

The trustees of the FMB made two decisions regarding work in Europe in its meeting of February 8-10, 1993. The trustees elected John Floyd as area director for Europe. He and his wife, Helen, had earlier served eleven years as FMB missionaries in the Philippines. Floyd was elected from his position as Vice President of Mid-America Baptist Theological Seminary in Memphis, Tennessee. In another action, the trustees voted to create a new Eastern Europe Area, thus dividing FMB administration in Europe into two areas. In the meeting in Hamburg, European Baptists had emphasized to the FMB delegation the importance of seeing all of Europe as one area and with European Baptists and FMB personnel working for unity in European Baptist work, in both fellowship and administration. The FMB delegation assured European Baptist leaders that they, too, saw all of Europe as one area and that they and FMB missionaries would work for unity in European Baptist life. The FMB failed to keep its promise to work for unity in European Baptist life.

Unity In EBF Threatened Over Role of Women in Leadership

In the summer of 1993, as the time neared for my service as EBF President to end and for Birgit Karlsson to be installed as President, a serious controversy arose that threatened the unity of the EBF. Birgit was General Secretary of the Baptist Union of Sweden, an ordained pastor and a woman. There had been no opposition to her election as Vice President. However, as the time approached for her to be installed as President during the EBF General Council meeting in Kishinev, Moldova, September 18-25, opposition to her installation arose in the Romanian Baptist Union and in some parts of the Euro-Asiatic Federation (CIS—Baptist Unions in areas formerly served by the All Union Council of

Evangelical Christians-Baptists of the Soviet Union). The problem, as they saw it, focused on the fact that Birgit was a woman who had been ordained to the gospel ministry as a Baptist pastor.

On July 1, the EBF office received a fax from the Romanian Baptist Union's Council which stated:

> In the meeting of the council of our Union, on June 16, 1993, we discussed the fact that a woman who is ordained as pastor will become the President of the EBF. The Council was unanimous in deciding that we consider the ordination of women as pastors unbiblical. Due to the fact that an ordained woman will be installed as President of the EBF in Kishinev, we decided that our Union will not be represented at that meeting.[1]

EBF leaders were saddened that Romanian Baptist leaders would not be represented in the Council meeting in Kishinev since they had been active participants in the fellowship, leadership, and life of the EBF for generations. They did not want Christian fellowship and unity in the EBF to be disrupted over such an issue and took the initiative during BWA General Council meetings in August in Harare, Zimbabwe, to get representatives of the various unions together with BWA and EBF leaders to seek reconciliation concerning the matter.

A meeting took place first with Romanian leaders. Karl Heinz Walter (Germany), David Coffey (England), Birgit Karlsson (Sweden) and I representing the EBF; Denton Lotz (USA) and Knud Wumpelmann (Denmark) representing the BWA; and Nic Gheorghita and Paul Negrut representing the Romanian Baptist Union met to discuss the problem.

There were important historical differences in the various countries that affected how they interpreted Scripture. Sweden had remained a neutral country during the Second World War and during the Cold War. It had a long history of freedom and free elections of leaders, and one of the highest living standards in the world. Politically, it used its neutrality as a leverage to further the causes of peace and freedom throughout the world. The Nobel Peace Prize was endowed by the Swedish inventor, Alfred Nobel, who invented dynamite. Realizing the potential destructiveness of his invention, he established the peace prize to honor those who make extraordinary efforts to achieve peace in the world.

Life had been very different for Romanians, Russians and all the other people in the former eastern Europe. Their nations and people had been ravished during World War II and brutalized during Communist rule. Their economies had collapsed under the weight of corruption and the costs of military armaments. Freedom to think and to speak openly had not been allowed under Communism.

In these circumstances, Baptist life took very different paths. Swedish Baptists recognized and respected the equality of spiritual gifts that God gives to both men and women. Swedish Baptists had been among the leaders in BWA and EBF life. Eric Ruden of Sweden served as EBF President in 1958-59, and as General Secretary 1959-65. His wife, Kerstin Ruden, gave strong and gracious leadership to the development of Baptist women's work throughout Europe, serving as both Secretary and President of European Baptist Women's Union (EBWU). She traveled with her husband and was invited to visit Baptist women's groups throughout Europe, including those in Communist countries. Capable women from Communist countries, such as Julia Gero of Yugoslavia, who later served as President of EBWU, helped build strong Christian work among women.

Baptists in Romania, Russia and throughout the former eastern Europe courageously evangelized and defended their faith against Communist oppression. Their leaders had been EBF leaders too. Both Alexei Bichkov of the USSR and Vasile Talpos of Romania had served as Presidents of the EBF. Most people in those countries had little time or energy to give to the cause of peace beyond their borders.

The group dealt with the complexity of the issue in Scripture, in church life and in the world family of Baptists. Both sides arrived at their points of view on the basis of Scripture and how they interpreted it. Although at that time the issue of women being ordained as pastor was focused on Birgit, it was much broader than any personality. She had offered to step aside and not be installed as President if her installation would disrupt the unity in Christ in the EBF. She said this was the first time in all her service for Christ that she was treated differently because she was a woman.

Two great principles were at stake. The first was freedom in Christ. Were individuals, churches and Baptist unions free to study Scripture and obey Christ as they believed the Spirit was leading them? The second was unity in Christ. Christ had accepted Romanians, Russians, Swedes and all others who believed in him into his one body. He had given all believers the same Holy Spirit. Should Swedish Baptists say to Baptists who were a part of the body of Christ and who thought differently about this issue, "We have no need of you. We cannot have fellowship with you?" Or should Romanian and Russian Baptists say the same about their Christian brothers and sisters in Sweden and other Baptists churches and unions that ordain women?

Could any of the EBF leaders say to any others, "You are not wanted or needed," when Christ had accepted them, just as he had us? The solution was love. We thought the greatest commandment, the highest law of Christianity, the law of love, could bridge the gaps of understanding and diversity of practice between

Baptist individuals, churches and unions across nations. We believed that through Christian love and acceptance and by obeying Christ, we could sustain Christian unity in the EBF.

We concluded that all believers in the EBF unions belonged to Christ and to his one body. Belonging to the one body of Christ, all belonged also to each other, although we might see some issues differently. We believed the plan to install Birgit as president was right from an EBF constitutional point of view and was morally and spiritually right because she was a highly respected Christian person, an ordained minister of the gospel, a leader in the EBF and in her own Baptist Union of Sweden. She had previously served as a Vice President of the BWA.

We appealed to Brothers Gheorghita and Negrut to do everything possible to help others in their Union to see the issue in light of freedom in Christ, unity in the Spirit, and Christian love. We urged them to try to get their union to send representatives to Kishinev, and to try "to keep the unity of the Spirit in the bond of peace" in the EBF. We prayed fervently for unity in the entire EBF.

Reporting on the meeting, Karl Heinz said:

It was a time of open sharing and the discussions took place in a very deep and spiritual, brotherly atmosphere. At the conclusion of the Harare meeting, it was stated, in particular by Gheorghita, that the Romanians felt their concerns had been heard and understood. The EBF leaders, on the other hand, had assured the Romanian brethren that no one would try to force any union in the EBF to accept the ordination of women. The EBF leaders further emphasized that Birgit Karlsson was elected EBF Vice President by reason of her position as General Secretary of the Swedish Baptist Union and in recognition of her leadership in Europe and around the world. The explanation of BWA Secretary Lotz in his letter to the Romanian Baptist Union seemed acceptable to all—that the position of President is *functional* and not sacramental.[2]

Karl Heinz, Birgit and I later met with Alexander Firisiuk, who represented the Euro-Asiatic Federation (CIS) and his interpreter to make the same appeals we had made to the Romanians.

Swedish Baptist leaders had a long and friendly relationship with Baptists throughout Europe. David Lagergren, Birgit's predecessor as General Secretary of Swedish Baptists, "once commented that their Union was able to exchange visits with all Eastern Unions during the 1970s and received almost annual invitations to the Soviet Union. He attributed this to the fact of Sweden's neutrality."[3]

During the meeting Birgit stated to Brother Firisiuk that during the days of the Cold War, she had visited many churches throughout the Soviet Union as a representative of Swedish Baptists and had always been invited to speak to the congregations. She asked why such a problem should now develop when she would preside over EBF business meetings. There were no easy answers to the question. Overall, the meeting was positive, just as the one with the Romanian Baptist leaders had been. I believe the love of Christ in all of us helped bridge the gaps of understanding and practice.

Birgit was installed as EBF President in Kishinev. No Baptist Union in the CIS refused to send representatives to the General Council meeting in Kishinev. Romanian Baptists sent no representatives to the meeting. However, during her service as EBF President, Romanian Baptists invited her to speak to their General Assembly, which she did. The love of Christ, the vision of BWA and EBF leaders and their strong desire to keep unity in the body of Christ prevented a serious division in the EBF.

THE BAPTIST Record
JOURNAL OF THE MISSISSIPPI BAPTIST CONVENTION

PUBLISHED SINCE 1877
NOVEMBER 14, 1996
VOL. 120
No. 40

Mississippi's Merritts leave mark on Europe

By Mike Creswell
SBC Foreign Mission Board

WIESBADEN, Germany — Draw a map of Baptist work in Europe and somewhere you'll have to put the names of Mississippians John and Elizabeth Merritt.

For more than 30 years these two Southern Baptist foreign missionaries have helped start and lead English language Baptist churches in Europe. As they retire and head home to their native Mississippi this fall, they leave a solid record — and a bit of their hearts — behind.

Since 1972 Merritt has served as general secretary of the European Baptist Convention (EBC), a fellowship of 66 English-speaking congregations across Europe. These nearly two and a half decades have included Cold War years in which most English-language churches were composed of American military personnel put in Europe to fend off an attack which never came.

The fall of communism in 1989 meant many of those soldiers and their families went back to the United States — and more than a dozen EBC churches closed for lack of members.

The EBC switched its emphasis to reaching international citizens for whom English is an important language. Amid dozens of other native languages, English continues to be the continent's most popular second language because of its heavy use in business, industry, and education. Every European city of any size has a population of English speakers — making English-speaking churches a viable proposition.

The Merritts

...been organized, including eight congregations in Eastern European capitals such as Moscow and Buda... as it became possi... rally support for s... churches in Easter...

"One of the th... for our plantin... Europe was the ... Baptist people ... Merritt said. Be... EBC had cont... assistance to ... with no strings ... ing, 10 years.

"We gave t... concern," he s... ation from th... and the natio...

In 1991 M... the Europ... umbrella or... unions acro... American ... Elizabet... that, while ... to suppor... identity. ... led pasto... the missi... years sh... and eve... ter for ...

But ... her v... ing wi... had th... people ... groun... get so... certa...

So she ... and earned a degree in ... counseling ... University of Southern Mississippi. ... she earned ... European pro... Ind. Her new skil... University in her ... helped her in her mi... worked wi... John in a natur...

up in Macedonia and Petal. Elizabeth was born in Mobile, Ala., but grew up in Chicora in Wayne County. The two met at youth revival John helped lead in Clara... ...with a cousin. "When I first ...music, I didn't...

The Merritts in front of the First Baptist Church, Vicenza, Italy, their first missionary assignment, 1964.

...aking Baptist Chu... retired ... of starting be g... ...and grew o... ... ...

...venes in the Sky Room ...red plan ... Annuity

...Columbus, ...otherhood ...emi-annual

...tist Foreign ...d across the ...st-war China ...work in China

The Italian Baptist Mission (organization of Southern Baptist missionaries in Italy), 1965.

SBC missionaries in Italy, 1966.

Merritt with European Baptist friends during visit to Soviet Union, 1976.

Merritt preaching in the Baptist church in Tallinn, Estonia, 1976.

The congregation of the Central (First) Baptist Church, Moscow, Russia, 1976.

Baptism of Russian converts in early 1970s. Picture given to Merritt during 1976 visit.

The European Baptist Convention celebrates its 25th anniversary during Annual assembly in Kaiserslautern, Germany, 1989.

Merritt welcomes George and Carolyn Robertson. Robertson was the first full-time, fully supported African-American pastor called by an EBC church. Also pictured, Ray Benfield, pastor of Trinity Baptist Church, Athens, Greece, 1989.

Newly elected European Baptist Federation officers, August 1989.
Left to right: Peter Barber (Scotland), President; Karl-Heinz Walter (Germany), General Secretary; John Merritt (EBC), Vice President.

EBC leaders and Bill Gray (right) during EBC-Texas Baptist partnership, 1990.

In 1993, the Merritts revisit the Italian Baptist Church they helped to plant in Casorate Primo, a suburb of Milan, in the 1970s.

To have a beautiful new church building was a reason for this congregation to celebrate and give thanks to God. The congregation met in a room in the home of Mr. and Mrs. Antonio Spezzacatena for 25 years. The family offered the room unconditionally until the church could own a meeting place.

Charles Cottle, SBC missionary administrator in Europe, congratulates the Merritts for their years of service in Europe, 1996.

Left to right: Victor Kulbich, Merritt, George Hayner, and Gregory Komendant. Kulbich and Komendant were leaders of the Ukrainian Baptist Union. Hayner was interim pastor of International Baptist Church, Kiev, 1996.

Merritt speaks to new EBC pastors and wives, 1994.

Merritt visits Baptist Union in Kiev, Ukraine, 1996.

Merritt reflecting on his missionary service after his last Interlaken Baptist Assembly, Switzerland, 1996.

The Germany Baptist Mission says "auf wiedersehen" to Calvin and Betty Hogue, John and Elizabeth Merritt, and Helen and Ray Reynolds in the spring of 1996.

The EBC staff sees the Merritts off on their final furlough before retirement in the train station in Wiesbaden, Germany, November 1996.

> Dear Elizabeth and John!
>
> You have given a longlife ministry to Jesus and the Baptist churches in Europe and so become part of the Europeans yourself.
>
> From the very beginning you have been involved with the European Baptist Federation and always supported this instrument of God in building His Kingdom. So it was quite natural to also become President of the European Baptist Federation.
>
> We want to thank you from all our heart for your committed leadership in this exciting but also challenging time. We express to you our deep and warm gratitude.
>
> May God bless you in the future and guide you with His spirit and be with you with joy and peace for ever.
>
> On behalf of the European Baptist Federation
>
> *[signatures]*
>
> Kishinev/ Moldova, September 1994

Letter to Merritts from Executive Committee of European Baptist Federation at the end of John's service as EBF President, 1994.

Merritt and Herbert Stout revisit EBC and church in Stuttgart, Germany in 2003. Stout and his twin brother, Herman, were co-founders of the Association which grew into the EBC.

Authority Over Church Offerings

The Southern Baptist Convention (SBC), meeting in Orlando, Florida, June 14-16, 1994, took actions that further excluded Southern Baptist churches and members who were not fully supportive of the fundamentalist leaders of the Convention. It also caused the collapse of any meaningful implementation of the Hamburg Agreement. Jim Henry, pastor of the First Baptist Church of Orlando, was elected SBC president. Because Henry was not the first choice of the fundamentalist leaders for election as SBC president, his election was interpreted by some Southern Baptists as a step toward reconciliation in the SBC.

However, any hopes of reconciliation in the SBC at that time were crushed when the Convention voted not to accept any funds from the CBF and instructed all SBC agencies and boards to refuse funds from the CBF. The fundamentalist leaders had already excluded and rejected the leaders of the CBF and their voices of concern and protest. In Orlando they went further by rejecting the tithes and offerings that Southern Baptists had given through their churches.

The policy that the SBC established in Orlando regarding the CBF crystallized the duplicity in the Convention and deepened the division. Rather than practicing what Scripture teaches and being obedient to Christ concerning reconciliation, the fundamentalist leaders tried to drive supporters of the Cooperative Baptist Fellowship out of the SBC. This action, in turn, imposed on all agencies, boards and institutions the responsibility of enforcing the Convention's actions in their areas of responsibility. Enforcing the Convention's actions was most difficult for administrators who wanted to obey Christ, promote Christian unity, and at the same time be servants of Christ in the Convention.

The action of the 1994 SBC concerning the CBF put missionaries, particularly those of us serving in Europe, directly in the line of the SBC controversy. Not only did it demonstrate that our Convention was not following Scripture and was not being obedient to Christ in the practice of reconciliation, it also put the FMB in conflict with the agreement it had signed in Hamburg. By that time the CBF had been operating in Europe for more than two years as a valued, needed and respected partner in missions.

Missionaries appointed by the FMB were working in full cooperation with European Baptist unions, some of which also had requested and were working with missionaries appointed by the CBF. I know of no FMB missionaries who at that time had any difficulty working with CBF missionaries, or vice versa. Before the defunding of Rüschlikon in 1991, all of us had served with the FMB. All of us knew the circumstances that had given birth to the CBF in Europe.

The SBC action in 1994 forced the FMB to try to follow two conflicting policies in its mission work. The Hamburg Agreement states:

The EBF representatives indicated their intention of working with both the Foreign Mission Board and the Cooperative Baptist Fellowship (CBF). The FMB representatives reported that, by official action, their Board had given the assurance that this would not adversely affect relationships with EBF. At the same time, the EBF representatives indicated their intention of discouraging any element of competition in developing relationships with both bodies.[4]

Duplicity comes from double-minded thinking. It is double-minded to think Southern Baptists can follow one policy in the churches, another in the Convention and still another overseas where we send missionaries to work. All SBC agencies, institutions and boards were expected to take the views toward the CBF and its people that were consistent with the views shown by the fundamentalist leaders and which they had led the Convention to adopt as policy. No Convention agency, board or institution, including the FMB, dared challenge or contradict the will of the fundamentalist leaders, who could not see that their own folly had created the climate which gave birth to the CBF. When the SBC took the action concerning the CBF in 1994, I was convinced that the Convention had clearly stepped off its sure foundation of truly believing the Bible and of obeying Jesus Christ and his teachings.

Another Christian principle agreed to in Hamburg concerned "Preserving Baptist Unity." It stated:

During the meeting it became clear that unity in Christ among Baptist churches and Unions in Europe was particularly important in the light of the divisions the continent had experienced in recent years. Members of the Consultation agreed to urge those they were representing to do everything in their power to avoid disrupting this unity; rather, *'to keep the unity of the Spirit in the bond of peace.'* (Eph. 4:3)[5]

While European Baptists were emphasizing the need for unity in Christ, Southern Baptists were marching headlong toward division. Both the FMB and CBF were sending missionaries to work in Europe. However, FMB administrators did not want SBC missionaries to have fellowship or work with CBF missionaries.

The action of the SBC in 1994 deepened the division within the SBC. It also imposed on many people in the Convention the burden of divided loyalties. As for me, I knew my highest loyalty was to Jesus Christ and his teachings. I wanted also to be true to the agreement we had made with our overseas partners, which FMB administrators and the entire Board of Trustees had voted to approve. I wanted to be loyal also to the SBC and affiliated churches that were supporting us. The loyalties had a violent collision. On one hand, Jesus commands us to love each other as he has loved us. He prays that we will be one with each other, just as he is one with the Father. The agreement with our overseas partners called on us to work for unity in Christ among Baptists. The crunch was on for all missionaries, particularly those of us who had administrative responsibilities. When I read about the SBC's vote concerning the CBF, I wondered, "How long will that take to catch up with us?" It didn't take long.

1994 Interlaken Baptist Assembly

During the EBC Summer Assembly in Interlaken in July, 1994, the effects of the action of the SBC in Orlando concerning the CBF became evident in the EBC in full force. Every evening before the sermon, we made a brief presentation on some aspect of EBC work. One evening that week the feature was on European Home Missions. Ray Benfield, SBC missionary pastor of the International Baptist Church of Copenhagen, Denmark, was chairing the Missions Committee and was responsible for the presentation on missions that evening.

The EBC was in partnership with the Baptist unions of the Czech Republic and Slovakia. One of our mission projects that year was to give financial assistance to the Bela Education and Retreat Center of the Czech Baptist Union. Kevin Rutledge was serving as a CBF missionary in the Czech Republic and was knowledgeable of the center the EBC was supporting. Kevin had been an FMB journeyman in Salzburg, Austria. He and his wife had been appointed later by the FMB. They had resigned the FMB and were appointed by the CBF following the defunding of Rüschlikon. Kevin was asked to present information on the Czech project to the assembly and was introduced as "a Southern Baptist missionary supported by the CBF."

A few days after the Assembly I learned that the introduction of Kevin as "a Southern Baptist missionary supported by the CBF" had offended and angered John Floyd, the FMB area director for Europe, who was also present at the Assembly.

The Ultimatum: Like It Or Get Out!

The EBF Congress met in Lillehammer, Norway, in late July, 1994. During the Congress, I gained further understanding of the division that was occurring in the SBC and the nature of "the Purge" that was being carried out by the SBC's fundamentalist leaders. John and Helen Floyd invited Elizabeth and me to lunch with them in Lillehammer on Friday, July 29. Although I had heard that John was not happy about the introduction of "a Southern Baptist missionary supported by the CBF," I had no idea of the severity of his opposition to such a statement.

During lunch we briefly discussed the Congress in Lillehammer, the SBC in June, and the Interlaken Assembly. In reference to the incident at Interlaken, John said that only the people appointed by the FMB should be called Southern Baptist missionaries. I told them that I had hoped there would be reconciliation in the SBC between SBC leaders and the CBF. Helen said there would never be reconciliation in the SBC. John said he believed things were getting better in the SBC, and informed us that SBC leaders thought and hoped that by the SBC voting to refuse funds from the CBF, the people with the CBF would leave the SBC. According to John, the SBC would be better off if those supporting the CBF left the SBC. John then leaned forward and said to me, "John, I know you don't like what has been going on in the SBC." I nodded in agreement that I didn't like it. Then he said, **"If you don't like it, get out!"**

I was stunned. Elizabeth was puzzled at such harsh words. Seeking clarification, she asked John, "We have been talking in generalities. Are you talking to us personally?" he confirmed that he was. I felt from then on that we must proceed with extreme caution. I remembered that Russell Dilday had recently been fired as president of SWBTS. I remembered also that in FMB policy, insubordination to administrators can lead to termination. I knew that we had more work to do and I did not want to be fired.

The atmosphere had become tense. John asked me whether the EBC was giving any money to support to the CBF. I replied that the EBC gave no money directly to the CBF, but that we continued to support the seminary in Rüschlikon as we had done before the defunding. I told him also that the EBC Executive Committee had agreed not to request missionaries from the CBF to serve EBC churches. The Committee had decided, however, that if a CBF missionary started or served an English speaking church in Europe and that church wanted to join the EBC, both the pastor and the church would be welcome in the EBC. I asked him for his response to the position the Executive Committee had taken in this regard. He said he thought it was reasonable and fair.

It was a difficult confrontation. After we had finished lunch and our discussion, Elizabeth and I returned to our hotel room, deeply troubled. We discussed the conversation with the Floyds and questioned whether we should consider resigning from the FMB or retiring earlier than we had planned. We decided we should do neither.

Many perplexing questions came to my mind. What happened to the agreement on unity and cooperation we had so carefully and prayerfully worked out and signed in Hamburg? Remembering the contents of Ron Wilson's letter, I asked,

One Missionary's Journey

Why should I like what the Lord hates? (Proverbs 6:16-19) Why should I like slander, deceit and false accusations? I wondered: Did the SBC's fundamentalist leaders provide SBC trustees information that was deceptive and false, expect them to believe it and spread it, use it to establish Convention policies, then tell Southern Baptists to '*like it or get out?*'

There were other disturbing questions concerning the Southern Baptist Convention. "Why would anyone want to drive other people out of the SBC?" "What kind of wall has been built between people in the SBC?" "Why has such a wall been built?" "How can Christian people say there will never be reconciliation in the SBC?" "What about the Southern Baptist churches that were electing trustees and supporting all the FMB administrators and missionaries? Did they have any idea about what was happening in the SBC?" I didn't believe they did. I had never been associated with a church that promoted such division.

It was at that time I first thought of appealing to the churches. I asked myself, "Are there leaders in the SBC who think they have the authority to drive others out? If so, where do they get their authority?" I remembered how the wall in Berlin had fallen, and how tyrants such as Ceauscescu of Romania had been toppled. Then this strong impression came to my mind: ***If there is anything the people of our generation should have learned it is this . . . walls fall and tyrants get toppled!***

Renewed Resolve

I knew we were working in conditions different from anything we had ever experienced. FMB administrators were compelled to implement SBC policies overseas. If they worked for the FMB, they had to implement the action of the SBC in Orlando regarding the CBF, even though to do so in Europe would bring division in the body of Christ, which both Scripture and the Hamburg Agreement denounced. All of us were in a tangled web. The EBC and I were clearly in a precarious position. In our hearts we were loyal to the SBC and to European Baptists. We had adopted the Hamburg Agreement as the basis of our working relationship with the FMB. The FMB had also adopted the Hamburg Agreement, but the SBC action in Orlando nullified the possibility of its implementation.

I faced a new dilemma. Convention authority, the power to make and implement policy, approving or rejecting requests for missionary personnel, and the use of SBC Cooperative Program and Lottie Moon funds for foreign missions all were fully at the discretion of FMB administrators. To discuss or disagree with the action of the SBC in Orlando was not allowed by FMB administrators. It could lead to being fired by the FMB.

It seemed that the majority of those who voted for those actions in Orlando were operating under the assumption that God had spoken in Orlando through godly people, and their decisions should not be questioned. It is also possible that many people in our Convention, including FMB administrators, believed the SBC action in Orlando was wrong, but they were in no better position to question it at that time than I.

We were deeply convinced that we should continue our work with the EBC and FMB since there remained much work to be done. To rebel against the policy regarding the CBF, even though I did not agree with it, would mean suicide as far as our missionary careers were concerned. I believed we were obeying Christ in our faith and that we were doing what Southern Baptist churches sent us to do. I thought that most FMB administrators believed those same things about themselves and about their call and service for Christ and for Southern Baptists. I decided that I must continue to work cooperatively, to support as much as possible FMB administrators, and to continue to lead the EBC according to the same principles we had established. I would continue to promote planting and nurturing international Baptist churches in great European cities. I would also have fellowship with CBF missionaries, convinced that they were true partners in the gospel. I decided that I would not provoke conflict with FMB administrators, but neither would I avoid it when principles were concerned.

I continued to serve both the EBC and FMB through the annual EBC convention in October 1996, after which our overseas missionary service ended and we began our final furlough. **I believed that unless the direction of the Southern Baptist Convention changed drastically, some day I would appeal to the churches!**

CHAPTER 6

The Gospel of Jesus Christ

Jesus went throughout Galilee, teaching in their synagogues, preaching the good news (gospel) *of the kingdom, and healing every disease and sickness among the people."* (Matt. 4:23) *"For in the gospel* (good news) *a righteousness from God is revealed, a righteousness that is by faith from first to last, just as it is written, `The righteous will live by faith.* (Romans 1:17 . . . emphases added)

The gospel of Jesus Christ is who Jesus is and what he prayed, preached, taught, commanded, did and promised. Jesus cannot be separated from his words. The gospel is the totality of Jesus Christ.

The gospel is also the further revelation of the teachings of Jesus Christ through the apostles in the early church. Jesus called disciples and trained them to understand and to spread his gospel. The writings of the disciples, later called apostles, applied the teachings of Christ to believers in Christ in the settings of the first local churches. The apostles wrote about the teachings of Christ and in the same writings applied those teachings to fellow Christians in the cultural, historical, political and religious environment in which they lived. The church as the body of Christ was in its infancy and was comprised of new Christians who were learning to follow Christ in their culture and environment.

The gospel of Jesus Christ continues throughout generations through Christians who are empowered by the Holy Spirit to continue Christ's work. Jesus said, *"All this I have spoken while still with you. But the Counselor, the Holy Spirit, whom the Father will send in my name, will teach you all things and will remind you of everything I have said to you."* (John 14:25-26)

The Voice of Jesus Christ

God speaks with one voice. Jesus Christ is God and speaks for God. The Father, the Son and the Holy Spirit say the same things, make the same promises, use the same weapons, have the same objectives, give the same power, and make the same commands. They do not contradict each other in what they say. Servants of Jesus Christ are called to speak and teach with the voice of Jesus Christ in the same spirit of humility and service with which Jesus spoke. The voices of Christians should not contradict the voice of Jesus Christ. In Scripture, when someone says something that on the surface gives a different message than what Jesus gave, an effort should be made to understand the circumstances that accompany the difference. What every Christian says should be judged and evaluated by what Jesus said.

Jesus said the words the Father had given him. *"For I gave them the words you gave me and they accepted them."* (John 17:8; 7:16-18) Jesus cannot be separated from what he said. He and his words are eternally inseparable. (Mark 8:38; John 12:47-50) Jesus said, *"Heaven and earth will pass away, but my words will never pass away."* (Matt. 24:35) his words are linked to eternal life. (John 6:63, 68) his words are the wisdom of the Father. (Matt. 12:42; Col. 2:3)

Jesus warned his followers not to listen to anyone who spoke with a voice other than his voice.

> *I tell you the truth, the man who does not enter the sheep pen by the gate, but climbs up some other way, is a thief and a robber. The man who enters by the gate is the shepherd of his sheep. The watchman opens the gate for him, and the sheep listen to his voice. He calls his own sheep by name and leads them out. When he has brought out all his own, he goes on ahead of them, and his sheep follow him because they know his voice. But they will never follow a stranger; in fact, they will run away from him because they do not recognize a stranger's voice.* (John 10:1-5)

The Spirit helps us know the sound and content of the voice of Jesus Christ. His voice speaks through his entire ministry and teaching. His voice speaks to us through the Bible. The ministry of the Spirit is to continue the work of Jesus Christ by reminding Christians of all of the above in order to empower them to speak with the same voice with which Jesus spoke. Christians should know very well what Jesus taught, be so clear about his teachings, and be so committed to them personally that everywhere and in every circumstance they will hear, recognize and obey the voice of Jesus Christ. This is what God meant when he said, *"I will put my law in their minds and write it on their hearts."* (Jer. 31:33; Hebrews 10:16)

The Authority of Jesus Christ

The authority of Jesus Christ is absolute and complete. *"Then Jesus came to them and said, `All authority in heaven and on earth has been given to me.'"* (Matt. 28:18) The authority that he has given to others derives from his authority.

Jesus prayed, *"Father, the time has come. Glorify your Son, that your Son may glorify you. For you granted him authority over all people that he might give eternal life to all those you have given him."* (John 17:1-2)

Jesus affirmed the authority and inspiration of Hebrew Scripture. He affirmed that what the prophets had preached and written, they had preached and written by inspiration of God. He said, *"Do not think that I have come to abolish the Law or the Prophets; I have not come to abolish them but to fulfill them. I tell you the truth, until heaven and earth disappear, not the smallest letter, not the least stroke of a pen, will by any means disappear from the Law until everything is accomplished."* (Matt. 5:17-18)

The Law and the Prophets Jesus spoke about were not the ceremonial laws held so reverently by the Jews, which he broke many times. He did not wash his hands as they said he must. He healed on the Sabbath, which they said he must not. He was condemned and crucified as a lawbreaker in their eyes, even though he affirmed to the end that he had broken no law at all. His view of the law was different from theirs. He dealt with God's highest moral and spiritual law, which has two parts, both of which are rooted in love. The first part is love, reverence and obedience to God. The second part is love and reverence for people, who are made in God's image. Jesus not only gave these two greatest and most important commandments, but he linked all other commandments to them by saying, *"All the Law and the Prophets hang on these two commandments."* (Matt. 22:40) Paul linked all the laws to the law of love. He wrote:

> *Let no debt remain outstanding, except the continuing debt to love one another, for he who loves his fellowman has fulfilled the law. The commandments, 'Do not commit adultery,' 'Do not murder,' 'Do not steal,' 'Do not covet,' and whatever other commandment there may be, are summed up in this one rule: 'Love your neighbor as yourself.' Love does no harm to its neighbor. Therefore love is the fulfillment of the law.* (Rom. 13:8-10)

The Authority of Jesus Christ in Scripture

Christians believe that both the Old and New Testaments are inspired (God - breathed). Jesus made it clear, however, that the Scriptures are about him. He did not equate what he said with what anyone else had ever said or with what anyone else would ever say. He quoted Scripture while at the same time he emphasized his authority in Scripture by use of terms such as: *"You have heard that it was said to the people long ago . . .* ***but I tell you.***" (Matt. 5:21-22; 27-28; 31-32; 33-34; 38-39; and 43-44: emphasis added) His words are in Scripture, where his teachings have supreme authority. The people who heard and believed him, believed he was God and that when he spoke to them, God was speaking to them. He spoke with authority. At the conclusion of the sermon on the mount, Matthew wrote: *"When Jesus had finished saying these things, the crowds were amazed at his teaching, because he taught as one who had authority, and not as their teachers of the law."* (Matt. 7:28-29) Jesus made an unmistakable connection between who he was and what he taught, promised, prayed and did. He cannot be separated from the authority and truth of his teachings. Neither can the Bible be separated from Jesus and his authority.

The apostles in the early church identified themselves as servants of Jesus Christ and recognized him as their final source of authority. Paul wrote about himself as *"a servant of Jesus Christ, called to be an apostle and set apart for the gospel of God."* (Romans 1:1)

The authority of Jesus was inherent in his being as was demonstrated when he calmed storms, winds and waves. He had authority over disease and death. Although he submitted to them in humility to fulfill the purpose of his coming, he had authority over all rulers and people in authority. *"Pilate said, `Don't you realize I have power either to free you or to crucify you?'* Jesus answered, *`You would have no power over me if it were not given to you from above.'* "* (John 19:10-11)

The submission of Christians and other citizens to any authority must take into account that all authority derives from God and is accountable to him. Obedience to the instruction of Paul to Timothy in this regard must be understood in the larger context. *"I urge, then, first of all, that requests, prayers, intercessions and thanksgiving be made for everyone — for kings and all those in authority, that we may live peaceful and quiet lives..."* (1 Tim. 2:1-2)

The early Christians lived with the reality that some people who called themselves Christians acted on their own authority. *"Some men came down from Judea to Antioch and were teaching the brothers: `Unless you are circumcised, according to the custom taught by Moses, you cannot be saved.'* "* (Acts 15:1) The problem with these people was that they were working against the process through which the Holy Spirit was leading the early church. Jesus had been their example in establishing a completely new view of what it meant to worship and serve God. The church was continuing the painful process of dismantling the ceremonial laws, which had been added by religious leaders to the laws given through Moses. Those additions also had become such a dominant part of their worship before the coming of Christ that the essence of God's laws had become obscure.

The teachers of the law looked to Abraham, Moses and the prophets as the authorities in everything they did. They studied their commandments and writings, which formed the basis of their worship. Christ dismantled even some of these ceremonial laws in order to clearly establish God's most important law. It was incomprehensible to the religious leaders that someone greater than Moses, Jonah, Solomon, and even greater than Abraham was alive, working and teaching in their generation.

> *At this the Jews exclaimed, 'Now we know that you are demon-possessed! Abraham died and so did the prophets, yet you say that if anyone keeps your word, he will never taste death. Are you greater than our father Abraham? he died, and so did the prophets. Who do you think you are? . . . Jesus answered, 'I tell you the truth. Before Abraham was born, I am!'* (John 8:52-53, 58)

They wanted to stone him, did not believe him, did not accept his authority, and could not comprehend the truth he was telling them.

The content of the message that Christians are authorized by Jesus to teach and preach has limitations and restrictions. No follower of Jesus has the authority to teach and preach anything that conflicts with what he preached and taught. Jesus gave his disciples specific instructions when he said " . . . *make disciples of all nations . . . baptizing . . . teaching them to obey everything I have commanded you.*" (Matt. 28:19-20)

Love: The Greatest Test of Christians

Love is at the center of Jesus' teachings. God's love for the world motivated him to send his Son in order that people might believe in him and have eternal life. It was the love of Christ that motivated him to endure the rejection of his people and the pain and shame of the cross that all who believe might have life in him.

The two greatest laws found in the Old Testament, in the teachings of Jesus, and in the minds of the apostles were laws of love . . . love for God and love for others. God commanded it to Israel. Jesus commanded it to his disciples. The apostle John wrote:

> *We know that we have passed from death to life, because we love our brothers. Anyone who does not love remains in death. Anyone who hates his brother is a murderer, and you know that no murderer has eternal life in him. This is how we know what love is: Jesus Christ laid down his life for us. And we ought to lay down our lives for our brothers.* (1 John 3:14, 16)

Love is the dominant theme that runs through the Bible. God has it, shows it and commands it. God is love. The most essential virtue for which Christ is known is his love. It is the highest value and virtue found among mankind. It is the greatest commandment we must obey. In light of all the emphases in the Bible on love, it is difficult to comprehend why the fundamentalist leaders exclude other Christians and do so in the name of "believing the Bible!"

The ultimate test of how much Jesus loved people was answered on the cross. His love was so complete that he died to save people he loved. He expected and required the same kind of love among his followers for each other that he gave for them. *"My command is this: Love each other as I have loved you. Greater love has no one than this, that he lay down his life for his friends."* (John 15:13)

The apostles learned that the love Jesus had shown for them was the same love they must show toward each other. The lesson was not learned easily. Instead, it was learned through the bitterness of their own failure. Not only did Judas betray Jesus and Peter deny him, *"... all the disciples deserted him and fled."* (Matt. 26:56) In the greatest time of testing, in the moment Jesus had pleaded with them to pray, stay and watch with him, they fled. After his death on the cross and after his resurrection, when he called them together again he still loved them. Only then did they comprehend the depth of his love for them. Only then did they understand that they were commanded to love each other just as Jesus had loved them.

Love and Christian Leadership

Christianity is a movement with one Head and one Leader, Jesus Christ. It is a movement that is always in the present tense, yet is always eternal; it is always local, yet always universal; it will always be attacked, yet it can never be defeated. All leaders in all expressions of Christianity, whether home, church, institution, denomination, mission agency or other, should follow the Leader, Jesus Christ. *"But they will never follow a stranger."* (John 10:5a) Any leader who does not follow Jesus is rejected by God and forfeits his role of leadership of other Christians. (John 15:1-2) he cannot expect other Christians to follow him.

Leaders who follow Jesus, who seek to have the mind of Christ, and who make a serious effort to lead like Jesus led are gentle and humble. Jesus said, *"Take my yoke upon you and learn from me, for I am gentle and humble in heart, and you will find rest for your souls."* (Matt. 11:29) Anyone who does not willingly wear the yokes of learning from Jesus, including his yokes of gentleness and humility, cannot lead as Jesus led.

Jesus taught that the road to greatness in his kingdom is different from the way people think about greatness. It is through humble service.

Jesus called them together and said, 'You know that the rulers of the Gentiles lord it over them, and their high officials exercise authority over them. Not so with you. Instead, whoever wants to become great among you must be your servant, and whoever wants to be first must be your slave—just as the Son of Man did not come to be served, but to serve, and to give his life as a ransom for many.' (Matt 20: 25-28)

Not so with you. Leadership for the followers of Jesus is to be achieved in a different way from the way the carnal and worldly mind achieves it. Jesus warned against trying to achieve greatness in any way other than through service. *"The greatest among you will be your servant. For whoever exalts himself will be humbled, and whoever humbles himself will be exalted."* (Matt. 23:11-12)

According to the apostle Paul, leadership is a gift of the Spirit along with the gifts of serving, teaching, encouraging and contributing. *"... if it is leadership, let him govern diligently."* (Romans 12:8) All gifts of the Spirit are given to build up the one body of Christ. No leader in the church can legitimately exert leadership which does not build up the body of Christ.

Christians are taught to respect, imitate and remember leaders whom God has chosen. *"Remember your leaders, who spoke the word of God to you."* (Heb. 13:7) At the same time we are taught, *"Dear children, do not let anyone lead you astray."* (1 John 3:7) It works both ways. Responsibility rests on leaders not to lead their followers astray and on followers not to let leaders lead them astray. (Col. 2:5, 8)

Warnings Against Presenting Another Gospel

The warnings in Scripture against presenting "another gospel" are clear and severe. No one has the authority to change the content and the spirit of the gospel taught and preached by Jesus Christ. He is The Prophet, above all other prophets. Moses wrote:

The Lord your God will raise up for you a prophet like me from among your own brothers. You must listen to him . . . I will put my words in his mouth, and he will tell them everything I command him. If anyone does not listen to my words that the prophet speaks in my name, I myself will call him to account. But a prophet who presumes to speak in my name anything I have not commanded him to say, or a prophet who speaks in the name of other gods, must be put to death. (Deut. 18:15, 18-20)

Paul called the Christians in the churches in Galatia to account for having turned to a "different gospel." he wrote:

> *I am astonished that you are so quickly deserting the one who called you by the grace of Christ and are turning to a different gospel—which is really no gospel at all. Evidently some people are throwing you into confusion and are trying to pervert the gospel of Christ. But even if we or an angel from heaven should preach a gospel other than the one we preached to you, let him be eternally condemned!* (Gal. 1:6-8) See also 2 John 8-11 and Jude 3-4.

While studying and applying Scripture in the context of the Southern Baptist Convention in our generation, we should listen to the voice of the Spirit who reminds us what Jesus taught and commanded. In this regard, we need to discern what the Spirit is saying to us today. We should remember that nobody has the authority to teach or preach anything that contradicts or rivals what Jesus taught. Jesus said, "*A student is not above his teacher, nor a servant above his master. It is enough for the student to be like his teacher, and the servant like his master.*" (Matt. 10:24-25a)

No one has the authority to change the eternal message of the gospel that Jesus taught so clearly. Anyone who presumes to do so is acting dangerously.

Unity in Christ

Throughout history people have longed to live in peace and harmony with their neighbors. The psalmist declared, "*How good and pleasant it is when brothers live together in unity! . . . For there the Lord bestows his blessing, even life forevermore.*" (Psalm 133:1, 3b)

The followers of Jesus understood well their role as peacemakers and reconcilers. They practiced these roles. They opposed division and promoted unity. They saw division in the body of Christ as something demonic and unspiritual. Division in the body of Christ was so unnatural that it alarmed them and compelled them to deal with the problem.

The theme of unity in the body of Christ runs throughout the New Testament. Paul wrote:

> *Make every effort to keep the unity of the Spirit through the bond of peace. There is one body and one Spirit—just as you were called to one hope when you were called—one Lord, one faith, one baptism; one God and Father of all, who is over all and through all and in all.* (Eph. 4:3-5) See also 1 Cor.1:13, Rom. 12:4-5, and Gal. 3:26-29

Unity among Christians is possible when Christians obey the command Jesus gave his disciples: "*My command is this: Love each other as I have loved you. Greater love has no one than this, that he lay down his life for his friends. You are my friends if you do what I command.*" (John 15:12-14)

State of the Southern Baptist Convention

If one looks at the Southern Baptist Convention today through some external indicators one could conclude that all is well. Cooperative Program receipts are high. New churches are being planted. Many churches are growing. Fundamentalist leaders point out that these indicators are proof that their movement is good and that God is blessing the Convention in remarkable ways under their leadership. To them, their purge and surge movement was necessary and they were led by God to lead it. To them, division throughout the Convention and the entire world of Baptists is well worth the price of doctrinal purity as they see it. Fundamentalist leaders welcome the division and fragmentation and interpret it as justification for their cause. When churches leave the Convention or churches, state conventions and associations divide, they count only those that do not leave and those that do not divide and exalt themselves for the effectiveness of their actions. When missionaries are fired, they count only those who are not fired and exalt themselves for purging the Convention's mission personnel. They believe they are on a mission for God and are winning a battle for God.

While they were successful in electing officers and trustees and in controlling the Convention's agencies, institutions and boards, deep divisions have occurred in Convention life. Opposition groups have been established and others are being formed in response to the lack of freedom to interpret the Scriptures that the fundamentalist leaders deny others.

Southern Baptists are colliding with each other throughout the Convention: SBC leaders with leaders of Baptist state conventions; pastors with their congregations; Baptist state convention leaders with pastors, associations and directors of missions; churches with other churches and their associations; and institutions and agencies with each other. The collisions continue between missionaries and IMB administrators and with each other. Baptist leaders in numerous countries who had been faithful partners with Southern Baptists for decades are colliding with IMB administrators and some missionaries about what it means to believe the Bible and what Christian missions means. SBC fundamentalist leaders have collided with Baptist World Alliance leaders.

The lay people in the churches are paying for all of these collisions with the tithes and offerings they bring to their churches and offer in worship to God and for the support of Christian missions throughout the world.

People cause divisions, fights and quarrels. (James 4:1-6) The collisions, divisions and fragmentation occurring in the SBC are seen by many as evidence of evil among leaders. The fundamentalist leaders see the collisions, divisions and fragmentation as their work to purge and purify the church.

The Cooperative Baptist Fellowship, the Alliance of Baptists, Mainstream Baptists, Global Women, and Missouri, North Carolina, Texas and Virginia Baptists have responded in various ways to the denial of freedom and the intoleration of diversity in church and convention life. Cooperative Baptist Fellowship and Mainstream Baptists networks are providing constructive alternatives to fundamentalism. The Cooperative Baptist Fellowship appoints and supports missionaries. Texas Baptists have adopted a strategy to assist missionaries who are fired by the IMB or who resign because they cannot serve a mission board that puts the rules of men above the commands of God.

Twelve new theological seminaries (See Appendix A) have been established and are attracting and training a new generation of Baptist leaders. Who knows how much more division and fragmentation lie ahead unless decisive measures are taken to heal the wounds in the Convention?

Deceptive Unity in Annual SBC Meetings

Annual meetings of the SBC are deceptively consistent in their unity. The fundamentalist leaders believe they have achieved their objectives. Their authority is so complete that few people offer serious challenges. When someone asks questions or raises objections, they are easily silenced.

The annual meetings are consistent also in what does not happen. No efforts are made toward reconciliation in the Convention. No calls are given for those who have been excluded from fellowship and participation in Convention life and leadership to be invited back into fellowship.

Although the leaders have falsely accused fellow Christians and deceived their followers, no calls for accountability, confession or repentance are voiced concerning these acts of evil by which the fundamentalist leaders have risen to their posts of leadership. Their recommendations concerning personnel, policies and budget are overwhelmingly approved by the messengers from the churches.

The leaders honor their followers by making certain that only those submissive to them are elected as trustees. Only those submissive to the fundamentalist leaders are elected to the highest places of honor and leadership in the Convention's agencies, boards and institutions. Disloyalty to the fundamentalist leaders results in being fired. The division in the Convention grows deeper and wider.

The 1997 Southern Baptist Convention Annual Meeting

I attended the SBC annual meeting in 1997, the last full year of active missionary service. The fundamentalist leaders were in full control, free to plan and bring any important issue before the convention, practically assured that the messengers would respect and follow their leadership. They controlled the process that brought all the recommendations on personnel to serve as trustees as well as on committees and how Cooperative Program money, which came from churches, would be budgeted and spent.

The leaders failed to bring any proposal that would bring reconciliation and unity in the Convention. The very opposite was true. Adrian Rogers was the keynote speaker for missions night. It was the time during the Convention to call on all present to be obedient to Christ and follow him wherever he might lead. During his message, Rogers made reference to the 1985 convention in Dallas, at which more than 45,000 messengers had cast ballots for president.

He said the 1997 meeting was much better than the one in 1985, although the attendance was about 13,000 compared to more than 45,000 in 1985. He mentioned also that he had served on the Peace Committee. He said that someone on the Peace Committee told him that if he didn't compromise, Southern Baptists would never get together, to which he had replied, "We don't have to get together." There were some who said "Amen" to his comment.

About 13,000 messengers to that convention went home to their churches having heard one of the most prominent Southern Baptist leaders of our generation say that unity in Christ is not important. According to Rogers, the messengers who heard him don't have to pay much attention to unity in Christ in their churches, associations, state conventions, the SBC and throughout the world of Baptists.

Such theology cannot be reconciled with the prayers of Jesus and the teachings on the one body of Christ throughout the New Testament. What a splendid opportunity Rogers had to call for reconciliation in the Convention; but by his attitude, his theology and his words, he promoted the division in the Convention. In that meeting, the fundamentalist leaders chose to continue to exclude and reject those who were not following them.

The 1999 SBC: Declaration of Complete Victory!

The Southern Baptist Convention met in Atlanta in June 1999, with 11,554 registered messengers from churches. In six of the previous seven SBC meetings, the president had been elected without opposition. **The fundamentalist leaders declared complete victory!** They were convinced they had achieved their goal of winning and declared that in SBC life, their victory was complete.

Adrian Rogers said, "We have won the battle for inerrancy of Scripture; let us not lose the battle for the authority of Scripture."[1] When I read his statement I asked myself whether this means that the SBC is headed for two decades more of wrangling over words about the authority of Scripture, as we have had about the inerrancy of Scripture! How does the authority of Scripture rank on the priority list of authorities in light of the declaration of Jesus Christ, "*All authority in heaven and on earth has been given unto me?*"

During the convention, Broadman and Holman Publishers presented to Paul Pressler a copy of his book, *A Hill On Which To Die*. "Paul Pressler, after receiving . . . a copy of his book about the Convention's conservative remodeling, said he waited until the victory was complete before penning the memoir."[2]

Again, there was failure to bring any proposal on reconciliation to the messengers. Instead, exclusion and rejection continued for those who would not submit to the authority of the fundamentalist leaders. The leaders were praised. People submitted to their authority, voted for the people they proposed, approved the budget they proposed, and endorsed the recommendations and resolutions they made. No one from within their movement opposed them or called them to accountability for practicing deceit.

The 2000 SBC: Authority Over Jesus Christ

After spreading confusion throughout the Convention on what it means to believe the Bible and excluding all those who would not submit to their authority, the fundamentalist leaders thought they had established an impregnable hierarchy of authority with themselves securely perched at the top. They seemed ready for their assault on the Convention's carefully prepared doctrinal statement, *The Baptist Faith and Message* (1963).

Before the Southern Baptist Convention met in Orlando in June, 2000, Committee Chairman Adrian Rogers wrote the cover letter for the report of the Baptist Faith and Message Study Committee to the Southern Baptist Convention, which included this statement:

> We have removed the statement that identified Jesus Christ as 'the criterion by which the Bible is to be interpreted' . . . Jesus Christ cannot be divided from the biblical revelation that is testimony to him. We must not claim a knowledge of Christ that is independent of Scripture or in any way is in opposition to Scripture. Likewise, Scripture cannot be set against Scripture.

The proposal of the Study Committee and the explanations they gave revealed critical errors in Christian thought in the minds of those making the proposals. Removing the statement that identified Jesus Christ as "the criterion by which the Bible is to be interpreted" was, in effect, an attempt to remove Jesus Christ from his authority in the Bible, beyond the Bible and, it seems, over those who made the proposal. They seem to really be saying that Christ has no authority over them, and that the Bible as they interpret it has become their authority. If that is so, it seems that Christ and his teachings have no authority over them and that the Holy Spirit speaking for Christ has no authority over them. To them, the Bible *as they interpret it* has become their authority.

The Study Committee wrote as if the Scriptures are God. God is three in One—not four in one. They do not distinguish between God the Father, who is God; God the Son, who is God; and God the Holy Spirit, who is God; and the Scriptures, which are *not* God. The Holy Spirit, who is God, was sent by Christ to remind his followers of what he said, to continue his work and to empower believers in Christ to be obedient to him. (John 14:25-26)

The early church lived by the Spirit, who is God, and the witness of the apostles who preached the gospel that Jesus had preached. They were witnesses of his resurrection. The first churches that were planted had only scarce written material about Jesus. They identified the Spirit as being Jesus himself, as in Acts 16:7: "*When they came to the border of Mysia, they tried to enter Bithynia, but the Spirit of Jesus would not allow them to.*" Much time would pass before written records would be collected and compiled into the Bible. The written record that tells what God did through those who obeyed him is not God. In the beginning was *God*. At no point in the past or in the present did the Bible ever become God. God speaks *in, through*, and *with* the Bible. Christians throughout the centuries have understood that the Holy Spirit enlightens them and empowers them to obey Jesus Christ.

Another error in the Study Committee's explanation was in their statement, "Scripture cannot be set against Scripture." The committee did what they said couldn't be done by setting Scripture against Scripture. Trying to establish the supremacy of men over women, they carefully selected parts of Paul's letters regarding women serving as leaders in local churches almost 2,000 years ago as the highest law governing churches today. Without taking into account the cultural and historical factors regarding women in society in Paul's time, they applied his writings to women serving as pastors in our time. In reality, they set Paul's teachings in his times above the greatest commandment of Jesus, against the prophecy of Joel 2:28, and against Peter's sermon at Pentecost in Acts 2:17. Both Joel and Peter prophesied that women will preach. "*I will pour out my Spirit on all people. Your sons and daughters will prophesy . . .* " A prophet is one who prophesies. According to Paul, Christians should desire spiritual gifts, especially the gift of prophecy. (1 Cor. 14:1) The purpose of prophecy is to strengthen, encourage and comfort Christians and to edify (build up) the church. (1 Cor. 14:3-4) Paul allowed women to pray and prophesy with their heads covered. (1 Cor. 11:5)

The committee ignored also the promises of Jesus in John 8:31-32 and 36 that Jesus sets people free. Not only was Scripture set against Scripture, but the Royal Law, which is the greatest commandment of Jesus and is in effect on all believers in all times, was also ignored. (Mark 12:28-31) The prayer of Jesus for unity in his body, the church, was ignored as well. (John 17)

The committee violated an appeal Paul made when he appealed to people not to divide themselves into parties following men, but to follow Christ and obey him. He appealed to the Christians in Corinth not to follow Apollos, or Peter, or even himself. According to Paul, all must follow Christ. (1 Cor. 1:10-14) The Study Committee made a proposal that was precisely what Paul appealed to Christians *not* to do.

Paul did everything he did in obedience to Christ. No one knew better than Paul that Jesus is God and that he had to obey him. No human being ever exalted the authority of Christ higher than did Paul. He wrote:

He (Christ) *is the image of the invisible God, the firstborn over all creation. For by him all things were created: things in heaven and on earth, visible and invisible, whether thrones or powers or rulers or authorities; all things were created by him and for him. He is before all things, and in him all things hold together. And he is the head of the body, the church; he is the beginning and the firstborn from among the dead, so that in everything he might have the supremacy, and through him to reconcile to himself all things, whether things on earth or things in heaven, making peace through his blood, shed on the cross.* (Col. 1:15-20)

No one respected and submitted to the authority of Christ more than Paul. No one needed to give lectures to him on the authority and power of Jesus Christ. He learned his lesson the hard way. After he was struck to the ground by the power of Christ and lay there blind and helpless, no one ever needed to tell him again not to try what he had tried. No one knew better than Paul the dangers and utter futility of trying to lead a movement in opposition against Christ, his authority and his power.

Paul was the master in the early church when it came to demolishing arguments and strongholds and "taking captive every thought to make it obedient to Christ." (2 Cor. 10:5) Christians today should follow his example.

According to Jesus, his disciples are commanded to obey him as the Holy Spirit reminds them of what he said. Christians, being reminded and empowered by the Spirit to obey Jesus, are entrusted with the keys of the kingdom. The Scriptures are written to correct us, to enlighten us, to equip us, to guide and instruct us, to rebuke us and to warn us. Jesus is God. Scripture is not God, but a witness about God. Jesus established his church. Scripture is not his church, but a witness about his church. Jesus established his kingdom and is its King. Scripture is not his kingdom, but a witness about his kingdom. Scripture is a witness about those who faithfully obeyed him and unlocked many doors with the keys he gave them. Scripture is a witness about how we, too, can keep unlocking doors with the keys he keeps on entrusting to those who obey him.

The new Convention law the Study Committee proposed was: "The office of pastor is limited to men as qualified by Scripture." That is a statement of male supremacy. Christianity is not a religion of male supremacy. Christianity is not a reformed caste system, similar to ancient Hinduism, in which males are born into a higher, fixed status than females. Males and females belong to one status, servants of one Lord and Master. God loves his daughters as much as he loves his sons. The Study Committee ignored the gender inclusiveness of God's commandments, of prophecy, of the beatitudes, of the indwelling and gifts of the Holy Spirit, and of the teachings, examples and promises of Jesus.

In Scripture, both men and women are called to submit to God and his purpose for them and his kingdom. When God decided that the time was right for his Son to be born, he sent the angel Gabriel to speak to Mary about what God was going to do in and through her. Gabriel told her that she was highly favored and that she would bear God's Son, whose kingdom would never end. Mary's humble reply was, *"I am the Lord's servant. May it be to me as you have said."* (Luke 1:38) Mary's song of submission, joy and praise to God is recorded in Luke 1:46-56. In fulfillment of Scripture, Mary prophesied.

In Scripture, it is written that Christians and churches must obey Jesus Christ as the Spirit leads them. *"Now the Lord is the Spirit, and where the Spirit of the Lord is, there is freedom."* (2 Cor. 3:17) When the Spirit calls a woman to prophesy, as the Scripture says will happen, and members of a Baptist church who are free in Christ and who believe the Spirit is leading their church to call that woman as their pastor, all the gates of Hell and all the laws, propositions and rules of men cannot keep that from happening.

The proposal of the Study Committee was approved overwhelmingly by messengers from Southern Baptist churches, thus changing the Baptist Faith and Message to include the new convention rule made by men.

The reasoning of the Study Committee, it seems, is that God is limited by Scripture about what he will do and can do. Regarding women, there is a problem for them in that they are saying God cannot do what Scripture says he will do. They believe that what Paul wrote to local churches 2,000 years ago in their culture and times limits what God can do. In reality, they and their followers have voted for the limitations of their own minds. They have voted into Convention law what they don't want to happen in their own minds and in their own churches. What God does in the minds of other people and in other churches is a different matter.

Partiality Toward Men

The Holy Spirit is sovereign in his work. (John 3:8) God alone knows perfectly what he will do and those who will obey him. He alone determines which gifts he gives to those who obey him. *"All these (gifts) are the work of one and the same Spirit, and he gives them to each one, just as he determines."* (1 Cor. 12:11) The partiality shown toward men over women in the new Convention law becomes personal when our own loved ones are involved. The members of the Study Committee and the messengers from churches are saying to their sons, "Obey God. Do what God calls you to do no matter what that might be." They are then saying to their daughters, "Obey God. Do what he calls you to do, *except serve as pastor of a church*!" God does not show partiality. Christians should not make laws which open doors of opportunity to their sons and close those same doors of opportunity to their daughters. Knowing that the Holy Spirit who lives in their daughters is sovereign, Christians should not tell their daughters that they can be wives, mothers, homemakers, executives, missionaries, church planters, teachers, CEOs of great corporations, administrators, governors, senators, philosophers, attorneys, heads of state, professors, surgeons or *anything else but pastors*!

Many Christians in our generation believe we are living in an era in which the promise of Jesus to make people free and the prophecies of Joel and Peter that the Spirit will be poured on sons and daughters and they will prophesy (preach) have become a reality to a greater degree than ever before. We are seeing a revolution of the awareness about the capacity of women as leaders. For Christian women, this revolution is something completely different from rebellion or simply pursuing a feminist liberation movement. It is fulfilling God's promise and purpose in developing his image in them. They are claiming the promise of Jesus that the Son will set them free indeed and that they will live by the Spirit.

Our daughters as well as our sons should be encouraged to submit themselves completely to Jesus Christ and to serve him any way the Spirit leads them. If a Baptist church believes it is obeying the Spirit and calls one of our daughters to serve as their pastor, she should not have to deal with the wrath of fundamentalist leaders who say, "You can't do that! Paul did not allow that in local churches 2,000 years ago!"

The history of the Bible is incomplete without the stories of women who had great faith in God and served him wholeheartedly. Miriam was a prophetess

(Exodus 15:20-21). Deborah was a prophetess who led Israel with such wisdom that *". . . the Israelites came to her to have their disputes settled."* (Judges 4:5) She was also the commander over Barak, the leader of Israel's army. (Judges 4) Esther was a courageous queen of Israel. She loved her people so much that she risked her life and disobeyed the king's command to save her people. (Esther 5:15-16).

If God in his sovereignty 2,000 years ago chose women to break to men the great news of the resurrection of his Son, God can also choose women in our generation to break the bread of life to men and women through preaching and teaching. It is happening, and we should be rejoicing that God is keeping his promise and that the Scriptures are being fulfilled. We should not quench the Spirit in those we love most. All of the women mentioned in the Bible who loved and obeyed God were somebody's daughter, mother, wife or sister. Will we jeopardize the joy of those we love most by limiting their freedom to be obedient to God? Will we surrender their freedom to live in obedience to Christ to fundamentalist leaders who do not walk in love, do not walk in truth and do not repent? Will we allow such men to set the boundaries of God's sovereignty over our sons and daughters, our homes, our churches and our mission throughout the world? Will we allow people who have locked freedom, love and truth out of their hearts to lock God's grace and sovereignty out of our churches and out of the lives of our sons and daughters in our generation and for generations to come? If the fundamentalist leaders in our Convention cannot obey Jesus Christ and walk in love and truth in their own lives, how can they make decisions for others regarding obedience to Christ?

The effect of the change in the Baptist Faith and Message is that the fundamentalist leaders and their followers are saying to other Christians and churches that they can be *free almost*, when Christ has promised his followers that they will be *free indeed*. (John 8:36) The change that the messengers made concerning the freedom of churches to call whomever God leads them to call falls far short of the promise of Jesus that they will be *free indeed*.

In fulfillment of prophecy and claiming the promise of Jesus that they will be free indeed, God is calling both men and women to preach in the Southern Baptist Convention, in many Baptist churches in other parts of the world, and in other denominations. We need to elect leaders in the Convention who love them, encourage them, equip them and include them in fellowship. Churches should be free to call them as pastors and ordain them to the gospel ministry when they believe the Spirit is leading them to do so. Instead, the fundamentalist leaders try to quench the Spirit of freedom in them, lock them out of fellowship, throw the weight of their hierachy of authority against them, refuse to train them and exclude them.

The fundamentalist leaders have a problem far greater than they can imagine. They led their followers to remove from the Baptist Faith and Message the statement that Christ "is the criterion by which the Bible is to be interpreted." They cannot remove from the Bible the many Scriptures that affirm the absolute authority of Christ. They cannot remove from the Bible the writings of the apostles that affirm that they believed all authority belongs to Jesus Christ. In more than 41,000 churches that claim a relationship with the SBC, pastors and teachers read, teach and preach that Jesus said, "*All authority in heaven and on earth has been given unto me.*" (Matt. 28:18)

Their problem might be even greater than that. God might be saying something to Southern Baptists similar to what he said through the prophet Amos:

> *I hate, I despise your religious feasts; I cannot stand your assemblies. Even though you bring me burnt offerings and grain offerings, I will not accept them. Though you bring choice fellowship offerings, I will have no regard for them. Away with the noise of your songs! I will not listen to the music of your harps. But let justice roll on like a river, righteousness like a never-failing stream.* (Amos 5:21-24)

Fortunately, there remains in the Baptist Faith and Message this important point: "As in the past, so in the future, Baptists should hold themselves free to revise their statements of faith as may seem to them wise and expedient." I believe, hope and pray that after our churches have seriously studied what it means to follow Christ and what the Spirit produces in believers, and have elected leaders who obey Christ in word and practice, the Baptist Faith and Message will be revised again. In my opinion, the most serious deficiency in the statement is that **it does not say clearly: Jesus Is Lord! We Must Obey Him!**

Authority Over Missionaries and Their Message

Having rebelled against God's highest law, that we should love each other as Christ loved us, and having established their own law as the highest law in the SBC, the fundamentalist leaders began enforcing their law of male supremacy throughout all the Convention's agencies, seminaries and boards. The International Mission Board, the North American Mission Board and all the seminaries supported by Cooperative Program funds submitted to the fundamentalist leaders. "International Mission Board (IMB) trustees voted January 24, 2001 in Augusta, Ga., to 'wholeheartedly' affirm the Baptist Faith and Message (BF&M) as revised by the Southern Baptist Convention (SBC) last June as the 'standard for carrying out the programs and ministries' of the 155-year-old agency . . . The board declined, however, to end its tradition of allowing some missionaries to serve even if they disagree on minor points, as long as they teach 'in accordance with and not contrary to' the confessional document even if they disagree on some minor points . . . "[3]

> The trustees also strongly affirmed the current overseas personnel and stateside staff members of the IMB by acknowledging that they already have been processed appropriately and that nothing more should be required of them. They strongly affirmed the personnel selection processes that have been used in the past and the people who have been selected . . . The board will continue its long-standing process of asking new overseas candidates to state whether or not they are in agreement with the *BF&M* and to explain any area of difference. They will be asked to commit themselves to carry out their responsibilities in accordance with and not contrary to the *BF&M* . . . [4]

IMB president Jerry Rankin later reversed the above policy and required all missionaries to sign the statement. Missionaries who cannot and will not in good conscience sign the statement are fired. (See Appendix B.) The action of Rankin and IMB trustees to try to prevent missionaries from working against the 2000 Baptist Faith and Message can be compared to the attempt of the Sanhedrin to tie the tongues of the apostles in order to prevent them from preaching in the name of Jesus. "*But to stop this thing from spreading any further among the people, we must warn these men to speak no longer to anyone in this name* (Jesus)." (Acts 4:17)

The fundamentalist leaders accused missionaries of not believing the Bible and of spreading heresy throughout the world. Now the real heresies of male supremacy and of exalting the rules of the apostles in local churches 2000 years ago above the eternal commandments of Christ can be clearly seen. Jesus said, "*I tell you the truth, no servant is greater than his master, nor is a messenger greater than the one who sent him.*" (John 13:16) The fundamentalist leaders thought they were in a position to spread their own rule throughout the entire world of Baptists and attacked the Baptist World Alliance.

SBC Fundamentalist Leaders Preach and Practice Another Gospel

Looking carefully at what the SBC fundamentalist leaders have preached and practiced for more than two decades, it appears that they are preaching and practicing **another gospel.** They cannot or will not correct their course and will not lead the Convention to solve the problem in relationships because, for the most part, **they are the problem! They cannot or will not stop deceiving, lying, slandering and will not repent!** Trustees cannot solve the problem because they are the disciples of the divisive fundamentalist leaders. Presidents of agencies, boards and seminaries cannot solve the problem because they are held accountable to divisive trustees. State Baptist convention leaders cannot solve the problem because of the aggression of the fundamentalist leaders who want to exert their authority over them. The pastors cannot solve the problem because they are hopelessly divided on the cause of the problem and don't know whom to believe. **Southern Baptist churches could solve the problems in the Southern Baptist Convention!**

CHAPTER 7

Appeal to the Churches

If your brother sins against you, go and show him his fault, just between the two of you. If he listens to you, you have won your brother over. But if he will not listen, take one or two others along, so that every matter may be established by the testimony of two or three witnesses. If he refuses to listen to them, tell it to the church; and if he refuses to listen even to the church, treat him as you would a pagan or a tax collector. (Matt. 18: 15-17)

In the confusion that prevails in our Convention, the advice of one of our great leaders of the past is appropriate for us today.

> L. R. Scarborough, the second president of Southwestern Baptist Theological Seminary, spoke of his last conference with B. H. Carroll. 'B. H. Carroll, the greatest man I ever knew, as he was about to die, a few days before he died, expecting me, as he wanted me, to succeed him as president of the seminary. I went in his room one day and he pulled himself up by my chair with his hands and looked me in the face. There were times when he looked like he was forty feet high. And he looked into my face and said, 'My boy, on this Hill orthodoxy, the old truth is making one of its last stands and I want to deliver to you a charge and I do it in the blood of Jesus Christ.' he said, 'You will be elected president of this seminary. I want you, if there ever comes heresy in your faculty, to take it to your faculty. If they won't hear you, take it to the trustees. If they won't hear you take it to the conventions that appointed them. If they won't hear you, take it to the common Baptists. They will hear you. And,' he said, 'I charge you in the name of Jesus Christ to keep it lashed to the

old Gospel of Jesus Christ.' As long as I have influence in that institution, by the grace of God I will stand by the old Book.[1]

Are today's Southern Baptist fundamentalist leaders "lashed to the old Gospel of Jesus Christ?" Or are they preaching and practicing *another gospel*?

Aspects of Another Gospel in SBC Fundamentalist Movement

Common Baptists in the churches can correct the course of the Southern Baptist Convention. I appeal to Southern Baptists and their churches to study the following themes and revelant biblical teachings that run throughout the Bible. Study the themes in light of the teachings of Jesus Christ, the author and finisher of our faith. (Hebrews 12:2).

1. Rebellion Against God's Greatest Commandments

God's greatest commandments are that his people love him with all their hearts, souls, minds and strength and love their neighbor as themselves. (Mark 12: 30-31) The fundamentalist leaders rebelled against God and his greatest law. A commandment is more than an appeal, a suggestion, a concept, or an ideal. **A commandment is an order, not an option! The King of the kingdom ordered his followers to love one another!**

Rather than obeying God's commandments to humble themselves and love and serve others, the fundamentalist leaders hardened their hearts, mixed good and evil, made their own law and excluded those who would not obey it. They are like the people who opposed Jesus and his message of love. Jesus told the Pharisees and the teachers of the law, "*Isaiah was right when he prophesied about you hypocrites; as it is written: 'These people honor me with their lips, but their hearts are far from me. They worship me in vain; for their teachings are but rules taught by men.' You have let go of the commands of God and are holding on to the traditions of men.*" (Mark 7:6-8)

The fundamentalist leaders chose to follow the ways and practices similar to those advocated by Niccolo' Machievelli, who lived from 1469 until 1527 in Florence, Italy. He was a brilliant political philosopher who advised the Magnificent Lorenzo de' Medici, a powerful and wealthy Florentine, on how to govern Florence and the Florentine empire, by giving him a copy of his writings entitled, *The Prince.* Later Machievelli wrote *The Prince and the Discourses*, which was a further development of his ideas. *Machievellianism* refers to the use of both good and evil in ruthless and unscrupulous ways to reach objectives. This is the uniqueness of Machievellian philosophy:

The renown of *The Prince* is precisely to have been the first and best book to argue that politics has and should have its own rules and should not accept rules of any kind or from any source where the object is not to win and prevail over others.[2]

Florence was a beautiful and wealthy city and the center of Italian art and culture. A great problem Florentine rulers faced related to its geographical location. Italy had not been united as a nation. Florence was located between the powerful Romans and the Pope to the south, the Lombards of Milan to the north, and the Venetians of Venice to the northeast. There were also the foreign powers, France and Spain. Florentines were vulnerable to the ambitions of conquest on the part of the leaders of all these powers.

Machievelli had studied the lives and reigns of many kings, princes, and other rulers who had lived in ancient times and up until his era. He studied how they became rulers and how they kept their domain. He studied how they expanded their domain or, in time, lost it. He developed the idea that political morality differs from and is not bound by the usual ethical norms and insisted that power is the decisive factor in political life.

In *The Prince* he gave advice to a new ruler on how to found a state and how to maintain himself in power.

> This has to be understood: that a prince and especially a new prince, cannot serve all those things for which men are held good, since he is often under a necessity, to maintain his state, of acting against faith, against charity, against humanity, and against religion. And he needs to have a spirit disposed to change as the winds of fortune and variations of things command him, and as I said above, not depart from good, when possible, but know how to enter into evil, when forced by necessity . . . So let a prince win and maintain his state; the means will always be judged honorable and will be praised by everyone.[3]

Whether the fundamentalist leaders intentionally followed Machievellian thought or not, a striking resemblance is there. Machievellian methods were used in the ways they gained and maintained their authority in the SBC. They used those same methods in making and enforcing their policies in mission work overseas.

2. Commitment of Evil Against Others, Especially Christian Leaders

The fundamentalist leaders gained their positions of leadership throughout the SBC by attacking other Christians, especially Christian leaders, whom they falsely accused, judged and slandered. They did the **opposite** of obeying the command of Jesus not to judge others before carefully judging oneself. *"Do not judge, or you too will be judged. For in the same way you judge others, you will be judged, and with the measure you use, it will be measured to you."* (Matt. 7:1-2) They did the **opposite** of following Paul's appeal for the way Christians should treat each other. *"Therefore, as we have opportunity, let us do good to all people, especially to those who belong to the family of believers."* (Galatians 6:10)

By removing Christian leaders from their offices, they were able to place themselves and those who were submissive to their authority in the vacated offices. In Machievellian thought, a prince could come to power in a variety of ways. One way was to inherit his position. Another way was through committing crimes against others. In the eighth chapter, *Of Those Who Have Attained A Principality Through Crimes*, he cited an example of this in Agothocles the Sicilian and how he established his power.

> (He) became king of Syracuse not only from private fortune but from a mean and abject one . . . He determined to become prince and to hold with violence and without obligation to anyone else that which had been conceded by agreement . . . one morning he assembled the people and the Senate of Syracuse as if he had to decide things pertinent to the republic. At a signal he had ordered, he had all the senators and the richest of the people killed by his soldiers. Once they were dead, he seized and held the principate of that city without any civil controversy.[4]

By refusing to love other Christians and by engaging them in spiritual warfare, the fundamentalist leaders did the **opposite** of proving that Christians are truly disciples of Jesus Christ. (John 13:35)

3. Failure to Live by the Truth

*Oh, what a tangled web we weave,
when first we practice to deceive.*

Shakespeare

God gives the Holy Spirit to Christians. The Holy Spirit, like Christ, is not divided. God does not give a Spirit of half truth or truth mixed with deceit, lies and slander to Christians. One of the gifts of the Spirit is that of distinguishing between spirits. (1 Cor. 13:10) When a person lies, deceives or slanders another person, it indicates that the person is unclean inside his heart. Jesus said, *"For from within, out of men's hearts, come evil thoughts, sexual immorality, theft, murder, adultery, greed, malice, deceit, lewdness, envy, slander, arrogance and folly. All these evils come from inside and make a man unclean."* (Mark 7:21-23)

Wholesome conversation and speech that builds others up should come from the hearts, lips and mouths of Christians. (Eph. 4:29-31; Col. 4:6) Machievelli advised that, when necessary, the prince should behave like a beast. Concerning the use of force, he wrote:

> How laudable it is for a prince to keep his faith, and to live with honesty and not by astuteness, everyone understands. Nonetheless one sees by experience in our times that the princes who have done great things are those who have taken little account of faith and have known how to get around men's brains with their astuteness; and in the end they have overcome those who founded themselves on loyalty. Thus, you must know that there are two kinds of combat; one with laws, the other with force. The first is proper to man, the second to beasts; but because the first is often not enough, one must have recourse to the second. Therefore it is necessary for a prince to know well how to use the beast and the man.[5]

Christian psychiatrist M. Scott Peck in his book, *People of the Lie: The Hope for Healing Human Evil*, makes the point that people who go on lying and deceiving do so because they are inherently evil. He wrote:

> The evil in this world is committed by the spiritual fat cats, by the Pharisees of our own day, the self-righteous who think they are without sin because they are unwilling to suffer the discomfort of significant self-examination . . . A predominant characteristic, however, of the behavior of those I call evil is scapegoating. Because in their hearts they consider themselves above reproach, they must lash out at anyone who does reproach them. . . . Evil, then, is most often committed in order to scapegoat, and the people I label as evil are chronic scapegoaters . . . Evil originates not in the absence of guilt but in the effort to escape it . . . all who are evil also take the law into their own hands, to destroy life or liveliness in defense of their narcissistic self-image.[6]

Peck equates the biblical "pride" to the psychiatric term "malignant narcissism," which is projecting onto others and contaminating others with one's own evil. He wrote about pride: "Being at the very root of evil, it is no accident that church authorities have generally considered pride first among the sins."[7]

People who go on being evil and keep on lying often confuse others, who are unable to work through webs of lies and half-truths and find the substance of truth. Peck wrote, "Lies confuse. The evil are 'the people of the lie,' deceiving others as they also build layer upon layer of self-deception."[8] Peck makes the point that psychiatrists themselves, in dealing with truly evil people, must be very careful not to become confused by what they are being told. They must attempt to help evil people "from a position of remarkable psychological and spiritual strength."[9]

Many evil people want to appear to be good. Peck emphasizes that evil people have a great desire to appear to be good, but lack compelling desire to be good. He wrote:

> Utterly dedicated to preserving their self-image of perfection, they are unceasingly engaged in the effort to maintain the appearance of moral purity. They worry about this a great deal. They are acutely sensitive to social norms and what others might think of them . . . The words 'image,' 'appearance,' and 'outwardly' are crucial to understanding the morality of the evil. While they lack any motivation to be good, they intensely desire to appear to be good. Their 'goodness' is all on the level of pretense. It is, in effect, a lie. That is why they are the 'people of the lie.'[10]

Evil people spend much energy trying to disguise the evil within. Peck wrote about disguise.

> Since the primary motive of the evil is disguise, one of the places evil people are most likely to be found is within the church. What better way to conceal one's evil from oneself, as well as from others, than to be a deacon or some other highly visible form of Christian within our culture? . . . I do not mean to imply that the evil are anything other than a small minority among the religious or that the religious motives of most people are spurious. I mean only that evil people tend to gravitate toward piety for the disguise and concealment it can offer them . . . It is only one kind of pain they cannot tolerate: the pain of their own conscience, the pain of the realization of their own sinfulness and imperfection.[11]

Truth is an essential element of God's righteousness. It cannot be manipulated or negotiated by anybody. It needs no defense because it defends itself. It cannot be decided by either majority or unanimous vote. It is like the scales in Daniel 5:27. One person telling the truth outweighs a multitude telling lies. It is like the plumb line in Amos 7:8. Truth does not measure itself by any person or group of persons. Instead, people are measured by truth.

Anybody who knowingly and willfully suppresses the truth runs the risk of having a headlong collision with the wrath of God! (John 3:19-21; Rom. 1:18; Eph. 5:11)

4. Rejection of the Ministry of Reconciliation

Christ commanded his followers to love others and to make serious efforts to be reconciled with them. Paul taught that Christians, as ambassadors of Christ, are given the ministry of reconciliation by God. Instead of taking seriously and practicing the ministry of reconciliation, the fundamentalist leaders rejected this important Christian ministry. In its place was their own practice of exclusion: **Like It Or Get Out.** Since the Holy Spirit was living in the hearts of the people they were excluding, in effect they were excluding Christ. Jesus said, *"I tell you the truth, whatever you did for one of the least of these brothers of mine, you did for me . . . whatever you did not do for one of the least of these, you did not do for me."* (Matt. 25:40, 45) Other Scriptures on reconciliation are Matt. 5:23-26 and 2 Cor. 5:18-20.

5. Quenching the Spirit and his Gifts in Themselves and Others

God gives the same Holy Spirit to everyone who believes that Jesus Christ is Lord. Paul appealed to Christians to *"Submit to one another out of reverence for Christ."* (Eph. 5:21) The spirit of submission to each other and the spirit to rule over others are different spirits. John wrote, *"Dear friends, do not believe every spirit, but test the spirits to see whether they are from God, because many false prophets have gone out into the world."* (1 John 4:1)

The Holy Spirit is the Spirit of wisdom, understanding, counsel, power, knowledge and the fear of the Lord. (Isaiah 11:2-3) It is the Spirit of truth and grace. (John 1:17) It is the Spirit of freedom. (John 8:31-36; Gal. 5:1) It is the Spirit of love, joy and peace . . . (Gal. 5:22)

While many Southern Baptists are trying to live in the Spirit and be submissive to each other in obedience to Christ, some fundamentalist leaders do not seem to know how to live in love, peace and submission with other Christians. They make war, not peace. They are peacebreakers, not peacemakers. They have not learned the lesson Jesus taught his disciples: " . . . *all who draw the sword will die by the sword."* (Matt. 26:52) Machievelli wrote that the prince must practice the art of war:

> Thus, a prince should have no other object, nor any other thought, nor take anything else but the art of war and its orders and discipline; for that is the only art which is of concern to one who commands.[12]

6. Closing the Door of Freedom Opened by God

God is the author of freedom and is on the side of freedom for people. Jesus promised freedom to those who continue to follow him and live in truth. (John 8:31-36) Paul and Peter lived in Christian freedom and appealed to others not to abuse the freedom Christ had given them. (Gal. 5:13; 1 Peter 2:16) John wrote that God had given his people an open door that no one could shut. (Rev. 3:7-8)

Unable to live in Christian freedom themselves, the fundamentalist leaders made a law of their own and convinced their followers to pass their law. They tried to coerce others to obey their law and used excommunication as a weapon to enforce it.

Fear is a powerful motivator. The fundamentalist leaders use their authority over others to create fear. People fear being falsely accused, slandered and excluded. People fear being fired from their jobs when they have given their lives to be obedient to Christ and to serve only him.

Missionaries are fired (the IMB will no longer employ or support them) if they do not sign the 2000 Baptist Faith and Message. Although it is a law written by men and contradicts God's highest law, the fundamentalist leaders enforce their law by creating fear.

Missionaries have committed their lives by faith to missionary service, fully confident that Southern Baptist churches would support them in prayer and material needs, but now they have learned they also must submit to the authority of the fundamentalist leaders or be fired by the IMB.

Most missionaries have no source of income other than that provided by the IMB, have no home in the United States to which to return, have no furniture except what they have overseas, have no personal automobile, and have no health insurance except that provided by the IMB. They do not have sufficient money readily available for the purchase of airline tickets for their family and shipment of their goods back to the United States and depend on the IMB to provide for their retirement. When faced with the alternative of signing the 2000 Baptist Faith and Message or face being fired, most missionaries signed it. Those who cannot and will not sign are fired.

Machievelli wrote about whether it is better for a prince to rule by fear or by love, concluding that it is better for the prince to rule by fear.

> From this a dispute arises whether it is better to be loved than feared, or the reverse. The answer is that one would want to be both the one and the other; but because it is difficult to put them together, it is much safer to be feared than loved, if one has to lack one of the two . . . And men have less hesitation to offend one who makes himself loved than one who makes himself feared; for love is held by a chain of obligation, which, because men are wicked, is broken at every opportunity for their own utility, but fear is held by a dread of punishment that never forsakes you.[13]

Christians are servants of the Prince of Peace, who rules by love. The fundamentalist leaders have not learned that, for many Christians, fear is no match at all for the compelling love of Christ. (2 Cor. 5:14)

7. Establishment and Enforcement of Partiality

God does not show partiality between people. (Deut. 1:17; Acts 10:34) Jesus used words showing impartiality such as all, anyone, everyone, and whosoever. The apostles taught against practicing partiality and showing favoritism in churches. (Col. 3:25; 1 Tim. 5:21; James 2: 1-4; 3:17)

Paul urged Christians to be humble and to consider others better than themselves. *"Do nothing out of selfish ambition or vain conceit, but in humility consider others better than yourselves."* (Phil. 2:3) Behaving in ways opposite biblical teachings, the fundamentalist leaders considered themselves better than others and demanded that partiality be shown **to them.**

They excluded everyone who would not show partiality **to them.** They excluded everyone who placed greater love and loyalty to Jesus Christ than **to them.** They practiced showing favoritism of men above women and of their sons above their daughters, claiming their practice was because they believe the Bible!

8. Refusal to Listen to the Church

God called on Israel to hear and obey him. (Deut. 6:3) Often Jesus said, *"He who has ears, let him hear."* (Matt. 11:15; 13:9) The fundamentalist leaders did not hear the voice of Jesus Christ in the Bible and refused to hear the voice of Christ speaking to them through the church.

They did not hear the church speaking through appeals of Baptist leaders not to politicize the SBC. They failed to hear the church when fellow Baptist leaders appealed to them not to be excluded. They did not hear the church speaking to them in the Peace Committee. They did not hear the church speaking to them when numerous new organizations, such as the CBF, the Alliance of Baptists, Mainstream Baptists, and Women in Ministry were established by people who could not and would not follow them.

They did not hear when a new Southern Baptist foreign missions sending agency was established and IMB missionaries resigned from the IMB because they refused to work under the authority of anyone except Jesus Christ. They do not hear when churches, state conventions and associations divide.

Paul warned Christians to watch out for people who cause divisions in the body of Christ. (1Cor. 16:7) He advised Titus:

But avoid foolish controversies and genealogies and arguments and quarrels about the law, because these are unprofitable and useless. Warn a divisive person once, and then warn him a second time. After that, have nothing to do with him. You may be sure that such a man is warped and sinful; he is self-condemned. (Titus 3:9-11)

The fundamentalist leaders do not hesitate to practice cruelty on others if it is necessary for them to rule and keep their movement united. Machievelli wrote:

> A prince, therefore, so as to keep his subjects united, and faithful, should not care about the infamy of cruelty, because with few exceptions he will be more merciful than those who for the sake of too much mercy allows disorders to continue, from which come killings or robberies; for these customarily harm a whole community, but the executions that come from the prince harm one particular person.[14]

9. Self Exaltation

In the Bible, only God is to be glorified and highly exalted. All people are commanded to humble themselves and to obey and praise God. The first requirement God made to Israel for their nation to be forgiven and healed was that they humble themselves. (2 Chron. 7:14)

The SBC fundamentalist leaders do not hear the call to humility and service. They do the **opposite** and exalt themselves as rulers. While they remain in their exalted positions, they apparently take no thought that they have led Christians to despise each other rather than love each other. While they hold on to the traditions of men and let go of the commands of God, they exalt themselves. While they quench the Spirit and his gifts in themselves and others, they exalt themselves. While they enforce their law based on partiality, they exalt themselves. While they do not tell the truth and do not live by the truth, they exalt themselves. While they reject the ministry of reconciliation and refuse to listen to the church, they exalt themselves. While the body of Christ is dividing and fragmenting, they exalt themselves.

In addition to self exaltation, they gather around them only those who will exalt them and submit to their authority. Machievelli wrote: "... and men are so simple and obedient to present necessities that he who deceives will always find someone who will let himself be deceived."[15]

10. Ignoring Biblical Warnings Against Disobedience to God

The fundamentalist leaders not only rebelled against God's highest law and disobeyed other commandments, they also ignored many clear warnings in Scripture against disobeying God. God created people free moral agents with freedom to make choices. From the Garden of Eden to the present day, the primary issues faced by all people are good and evil, which people are free to choose. They are

not free to choose the consequences of their choices. The consequences are built into and are inseparably connected to the choices people make.

When the SBC fundamentalist leaders chose to preach and practice **another gospel,** apparently they were blind to the consequences of the choice they made. The connection between obeying Jesus Christ and the consequences of refusing to obey him are found in John 15:1-2 and 1 John 2:3-5. Consistency in Christian living and continuing to do what Jesus did is rooted in John 14:12.

The discrepancy between claiming to follow Christ and despising other Christians is found in 1 John 2:9-11. The seriousness and consequences of falsely accusing and speaking any kind of evil against others are found in Deut. 19:15-21 and Matt. 5:21-22. The consequences of exalting oneself are found in Psalm 18:27; Matt. 23:12; and Luke 14:11.

The Only Legitimate Division

There is only one legitimate division authorized by Christ. Jesus and the early church leaders prayed and worked to keep unity and prevent division within the church, which is the body of Christ. Jesus said:

> *Do you think I came to bring peace on earth? No, I tell you, but division. From now on there will be five in one family divided against each other, three against two and two against three. They will be divided, father against son and son against father, mother against daughter and daughter against mother, mother-in-law against daughter-in-law and daughter-in-law against mother-in-law.* (Luke 12:51-53)

In this division Christ himself is the divider. Other passages dealing with this division are in Matt: 10:34-42; and Luke 12:49-53. In these passages Jesus deals with the division that exists between those who believe in him and obey him and those who don't. Jesus cannot be divided from the values and virtues that derive from him and his name, such as love, light, grace, mercy, and truth.

No one has the authority from Christ to use his name if the values and virtues associated with his name are not exalted! Jesus said, *"If a kingdom is divided against itself, that kingdom cannot stand. And if a house is divided against itself, that house cannot stand."* (Mark 3:24-25)

The division Christ predicted and authorized cuts through all ties and relationships, even through families. Nothing and nobody must separate anyone from Christ and obedience to him. We should have leaders in the SBC who make every effort possible to keep the Convention united in Christ and in the values and virtues inherent in him.

Appeal to the Churches

Conflicts of Accountability

The SBC fundamentalist leaders want others in the Convention to be accountable to them for doctrine. Convention officers, trustees, leaders of agencies, boards and institutions have submitted to their authority and are now accountable to them. Anyone who questions their authority is fired.

The fundamentalist leaders have devastated the agencies, institutions, boards and relationships with Baptists throughout the world by imposing a gospel in which their Bible is exalted above Christ; love is not the theme; truth is suppressed; freedom is lost; and division is praised as victory. They have led the Convention into ruin. They see victory through Machievellian eyes. He wrote:

> When those states that are acquired, as has been said, are accustomed to living by their own laws and in liberty, there are three modes for those who want to hold them: First, ruin them; second, go there and live personally; third, let them live by their own laws, taking tribute from them by creating within them an oligarchical state which keeps them friendly toward you . . . For in truth there is no secure mode to possess them other than to ruin them . . . Hence it should be noted that in taking hold of a state, he who seizes it should examine all the offences necessary for him to commit, and do them all in a stroke, so as not to have to renew them every day and, by not renewing them, to secure men and gain them to himself with benefits.[16]

The Coming Crash

Every time the fundamentalist leaders sinned against other Christians, they sinned first against God, secondly against themselves, and lastly against others. Jesus spent about three years teaching the eternal wisdom of the Father. Everyone who believed what he said and practiced what he commanded was like a wise man who built his house on a rock. (Matt. 7:24-25) Everyone who heard what he said but did not believe him and did not put his teachings into practice was like a foolish man who built his house on sand. *"The rain came down, the streams rose, and the winds blew and beat against that house, and it fell with a great crash."* (Matt. 7:27)

Jesus called disciples who put his teachings into practice **every day.** *"Then he said to them all: If anyone would come after me, he must deny himself and take up his cross daily and follow me."* (Luke 9:23) Peck quoted C. S. Lewis on daily commitment to Christ: "There is no neutral ground in the universe: every square inch, every split second is claimed by God and counterclaimed by Satan."[17]

For more than two decades, the SBC fundamentalist leaders have opposed and worked *against* the authority of Christ, *against* love, *against* truth, *against* unity in the Convention, and *against* people and churches who would not submit to their authority.

Perhaps the most crucial question Southern Baptist churches have ever faced regarding their relationship to the Southern Baptist Convention is whether they will be accountable to the fundamentalist leaders for doctrine, or **whether they will hold the fundamentalist leaders accountable for preaching and practicing another gospel!**

According to Jesus, a great crash awaits them and their followers, all of whom have been clearly warned in Scripture not to challenge the authority of Jesus Christ, not to disobey him, and not to let themselves be deceived.

Southern Baptist churches and the messengers they send to the SBC hold the keys concerning the future of the SBC. If they continue to elect messengers who submit to the authority of divisive leaders and continue to send financial support to be administered by divisive leaders, more division awaits churches, associations, state Baptist conventions and the SBC. Churches will crash too.

If churches wake up, commit themselves to believing and practicing the teachings of Christ, fan the flame of the gift of the Spirit God has given to all believers, unite in their obedience to Christ, and elect leaders who are obedient to Christ, an entirely new future awaits churches, associations, state Baptist conventions and the Southern Baptist Convention.

CHAPTER 8

Actions for Churches

Why do you call me, 'Lord, Lord,' and do not do what I say?
(Luke 6:46)

The Southern Baptist Convention has come full circle. The Convention was organized when it was impossible for owners of slaves to be appointed as missionaries. Now it is impossible for IMB missionaries to be appointed or to continue in missionary service unless they submit to Convention leaders who are enslaved to deceit, lies and slander and who suppress the truth. (Rom. 1:18) *"Don't you know that when you offer yourselves to someone to obey him as slaves, you are slaves to the one whom you obey—whether you are slaves to sin, which leads to death, or to obedience, which leads to righteousness?"* (Rom. 6:16)

Southern Baptist churches could correct the course of the Southern Baptist Convention. Discipline in study and prayer and decisive actions could lead to decisive changes in the Convention. Based on sound doctrinal and theological foundations, individuals and churches should practice daily in their personal lives, churches and relationships what they have learned. While some Convention leaders aggressively attack other Christians and churches and thrive on controversy, other pastors and lay persons who are obedient to Christ, love other Christians and love the Convention could lead churches to resolve the problems. I offer these suggestions to churches.

Study and Ask Questions About the Bible

One of the most effective teaching methods of Jesus, the master Teacher, was to ask questions. He required his followers to think and give answers to searching questions. *"Who do you say I am?"* (Matt. 16:15) *"You do not want to leave too, do you?"* (John 6:67) *"How can you say to your brother, Let me take the speck out of your eye, when all the time there is a plank in your own eye?"* (Matt. 7:4) *"What good will it be for a man if he gains the whole world, yet forfeits his soul? Or what can a man give in exchange for his soul?"* (Matt. 16:26) *" . . . What is that to you? You must follow me."* (John 21:22)

Christians will ask questions until they die, often without ever gaining complete knowledge of all the answers. It is important to live by faith and in obedience to Christ *while one is asking questions.* While studying the Bible, hiding it in our hearts and asking the Holy Spirit for guidance, ask questions.

The doctrine of the priesthood of the believer is based on the belief that every person who repents of his sin and believes in his heart that Jesus is Lord receives the gift of the Holy Spirit. The Spirit enables the believer to obey Jesus. Historic Baptist practice affirms the priesthood of individual believers in Christ and their freedom to study and interpret the Bible individually.

This does not mean that one should retreat into isolation and study only by and for oneself, but rather that the entire body of Christ serves as an important resource for learning for all Christians. Christians should study the Bible, ask questions about it and learn from each other in groups. We should love and respect others who are studying and asking questions, just as we want them to love and respect us. Different opinions and beliefs should not lead to division among people who are led by the Spirit, love and respect each other and are obedient to Christ.

Since the Southern Baptist Convention is embroiled in a controversy concerning the role of women in church and home, it is timely to study biblical teachings on this issue. Jesus distinguished clearly between the commands of God and the traditions of men. (Mark 7:9) The apostles were citizens of the kingdom of God and had learned their doctrines from the teachings of Jesus. They were also citizens of the world of their times and were concerned about current events and issues that affected their lives. They had deep and strong beliefs and convictions about both the kingdom of God and about issues of their times.

Those who wrote what later became the Bible did not always clearly distinguish in their writings which were eternal commands of God and which applied mostly to their times. We see some of the complexity of this matter in Paul's writings to the Christians in Corinth. *"To the married I give this command (not I, but the Lord) . . ."* (1 Cor. 7:10). Then he writes, *"To the rest I say this (I, not the Lord) . . ."* (7:12) *"In my judgment, she is happier if she stays as she is—and I think that I too have the Spirit of God."* (7:40)

Those who lived in their times probably understood better than we who live 2000 years later what the apostles meant. We have the teachings of Jesus and the leadership of the Holy Spirit to help us discern which teachings are more concerned with the commands of God and which are more concerned with the traditions of men, recognizing that all of the first disciples and apostles were Jewish men who had strong traditions concerning the dominant role of men in families and society.

Are Paul's desires concerning how women should dress, wear their hair and use decorative ornaments more on the side of the commands of God for all people of all times or more on the traditions of his times? (1 Tim. 2:9) Is his strict position on women not teaching, not having authority over a man and remaining silent more on the side of the commands of God for women of all times or more on the side of the traditions of his times? (1 Tim. 2:11-12) Are the applications Paul made about men not covering their heads and women covering their heads more about the commands of God or more about the traditions of the first century? (1 Cor. 11:4-7)

The fundamentalist leaders of the Southern Baptist Convention fall short of trying to reconcile the prohibitions Paul placed on women with his positive appeal to men to "*love your wives, just as Christ loved the church and gave himself up for her . . .*" (Eph. 5:25). The fundamentalists also overlook the fact that the apostles were only men, just as we are, not gods.

Paul and Barnabas asked "*Men, why are you doing this? We too are only men, human like you.*" (Acts 14:15) They overlook the complexity of these matters, which Paul dealt with by writing: "*In the Lord, however, woman is not independent of man, nor is man independent of woman. For as woman came from man, so also man is born of woman. But everything comes from God.*" (1 Cor. 11:11-12)

Who decides how we deal with these issues today? Can Christians in local churches decide these matters, or should Convention leaders from outside the churches tell Christians in the churches that they do not believe the Bible and should get out of the Convention if they do not believe as the fundamentalists believe? Are differences of opinion on these issues great enough to cause division in a group that is sincerely studying the Scriptures and wanting to be true to Christ in our generation? Should a church, or association, or state convention or the Southern Baptist Convention or the Baptist World Alliance divide because some people have different views on applying the commands of Christ in our day? Should the members of a local group be so set in their opinions and hostile to the opinions of others that they would try to drive them out of the group, or church, or association, or state convention or the Southern Baptist Convention? How does our freedom in Christ affect our views on these matters? (John 8:31-

32,36) The Holy Spirit lives in and gives freedom to all believers. *"Now the Lord is the Spirit, and where the Spirit of the Lord is, there is freedom."* (2 Cor. 3:17)

Does the command of Christ that we love one another as he loved us override differing opinions about less important matters? Do the prayers of Jesus that his body be one carry more weight than the opinions of people about less important matters? (John 17)

An appropriate question to ask as we study the Scriptures is: *"If God is for us, who can be against us?"* (Romans 8:31) Or, as the case might be, "If God is for a value or virtue, who could be against that value or virtue?" We know that he who is against God and what God is for is especially against Christians loving each other and being united with one another.

Study and Ask Questions About Your Church

Is the entire church, including the leaders and lay persons, united in obeying the great commission of Jesus Christ? *"Therefore go and make disciples of all nations, baptizing them in the name of the Father and of the Son and of the Holy Spirit, and teaching them to obey everything I have commanded you . . ."* (Matt. 28:19-20a) How can people teach others to obey Christ if they themselves are not wholeheartedly committed to obeying him?

Have some members of your church abandoned the great commission of Jesus Christ in favor of the world vision of Southern Baptist fundamentalist leaders, which was stated by FMB Trustee Ron Wilson? *"If we cannot address liberalism and the mistakes of Europe, we will never be able to address liberalism and other problems in other parts of the world."* How can people who cannot solve their own problems solve the problems of people in other parts of the world? Which of these visions does your church view as its primary mission? If some members of the church want the church to abandon the great commission of Christ in favor of another commission, have the church vote on it so that all members will know the church's intentions.

Have some of the leaders of your church fallen for the hoax of the Southern Baptist fundamentalist leaders by abandoning the Bible in favor of a theory about the Bible? Do they practice double-minded thinking by saying they believe the Bible in your church, but go to Southern Baptist Convention meetings where believing a theory about the Bible is called believing the Bible? If there is not a clear consensus on this issue, lead the church to study this question and vote on whether the Bible or a theory about the Bible is the church's textbook of faith.

Have some church leaders tried to apply the fundamentalist tactic of *Like It Or Get Out* in your church? Have they tried to rule over dedicated Christian men and women who gave many years to building up a fellowship rich in love and faith and committed to Southern Baptist mission work throughout the world? Have church leaders shown no compassion when such dedicated people were forced into silence or left the church they helped to build?

How does your church make decisions? How is information handled by church leaders? Is the entire church fully informed about issues affecting the life of your church, including those about the Southern Baptist Convention? Do church leaders view themselves as rulers or as servants of the church? Are all members, men and women, boys and girls, encouraged to develop all the gifts the Holy Spirit has given them? Do church leaders believe that giving of spiritual gifts is under the sovereignty of the Holy Spirit? (1 Cor. 12:11) Are all places of church leadership open to all who have developed the gifts of the Spirit, or do church leaders practice partiality? If your church practices partiality, does it join with other churches that practice partiality and exclude churches that do not practice partiality? Are church members encouraged to study and discuss these issues openly and in freedom?

Hold Church Leaders Accountable to the Church

Do your church leaders view their primary accountability to the church, which they have been elected to serve, or to people outside your church? Hold church leaders accountable for telling the truth about any communication or involvement from outside the church that encourages any belief or action that is in conflict with the teachings of Christ, the leadership of the Holy Spirit and a good conscience. Ask them to record and report any such communication from outside the church, including means of communication, dates and names of persons who are interfering in the life of the church.

Hold your church's messengers to associational, state convention and SBC meetings accountable to your church. Elect messengers from your church who have participated in serious Bible study with others and who are willing to learn that all Christians who love Christ devotedly and study the Bible faithfully believe differently about some important issues. One of those issues is that some churches today practice their freedom in Christ by electing gifted women to all positions of church leadership? Have messengers from your church voted to exclude other deeply committed Christians from full fellowship in the association, state convention or Southern Baptist Convention? Will they listen to and learn from other Christians as they explain why they believe and practice as they do?

Hold church messengers accountable to the church for their votes on programs, election of leaders and budgets in associational, state convention and

Southern Baptist Convention meetings. Ask the messengers pertinent questions. Church members who support the church are entitled to know how their messengers vote on issues that affect the church and its mission to the world.

Study and Ask Questions About Your Church and the Cooperative Program

For more than a century Southern Baptists had confidence that when they brought their tithes and offerings to their church, and their church sent part of the offerings to the Convention to support the work of Christ, leaders of the Convention would administer those offerings to promote the kingdom of God. One of the primary objectives of SBC fundamentalists was to gain control of the millions of dollars Southern Baptists send annually to the SBC through the Cooperative Program. When they achieved their objective, they skillfully selected targets to defund that might challenge their claims to authority over others in believing the Bible. **Southern Baptists elected leaders with corrupted minds and consciences who have corrupted the Cooperative Program!** (Titus 1:15) The result of the ways they used Cooperative Program funds to exclude individuals and churches is division in the Convention.

Southern Baptist churches and individuals should study carefully whether their offerings that are sent to the Convention today through the Cooperative Program are supporting the work of Christ or supporting corrupt leaders who deceive, lie and give false reports. These leaders deny the freedom of churches to study the Bible under the leadership of the Holy Spirit and to love and unite with other churches that want to obey Christ. **They exclude churches that do not accept a theory of the Bible above the Bible and churches that do not show partiality among the members!**

As fundamentalists used defunding for wrong reasons, Southern Baptists can use defunding for right reasons. Defunding might take the course of a sudden and complete defunding, as FMB trustees did to the seminary in Rüschlikon in 1991. It might take the course that the International Baptist Church of Brussels took to defund the European Baptist Convention, in which all funds were withheld except a small amount to cover basic administrative costs.

Any individual or church that blindly sends money to the Cooperative Program today indicates an unawareness of the hoax that fundamentalist leaders used to gain control of the SBC. Instead, the individual or church supports divisive leaders who are leading the SBC and local churches into division, surrenders the biblical and historic Baptist principle of the priesthood of the believer, and reinforces the fundamentalists' practice of obeying men rather than God. They are also at the same time and with the same money supporting the firing of missionaries who will not yield to pressure to obey men rather than God. Blind support of the Cooperative Program today is used to finance the peacebreakers and fire the peacemakers. Intelligent Southern Baptists are fully capable of deciding how to use their tithes and offerings to promote the kingdom of God.

Create Open Forums of Discussion

One of the ways individuals, churches and Southern Baptist leaders could help promote understanding and unity in churches and the Convention would be to organize public forums for discussion. While churches and the Convention are dividing, the people in the churches who are paying for the division are entitled to know the reasons for the division. When the church in Jerusalem faced a serious doctrinal question, the apostles and elders hosted a council to discuss whether Gentile Christians were required to keep the ceremonial laws of Moses in order to be accepted fully into Christian fellowship with Jewish Christians. (Acts 15:1-21) After debating and deciding the issue in Jerusalem, in order to keep unity with other churches, those leaders decided to get the Christians in Jerusalem and Antioch together for further discussions.

> *Then the apostles and elders, with the whole church, decided to choose some of their own men and send them to Antioch with Paul and Barnabas. They chose Judas (called Barabbas) and Silas, two men who were leaders among the brothers. With them they sent the following letter: The apostles and elders, your brothers, to the Gentile believers in Antioch, Syria and Cicilia: Greetings. We have heard that some went out from us without our authorization and disturbed you, troubling your minds by what they said . . .* (Acts 15:22 ff)

Throughout their history, Baptists have practiced open debate to answer false accusations and resolve complex issues. An example of Baptists calling for "Public Disputations" occurred in England when Baptists were accused of being heretics and of belonging to a sect.

> Perhaps no group in England made more use of public disputations than did Baptists. Between 1641 and 1700 at least 109 such public debates involving Baptists were held in England, with 79 of these between 1641 and 1660. These debates pitted one or more Baptist champions against opponents from Anglican, Quaker, Independent, or, sometimes, Roman Catholic groups. Baptists welcomed these occasions, for they gave opportunity for declaring the gospel to large crowds, helped defend Baptists against unjust slanders, and often led

to numerous conversions and the planting of new churches. Many leading Baptists of that time were converted at public disputations, such as John Tombes, Henry Jessey, and Christopher Blackwood. All of these became popular disputation leaders themselves, along with other Baptists such as William Kiffin, Jeremiah Ives, and John Bunyan.[1]

Discussions in churches should follow the example of the early church: *"Let all things be done decently and in order."* (1 Cor. 14:40 . . . KJV) Increasing Christian faith and knowledge should be the goal of the discussions. *"But in your hearts set apart Christ as Lord. Always be prepared to give an answer to everyone who asks you to give a reason for the hope that you have. But do this with gentleness and respect . . . "* (1 Peter 3:15)

No coercion of other's opinions, no insulting language, no manipulative tactics nor anything else that might hinder the freedom and rights of people to speak, be heard and learn should be allowed. Those who are sincerely seeking the truth are entitled to hear the various points of view and make decisions for themselves and their churches. The Southern Baptist Convention belongs to the churches, which belong to Christ. Any other view is a departure from the authority of Jesus Christ, other biblical teachings and historic Baptist practice.

Author Available For Discussions

The author would be honored and pleased to participate in fair, free, and open forums of discussion intended to overcome the divisions and bring unity to our Convention. Discussions could be sponsored by individuals, churches or groups of churches. He can be contacted at ejmerritt@aol.com *or through the publisher at* www.rbrent.com.

CHAPTER 9

A New Vision for a New Future for Southern Baptists

Where there is no vision, the people perish.
(Proverbs 29:18 . . . KJV)

Vision is important to any endeavor, whether secular or spiritual. Vision involves what one sees, foresight, and the ability to visualize. Without vision people flounder and lose hope. The vision of Jesus was remarkable in that he saw people not only as who they were but also as who they could become. He had the unique ability to know what God created people to be in the beginning and the unique power to recreate people according to God's original intention for them. God's Spirit in believers is the enabling force that can make that happen.

The foundation of the vision of Jesus was the Father, who was his primary, unwavering and positive point of reference. Everything he did and said was rooted in the character of the Father who sent him. He came to earth because the Father loved his people. He taught people how to live full and meaningful lives because his Father loved his people. He forgave their sins, healed them, died on the cross, was raised from the dead and ascended to heaven because the Father loved his people. He is preparing an eternal home for his people because he loves them. His eternal plan, purpose and will have two dimensions. The first is that all the people in all the world know God and love him. The second is that all the people in all the world love each other.

The other point of reference for Jesus was evil and the evil one, Satan, who has been God's enemy from the beginning. He tries to distort God's character, demolish his plans and destroy the influence of God's people in the world. Everywhere Jesus encountered evil on earth, he attributed it to its one and only source, Satan, a murderer, a liar and the father of lies. (John 8:44) Jesus came *"so that by his death he might destroy him who holds the power of death— that is, the devil—and free those who all their lives were held in slavery by their fear of death."* (Hebrews 2:14-15)

One of the tasks every generation faces is that of rebuilding from ruin caused by themselves, others or nature. The writer of Ecclesiastes said "... *There is a time to tear down and a time to build* ..." (Eccle. 3:3) Israel sometimes faced the task of rebuilding walls, cities and the temple. (Isa. 61:4) Southern Baptists in this generation face the most gigantic task of rebuilding from ruin ever faced in our history. When ruin is so complete, people have a unique opportunity to study carefully why the ruin occurred, to learn from past mistakes and to build something better than what existed before. One of the most valuable resources God makes available to the world is the minds of bright people enlightened by the Holy Spirit. Such leaders can help churches, associations, state conventions and the Southern Baptist Convention rebuild from the ruin of the past two decades.

Our Convention will never again be just like it was. It never was and never will be perfect. Those who tried to purge it and make others like themselves made it worse. It could be rebuilt stronger than it was in the past. The lessons of the past could help us learn from our errors and avoid many of them in the future.

We are divided in many places and in many ways. We cannot now see perfectly the shapes and structures that will serve us better in the future, but we could start. Relationships could be healed. Trust could be rebuilt. Promises could be kept. Possibilities could be seen and pursued through people who seek to have the mind of Christ and who do the will of God as a new vision is revealed.

Potential in Ourselves

Jesus did not waver in pursuing his mission and his vision, which were identical. Followers of Jesus can be shaped by his mission and his vision. His mission is stated in Isaiah 53 and 61, Matthew 4:12-17, 23-25, and Matt. 11:5-6: *"The blind receive sight, the lame walk, those who have leprosy are cured, the deaf hear, the dead are raised, and the good news is preached to the poor. Blessed is the man who does not fall away on account of me."*

The first followers of Jesus first gave themselves to him. The vision of Christians for themselves can be comprehensive enough to embrace not only who we are but also who we can become when fully alive and empowered by the Spirit. When the Holy Spirit lives in believers, Jesus Christ lives in them. Paul wrote with confidence: *"Don't you know that you yourselves are God's temple and that God's Spirit lives in you?"* (1 Cor. 3:16) and *"Christ in you, the hope of glory."* (Col. 1:27)

Christians can, with perseverance, pursue the goal of becoming like Jesus Christ. Christians are tempted to accept the compromises Satan offers. They are tempted to compare themselves with themselves, which Paul said was not wise. (2 Cor. 10:12) They are tempted to be content to call Jesus *"Lord, Lord"* and refuse to obey him (Luke 6:46), to preach the gospel but refuse to practice it, and to get what they want by trampling on others. God does not accept such compromises. With him it is all or nothing at all.

The vision of Jesus is broad and sweeping enough to encompass all the earth, yet so specific that it includes everybody and everything, with great attention to details. He did not come on half a mission to save half the people in half the world from half their sins, but to save everybody in all the world from all their sins. The vision and objective of Christians can be shaped by the vision and objective of Jesus.

New Southern Baptist Convention Leadership

Whether an organization flourishes or flounders depends greatly on its leaders. Leaders largely determine whether an organization will pursue noble and worthy goals or be satisfied with mediocrity, whether the work environment will reflect stability or be torn by strife, whether the workers within the organization will follow dependable and visionary leaders or whether fragmentation and selfish ambition will lead to chaos and failure. In a Christian organization whose primary task is to work for good and against evil, it is essential that leaders live exemplary lives in this regard.

Southern Baptist leaders need to know well the difference between our friend and our foe, know well the difference between good and evil, and be committed to trying to be good and do good. They need to be clear about their role of servant, not ruler. They need to understand well the principles of the gospel and stand for them in all areas of the Convention's life. They need to be leaders who cherish their own freedom in Christ, who accept and respect the freedom of others, and who accept and respect the freedom of churches. They need to love others enough to listen to them and try to understand their deep convictions concerning the Bible. They need to realize the importance of truth and not practice deceit. Leaders are needed about whom it can be said, as God said about David, *"I have found David son of Jesse a man after my own heart; he will do everything I want him to."* (Acts 13:22) The Southern Baptist Convention is in desperate need of new leadership, including new trustees, new heads of boards, seminaries and agencies.

Unity in the Southern Baptist Convention

When life itself seems lunatic,
Who knows where madness lies?
Perhaps to be too practical is madness.
To surrender dreams — this may be madness.
To seek treasure where there is only trash.
And madest of all, to see life as it is
And not as it should be.[1]

           Don Quixote

If life were as it should be, Christians would love each other and all would be peacemakers. One of the most tragic developments in the history of Christianity is the multitude of divisions that have occurred. The New Testament was written before the body of Christ was crippled by serious division. The apostles urged Christians to love and pray for *all the saints.* (Eph. 6:18; Col. 1:4)

The crucifixion of Jesus was still fresh on the minds of believers and the power of his resurrection had energized their entire being. The apostles preached that followers of Jesus should crucify themselves and their sinful desires and present themselves as *living sacrifices* for Christ and his kingdom. (Rom. 6:6; Gal. 2:20; 5:24). They realized that the danger of division in churches was real and confronted the danger openly, with clear insight, frank language and decisive action. They viewed division in the body of Christ as demonic and unspiritual. Those who fell away from Christ and faith in him were denounced: ". . . *to their loss they are crucifying the Son of God all over again and subjecting him to public disgrace."* (Heb. 6:6)

In the Revelation, the apostle John wrote to seven young churches, all of which were dealing with corruption in various forms *in people who professed to be Christians and who were in the churches*. Christians cannot afford to underestimate the power of Satan to lead believers astray. Some of the problems the apostle John addressed when he wrote to the young churches in the Revelation concerned Christians *forsaking their first love* (Rev. 2:4); *slander and belonging to the synagogue of Satan* (Rev. 2:9); *tolerating sexual misconduct and refusing to repent* (Rev. :20-21); *having a reputation of being alive, but in fact were dead* (Rev. 3:1); *liars* (Rev. 3: 9); and *being neither cold nor hot.* (Rev. 3:15).

Sin was taking its toll on churches. When corruption in churches threatened the purity of their witness, the prevailing appeal to all the churches became: *"He who has an ear, let him hear what the Spirit says to the churches."* (Rev. 2:7, 11, 17, 29; 3:6, 13, 22) **The Spirit says what Jesus said! The Spirit commands what Jesus commanded! The Spirit teaches what Jesus taught!** (John 16:5-15)

Sin can take its toll on any church and on any human relationship. Getting along with others has never been easy or simple in church or family matters. Murder occurred in the first family when Cain killed his brother, Abel. God's own chosen nation of Israel divided into two kingdoms, Judah and Israel. Nations and people are still dividing, and division is often easier and more common than reconciliation, which requires hard work and patience. Marriages between two people who make promises of love and loyalty to each other often do not endure. Disagreements and disputes between people are inevitable, but division is even more devastating. Division occurs when someone or something is allowed to get *between God and his people or between people.* Isaiah told Israel that their iniquities had separated them from God. (Isa. 59:2)

Divisions between Christians are more tragic than any other kind of division, because Christians have the potential to get along with others. There are many good reasons for Christians to stay united. The structures and symbols that Christians adopt to express and extend faith varies among churches and denominations. However, the substance of faith, which affirms that God has revealed himself as Father, Son and Holy Spirit, is the same for all Christians. The Bible is God's inspired word of instruction that helps equip Christians to become " . . . *a chosen people, a royal priesthood, a holy nation, a people belonging to God, that you may declare the praises of him who called you out of darkness into his wonderful light.* " (1 Peter 2:9)

God's greatest commandment focuses on how people are to get along with other people: *"Love your neighbor as yourself."* (Matthew 22:39) Everybody is everybody else's neighbor. His final commandment was " . . . *you will be my witnesses in Jerusalem, and in all Judea and Samaria, and to the ends of the earth."* (Acts 1:8) These two commandments endure eternally and are always in effect in all who belong to Christ.

Potential Destinies

The possibilities of two entirely different destinies lie ahead of Southern Baptists. The Bible is clear that people must choose between two masters, two roads, two kinds of weapons, two directions and two destinies. All of these are completely incompatible with each other and are opposites of each other from start to finish.

The choices churches make are the result of what the members of churches choose. God inspired Jeremiah to say to the people of his day, *"But they did not listen or pay attention; instead, they followed the stubborn inclinations of their evil hearts. They went backward and not forward."* (Jeremiah 7:24)

Whether Southern Baptists go backward or forward depends greatly on how much we think and act like Christ. The question of whether we go forward or backward is both a question for individuals and a collective question, involving which direction we go together. When we think like Christ, we have a good measure of his vision. He keeps his promise to make us free just as surely as he keeps his promise to be with us always.

Paul's vision for the church was that the church would go forward. He believed God gave the spiritual gifts to church leaders to *"prepare God's people for works of service, so that the body of Christ may be built up until we all reach unity in the faith and in the knowledge of the Son of God and become mature, attaining to the whole measure of the fullness of Christ."* (Eph. 4:12-13).

Change is inevitable. Change for the best is possible, but not inevitable. The controversy of the past two decades should not dictate the future of our Convention. It is possible for us to achieve a great degree of unity in the Convention that is now divided and fragmented. It is important that we do so for Christ and his kingdom. Jesus said, *"... but with God all things are possible."* (Matt. 19:26) When Jesus Christ is praying that his followers be one as he and the Father are one, it is important. When he says that all things are possible with God, and when he prays for his followers because they are important, we can believe that unity in Christ in our Convention is both possible and important.

It could be helpful for us to take a long, serious look at the potential of our Convention. What could we become? What could we achieve if we wholeheartedly obeyed Christ, were filled with the Holy Spirit, truly loved each other, were united in Christ, and were focused on fulfilling his purpose for us and for the world?

Hope is one of the most powerful of the Christian gifts. It is the twin of faith and is essential in Christian leaders. Its power runs throughout Scripture. The psalmist wrote: *"I am still confident of this: I will see the goodness of the Lord in the land of the living. Wait for the Lord; be strong and take heart and wait for the Lord."* (Psa. 27:13-14)

One of the most serious mistakes Southern Baptists could make would be to become so accustomed to controversy and talk of division that we believe it is inevitable and normal. It is abnormal to accept as normal that which is abnormal. It is abnormal for Christians to be divided from each other. It is abnormal for Christians to slander others, falsely accuse others, use insulting language against others and refuse to repent. It is abnormal for Christians not to recognize the evil in such conduct. Life for Christians doesn't have to be like this. Christians do not have to tolerate that which is intolerable when people live under the lordship of Christ. Christians should not be satisfied with less than unity in Christ throughout our Convention. Only those who exemplify Christian values and virtues, who are committed to doing the will of God and who have a vision for unity throughout the Convention should be elected as Convention leaders.

Differences, difficulties and disputes are inevitable because people are different and see some issues differently. Only Satan can drive Christians away from each other. Intelligent, reasonable people who love each other and who work under the leadership of the Spirit could lead our Convention through this difficult period when complete division threatens us.

Churches produce leaders. If God is to make unity in our Convention a reality, he will do it through people. He will do it in individual lives, in homes, in churches, in associations, in state conventions and throughout the Southern Baptist Convention. He will do it through leaders who believe it is both important and possible. Paul wrote, *"Make every effort to keep the unity of the Spirit through the bond of peace. There is one body and one Spirit . . ."* (Eph. 4:3-4a)

Everybody who is elected as a leader in any part of the Convention should believe unity in Christ is not only important and possible, but should also work to make unity in Christ a reality. No one should be elected as a Convention leader who will oppose, work against, or put obstacles in the way of the objective of achieving unity in Christ in the Southern Baptist Convention.

Will Southern Baptists through their churches in our generation stand for, fight for, defend and contend for the gospel? I believe, hope and pray they will. I believe their convictions on the issues of faith are important enough for them to fight for. I am confident in Southern Baptists just as Paul was confident in the believers in Philippi, to whom he wrote, *"Being confident of this, that he who began a good work in you will carry it on to completion until the day of Christ Jesus."* (Phil. 1:6)

Inclusiveness of Genders and Generations

The prophet Joel's vision, quoted by Peter at Pentecost, included everybody . . . sons and daughters, men and women, old men and young men. (Joel 2:28-29 and Acts 2: 17-18) Everybody who has been redeemed by Christ has something to say and something to contribute to make to the kingdom of God a reality where he or she lives. God is the God not only of Abraham, Isaac and Jacob, but also the God of all generations. (Exodus 3:15) Churches serve people better when their leaders realize that God leads people to love and care for others from the cradle to the grave.

According to Joel's prophecy, God's intention was that both men and women receive salvation, receive the Holy Spirit and prophesy. Prophesy means "to speak before" or "to speak for." It is an important way to witness, which all Christians are commanded to do. There are several references to prophetesses in the Old Testament, including Miriam (Exodus 15:20-21); Deborah, who was both a judge and a prophetess (Judges 4-5); and Huldah (2 Kings 22:14-20). In the New Testament, Anna was a prophetess (Luke 2:36-38); as were the four daughters of Philip the evangelist (Acts 21:9). Just as there were true and false prophets, there were true prophetesses, as those above, and false prophetesses, as Noadiah (Nehemiah 6:14) and Jezebel, who called herself a prophetess (Revelation 2:20). Moses wished for all the Lord's people to be prophets. (Numbers 11:29)

Jesus said to the Samaritan woman whom he met at the well, "*Yet a time is coming and has now come when true worshipers will worship the Father in spirit and truth, for they are the kind of worshipers the Father seeks. God is Spirit, and his worshipers must worship in spirit and in truth.*" (John 4:23-24) On another occasion Jesus answered his critics who were plotting to kill him, "*I tell you the truth, a time is coming and has now come when the dead will hear the voice of the Son of God and those who hear will live.*" (John 5:25) Just before his arrest, trial and crucifixion, Jesus told his disciples, "*But a time is coming, and has come, when you will be scattered, each to his own home. You will leave me all alone. Yet I am not alone, for my Father is with me.*" (John 16:32) In all three instances, Jesus emphasized, **"The Time Has Come!"**

This was a point Jesus did not want the people to miss. All of the accumulated prophecies, hopes and expectations of the people for generations and even centuries had come to pass in their generation, right before their eyes and ears . . . in their presence . . . in a Person . . . in God's Son . . . in Jesus of Nazareth . . . in this man . . . in this Deliverer . . . in this Savior! Jesus brought the kingdom of Heaven to earth and said, the time is coming AND HAS COME!

The kingdom of God intersects every culture and person where the gospel is preached and taught. The kingdom of God intersected the people in the generation in which Jesus was born as well as every generation and community since that time where the gospel has been preached. People change and their perceptions of the gospel may change. The gospel has never changed and will never change! The writer of Hebrews expressed this truth: "*Jesus Christ is the same yesterday and today and forever.*" (Heb. 13:8)

The kingdom of God does not change. From generation to generation, from culture to culture, and from nation to nation there is one God, one Son and one Spirit, all of whom are God. In the Bible, the Holy Spirit is always singular.

Jesus promised to send *"The Counselor . . . I will send him to you . . . when he comes . . . He will convict the world of guilt . . . sin . . . righteousness . . . and judgment."* (John 16:7-8)

Paul wrote of many gifts of the Spirit coming from the same Spirit.

There are different kinds of gifts, but the same Spirit. There are different kinds of service, but the same Lord. There are different kinds of working, but the same God works all of them in all men . . . To one there is given through the Spirit the message of wisdom, to another the message of knowledge by means of the same Spirit, to another faith by the same Spirit, to another gifts of healing by that one Spirit . . . All these are the work of the one and same Spirit, and he gives them to each one, just as he determines. (1 Cor. 12:4-11)

In contrast to one Father, one Son and one Holy Spirit, who are always the same, people are not the same as other people. No two people have the same fingerprints or DNA. Everyone doesn't look, talk or think alike. Differences between people are real. Given these realities, differences, disagreements, disputes, and divisions occur among people. Divisions can get very ugly and can result in people's hating each other and even killing each other.

In church life among Christians, it doesn't usually result in some people's killing each other, but hurtful accusations and insults do occur. When these things are not corrected and overcome, deep and wide divisions can develop. Regrettably and strangely, sometimes those outside the church manage disagreements better than those inside the church. Churches are in deep trouble when peacebreakers and troublemakers are elected leaders in churches. It is often difficult to get them out of the positions they occupy.

Gender Barriers

Perhaps there is no area in the life of many Baptist churches in which it has been more difficult to break through a barrier of tradition than in the area of gender. What do churches allow, encourage and elect women to do? It appears that the major conflict in the Southern Baptist Convention, state conventions, associations and local churches centers on our understanding of two periods of time in the development of Christianity.

The first period was during the ministry of Jesus as he was building his kingdom and establishing his church. Jesus was the only Leader during this period. When Jesus was building his church, both men and women were included and involved in his plan. The angel Gabriel announced to a woman, Mary, that she would bear the child who would be the Savior of the world. She submitted to

God's purpose for her. (Luke 1:26-38) Then she broke into her great song of praise to God. (Luke 1:46-55)

Jesus spent about three years building his church. During this time, he taught and preached to the multitudes of people. He treated everybody in the crowds the same and taught all of them. When he healed people, he healed anybody who pleaded with him for healing . . . Jew, Gentile, man, woman, child, military officer, leper, blind, and the demon-possessed. Some of those who were healed of diseases and out of whom Jesus cast evil spirits were women. " . . . *The Twelve were with him, and also some women who had been cured of evil spirits and diseases . . . These women were helping to support them out of their own means.*" (Luke 8:1b-3)

He wanted everybody to believe him and serve him. He called twelve to be disciples, to receive his special training, and to be leaders after his ascension to heaven. He gave specific instructions and requirements on what it would take to be his disciples and warned them of many dangers they would face. Many people followed him. One woman who believed in him became an evangelist. "*Then, leaving her water jar, the woman went back to the town and said to the people, 'Come, see a man who told me everything I ever did. Could this be the Christ?' They came out of the town and made their way toward him.*" (John 4:29)

Women believers were the first to whom Jesus revealed himself after his resurrection. He instructed those women to tell the male disciples what to do and where to go to find the resurrected Lord. (Matthew 28:1-1-10)

The second period of time was after his ascension to Heaven, when the first local churches were established under the leadership of the Holy Spirit through the apostles. The kingdom of God met their culture when true democracy in any part of the world was more than 1700 years into the future, when slavery of many people by other people was legal, and when many women were regarded as not much higher than slaves. Christians knew they lived in the world of their culture *and that they truly belonged to another world in which Christ was King.* They were in the world but not of the world. It was during this period that Jewish Christian leaders developed in local churches restrictions and rules on the roles and conduct of men and women in churches. Jesus said: "*...Salvation is from the Jews."* (John 4:22) Salvation came first to Jews and from Jewish believers to Gentiles.

All of the first apostles were Jewish men, who believed in and practiced living in a hierarchy of authority with men having authority over women, men with authority in the church and women submissive to men according to Jewish laws, culture and tradition. In their generation they did not completely transform their culture into the image of Christ, but they made enormous progress, so much so that Paul wrote: "*For there is neither Jew nor Greek, slave nor free, male nor female, for you are all one in Christ Jesus. If you belong to Christ, then you are Abraham's seed, and heirs according to the promise."* (Gal. 3:28-29) The practice of the early Christians of accepting and loving everybody was so radical and revolutionary that they were accused of turning the world upside down. (Acts 17:6)

Jesus gave his disciples great responsibility when he said: *"I tell you the truth, whatever you bind on earth will be bound in Heaven, and whatever you loose on earth will be loosed in Heaven."* (Matt. 18:18) The first generation of Christians were authorized, called, commanded and empowered by Christ to accomplish some primary tasks: 1) To be personal witnesses of Jesus Christ; 2) To establish local churches to be witnesses of Jesus Christ; 3) To initiate a world wide missionary movement; and 4) To break down the barriers between Jews and Gentiles.

In reality, God broke the barrier on the spiritual level by giving the Holy Spirit to all believers, but people had to break the barrier on the personal and fellowship level. Breaking the barrier between Jews and Gentiles is recorded in Acts 15:6-11. We should note that it took Jesus about three years to break the barrier between God and man. It took the Jewish apostles one generation to break the barrier between Jewish and Gentile believers. Gentile Christian men have been stumbling for 2,000 years on fully breaking the barrier between Christian males and Christian females! When some Christians and churches break through the barrier, they are excluded by other Christians and churches and accused of not believing the Bible! It has been a long, uphill struggle for both men and women to fully live in the promises of Jesus: *"You will know the truth and the truth will set you free"* . . . and *"So if the Son sets you free, you will be free indeed."* (John 8:32, 36)

For centuries, Christian men have limited and often locked the doors of opportunity of service for Christ from women. Carefully selecting some passages in the Bible to support their positions and ignoring other important passages that support the opposite view, men have tried to think for women and speak for women when they are fully capable of thinking and speaking for themselves. Rather than studying this issue with compassion and vision for women, men have slept through generations and have been content to perpetuate the traditions of the past that do not really fit in the kingdom of God. On this issue, men have out slept Rip Van Winkle, who slept through a generation during the Revolutionary War.

In dealing with this complex issue, some guidelines and principles in interpreting the Bible are helpful. 1) The sovereignty of God, in which the Spirit is sovereign and does what he pleases to accomplish God's plan and purpose (John 3:6-8); 2) The teachings of Jesus and his example of how he related to men and women; 3) The cultural and historical context in which the Scriptures were written; 4) The people to whom the Scriptures were written; 5) The teachings of other Scriptures which shed light on the subject; 4) Consideration of what other

Christians believe the Spirit is teaching them on the subject; 6) The importance of unity in the body of Christ; 7) The fulfillment of prophecy, which affirms that both men and women will prophesy; 8) The fulfillment of the promises of Jesus on freedom; and 9) The greatest commandment of all, that we love each other as Christ loved us.

Southern Baptists are living in these two different worlds and are deeply divided. Some are living more closely to the world in which both Christian men and women are free in Christ to exercise all of their gifts, including the gifts of leadership. Other Southern Baptists are living more closely to the world of the first churches in the first century, in which Christian men hold and refuse to relinquish the positions of prestige and power. The Southern Baptist Convention is in desperate need of courageous and visionary leaders to lead us through this dark period.

A Vision for the Nations of Love and Inclusion

A vision for the nations begins with a vision for one's own nation. This is a complex and difficult issue, particularly for American Christians, since it involves various interpretations of the meaning of freedom of religion. Baptists have been leaders in appealing to all governments and people throughout the world to grant to all people the freedom to make religious issues a matter of the individual's conscience. No person should be coerced by any church, government or other entity to disobey his conscience in matters of religion. With this deep conviction, Baptists have been leaders in appealing to government leaders throughout the world to grant to all people the right to obey their conscience in matters of religion and to be free to exercise this right. This conviction has motivated Baptist leaders to appeal for the separation of church and state in all nations. Jesus recognized that both God and human government have respective roles in the lives of people and said, *"Give to Caesar what is Caesar's, and to God what is God's."* (Matt. 22:21)

The call of Jesus to eternal life was given to all who heard him. Some believed him and continued to follow him, even to their death. Others did not believe and did not continue to follow him. Reluctantly, he allowed those who did not believe to leave him. *"From this time many of his disciples turned back and no longer followed him."* (John 6:66) Freedom meant the freedom *to follow or not to follow Jesus*. God wants everyone to have eternal life, yet it is not his way to coerce people to follow him. *". . . Your Father in heaven is not willing that any if these little ones should be lost."* (John 18:14)

Careful attention needs to be given to what freedom of religion means and what it does not mean. When the New Testament was written, those who wrote about freedom were clear about the primary meaning of freedom, which was freedom to love and service and freedom from sin. When Jesus spoke about freedom and promised to make people free, he was speaking primarily about the power to live fruitful and peaceful lives and to overcome the evil that exists in every person. He said, *"I tell you the truth, everyone who sins is a slave to sin . . . so if the Son sets you free, you will be free indeed."* (John 8: 34, 36)

Freedom did not mean that Jesus would force owners of slaves to free their slaves. In time, as his followers lived in obedience to his commandments, they would realize that love motivates believers to treat others as they would like to be treated. When the command of Jesus to *"love others as you love yourself"* is put into practice, if one would like to be free, love motivates him to make efforts to help others be free. This is what Jesus meant when he said:

> *I tell you the truth, anyone who has faith in me will do what I have been doing. He will do even greater things than these, because I am going to the Father. And I will do whatever you ask in my name, so that the Son may bring glory to the Father. You may ask me for anything in my name, and I will do it.* (John 14: 12-14)

When people live in freedom, good people are free to do good. Evil people are free to do evil. The opposing forces of good and evil are always colliding with each other. In our generation the collisions are both national and universal and are so violent that they are shocking to many people. The minds of some people work to destroy some aspects of civilization that many generations have tried to build.

What a time of opportunity Christians in our generation have to practice the love, peace, grace and forgiveness of Jesus Christ and his gospel! What a time it is to be *living sacrifices* for his kingdom! There has never been a time in history in which the Prince of Peace and the principles by which he governs his kingdom are more needed and more attractive than in our generation. Isaiah prophesied about the influence and power of the Prince of Peace:

> *He will judge between the nations and will settle disputes for many peoples. They will beat their swords into plowshares and their spears into pruning hooks. Nation will not take up sword against nation, nor will they train for war anymore.* (Isa. 2:4)

Isaiah's vision seems like a dream too obscure and irrelevant to become a reality in our generation. But is it? Love is the greatest antidote to war the world has ever known. Practicing the principles of life given by the Prince of Peace leads people to love other people. Loving people and trying to destroy them are completely incompatible practices. The first and most important gift of the Holy

Spirit to believers is love. Nothing draws people together more powerfully than love. Nothing repels people and drives them away from each other with more certainty than rejection.

Christians need to be clear about their motivation for going throughout the world with the gospel. The foundation of our motivation is *"For God so loved the world"* and *"We love because he first loved us."* (1 John 4:19)

A vision for the women of the nations is an important aspect of any comprehensive vision. In some parts of the world, women are openly oppressed and sometimes murdered by ruthless men in the name of religion. Some women are stoned to death for committing adultery while adulterous males go free. The example of how Jesus treated women and how completely those women became devoted to him for what he had done for them can offer genuine hope for love and value to all women throughout the world. Christian women can be witnesses for Christ to non Christian women in ways that men cannot do.

IMB Fires Missionaries

Trustees of the Southern Baptist Convention's IMB, meeting in Framington, Massachusetts on May 7, 2003, fired 13 Southern Baptist missionaries who refused to sign the 2000 "Baptist Faith and Message."

> It is believed to be the largest group of SBC missionaries ever fired at one time . . . Another 20 missionaries resigned in recent days rather than sign the doctrinal statement and 10 more took retirement, according to the IMB. They join at least 34 missionaries who resigned last year in protest of the requirement to sign. That means at least 77 IMB missionaries have left the mission field because of the new faith statement, presumably the agency's largest exodus ever over one issue.[2]

The missionaries who were fired or resigned because of the pressure from the IMB did so after writing extensively to the IMB that they could not sign the statement because to do so would violate their conscience and would be contrary to the leadership of the Holy Spirit. These reasons got no hearing from IMB administrators and trustees.

New initiatives are now underway to support missionaries who have been fired or who cannot work under authoritative leaders who do not obey Christ. Some are raising their own support from churches and individuals and returning to the fields of service to which they believe God has called them. The Baptist General Convention of Texas (BGCT) has created a "missionary transition fund" to help missionaries. E. B. Brooks, coordinator of the BGCT church missions and evangelism section, said: "We are making it possible for churches and individuals to support missionaries whose ministry was taken away from them by the International Mission Board. We are doing this at the request of our churches who want to support their continued ministry."[3]

2003 SBC Defunds Baptist World Alliance

The Southern Baptist Convention met in Phoenix, Arizona June 17-18, 2003. "The 7,077 messengers who gathered in Phoenix June 17-18 constituted the smallest annual meeting since 1956, when 6,493 messengers met in San Francisco."[4]

As in past years under the leadership of Southern Baptist fundamentalists, those leaders brought no proposal for reconciliation in the Convention. Instead, they took their movement a giant step further toward isolation and from biblical and historic Baptist principles by leading their followers to vote to defund the Baptist World Alliance. The messengers voted to reduce the Convention's annual contribution of $425,000 to the Baptist World Alliance to $300,000. For almost a century the Baptist World Alliance has been the most unifying voice of the world Baptist family for the lordship of Jesus Christ and his message of salvation, peace and reconciliation.

BWA General Secretary Denton Lotz, a strong advocate of reconciliation among Baptists, said "We Baptists . . . want to stick together . . . we stick together because we belong to Christ."[5]

> The SBC is the largest and wealthiest affiliated convention in the BWA. Its 30 percent cutback in funding reflects strong disapproval of the BWA's openness to consider accepting the Cooperative Baptist Fellowship as a member.
>
> The Fellowship left the SBC 12 years ago, its members disenfranchised by the increasingly fundamentalist nature of the convention. Now, the Fellowship has petitioned to join the BWA, whose membership has slated the request for consideration this summer. SBC leaders claim they are pulling money from the BWA because they aren't being "heard adequately" and because they disagree with the process the BWA membership committee used in considering the Fellowship's petition. The bottom line, however, is SBC leaders despise the Fellowship and are furious the BWA might allow the upstart organization to join.[6]

Baptist World Alliance Accepts CBF into Membership

The General Council of the BWA voted on Friday, July 11, 2003, to accept the Cooperative Baptist Fellowship into membership.

The CBF received a majority vote of 75 of the 105 voting Council members who, after a long, but calm debate, cast their votes in a separate, secret ballot to include the group and end a three-year long process . . . 'We commit this decision to you,' prayed BWA President Billy Kim to end the Council session.

Following the session, BWA President Kim and General Secretary Lotz emphasized 'This decision to accept CBF was based upon the facts that CBF met the requirements for membership. It was not a decision against the SBC, but a democratic vote of the Council to affirm our Baptist family . . . We love our Southern Baptist brothers and sisters and want them to remain active and full participants in all our meetings as we affirm together our unity in Christ.'[7]

SBC Votes to End Membership in Baptist World Alliance

A study committee comprised of SBC fundamentalist leaders recommended that the SBC withdraw from the Baptist World Alliance. SBC leaders who use deceit, false accusations, slander and who suppress the truth in their work accused BWA leaders of "advocating aberrant and dangerous theologies and refusing to hear Southern Baptist objectives."[8]

The committee members are following the practice of more than two decades of accusing Baptists who do not follow SBC fundamentalist leaders of being "liberal." BWA General Secretary Denton Lotz labeled the proposal "a sin against love" and warned that the recommendation "will bring a schism within the life of our worldwide Baptist family . . . The BWA does not have a liberal agenda, but we pray that we have a biblical agenda of following in the footsteps of Christ to win the world to his leadership. We have rejected the theology of liberalism."[9]

The study committee's report was approved by the SBC Executive Committee on February 17, 2004, by a vote of 62-10.

> The plan approved by the Executive Committee calls for creating a worldwide network of 'conservative evangelical Christians' which likely would be run by the Executive Committee. Some of the more conservative Baptist bodies around the world have already expressed interest in the new SBC-led organization, the Executive Committee was told, raising the possibility of two competing worldwide organizations of Baptists.

> The hour-long debate was limited to Executive Committee members only. Denton Lotz, BWA General Secretary, was present but not permitted to speak to the recommendation.[10]

The issue was presented to messengers for approval at the Southern Baptist Convention's annual meeting in June 2004. The messengers approved the recommendation and the SBC terminated its membership and funding for the BWA effective October 1, 2004.

One of the most tragic results of the fundamentalist leadership of the past two decades is the way they have ruined relationships within the Southern Baptist Convention, with our own Southern Baptist missionaries and with Baptists throughout the world with whom previous leaders had worked cooperatively and respectfully for more than a century. The pattern of authoritative leadership that has characterized the Convention for two decades is being forcefully implemented in our work overseas.

When a board, agency, or institution has authoritative leadership, the convictions, opinions, experiences, and ideas of those who work under such leaders have little weight. The organization of missionaries in local "missions" for fellowship, inspiration, and decision making, which was an important element in Southern Baptist missionary work, has now been largely dismantled. The mission served an important purpose in respecting the convictions and opinions of missionaries.

Their knowledge and experience had been shaped in part by their knowledge of the people and the cultures where they worked and by their vision for their particular work. It was an important link in good communication between missionaries and IMB administrators. Knowing that their voices were heard by IMB administrators was an important element in their morale. Their voices were heard by their freedom to speak and vote on important issues regarding budgets, personnel and strategies.

The dismantling of organizations of missionaries as important parts of foreign missions vision and strategy is now called "liberating the missionaries" by IMB administrators. One has to stretch the meaning of "liberating" very broadly for the concept to mean taking away the voices and votes of the people who have been liberated.

Missionaries have been liberated from meaningful participation in making important decisions about how mission work should be done. Their understanding of mission work develops over years of experience on the field. To a great degree their mouths are now muzzled on issues of strategy and they must submit to the strategies of IMB administrators and trustees. Now they must surrender their voices regarding whether the promise of Jesus that he would make people *free indeed* applies equally to women and to men. Many of them are expected to produce results that can be tabulated immediately in terms of numbers, such as the number of churches started. These are important. It is also important that they know they are valued and respected. It is particularly important that they know they are loved by IMB administrators.

When the important elements of freedom in Christ and love are diminished, the situation of missionaries is not completely unlike that of the Israelites who were required to make more bricks in Egypt. Bricks could be counted. The brick makers were not required to do much thinking. If they had good thoughts, the Egyptians never knew. Their job was to count bricks.

What about Southern Baptist missionaries? Do Southern Baptist churches want them to be called by God, sent by him, filled with his Spirit and obedient to him above all? Or do churches want them to obey men rather than God? What kind of overseers of missionaries do Southern Baptist churches want IMB administrators to be? Do churches want them to obey God rather than men just as missionaries should? Do the churches want trustees and administrators of their missionaries to oversee their work by fear, or by love, grace and truth?

Rebuilding Relationships with Baptist Partners

One of the most important functions of missionaries was to serve as "links of love" between Southern Baptists and our partners in missions in the countries where we did mission work. Ideally, the link of love connected Southern Baptist churches to IMB administrators, missionaries, and our partners overseas. The link of love worked in reverse as well.

We did mission work because we had been called by God and sent by him and by Southern Baptist churches who were obeying Christ and his great commission. Missionaries were one in Christ and with one another, with the sending churches, with IMB administrators, and with our partners overseas, all of whom were trying to be obedient to Christ. No one can pretend that all the links were perfect or ideal.

There were people involved in every link who had strong convictions and strong personalities. There were disputes and disagreements about important issues. However, because of the compelling power of love, divisions were rare.

Fundamentalist Southern Baptist leaders, by their obsession with their own authority, are destroying the bridges of love and cooperation with Baptist partners overseas. From their pedestals of arrogance they have insulted Christian leaders, falsely accused them and rejected them. By rejecting the leaders they have rejected the people who elected them. They have disengaged our missionaries from genuine partnerships that result in unity in Christ throughout the world in favor of isolationism or parallelism.

Parallelism is different from unity. At its worst, it can be the fruit of arrogance, ignorance and Phariseeism. In its effect, it can say that we are superior to you and our work is superior to yours. It can say we know, understand and believe the Bible better than you do and we know more about how mission work ought to be done than you do. It can say we are bigger, more powerful and richer than you, so you do what we say.

At its best, in its effect parallelism says that we work in your country whether you like it or not. We do not need you because you are not important to us. It says we do our thing and you do yours; we go our way and you go yours; we develop our people and you develop yours; we work by our strategies and you work by yours; we plant our churches and you plant yours. It says we are not one in Christ!

In its effect, unity says we are all one because Christ has made us one. We are only servants, his servants. There is only one body of Christ. The work we do is in obedience to Christ. We love each other in obedience to Christ. The churches we plant belong to Christ. We come from different nations and cultures and speak different languages, but the Spirit helps us agree on the most important issues regarding the work of Christ. We will consult, cooperate, plan and work in obedience to Christ. We will do some things separately, but everything all of us do contributes to God's plan of unity and wholeness. Even when we do not agree on some issues, the love of Christ will bind us together. We will not destroy or devour each other.

We are paying a high price for pursuing parallelism rather than unity. We reap what we sow in missions just as we do in every other aspect of life. If we draw and use the sword against our partners in missions, we will die by the sword. We are treated by others just as we treat them. What we say to others, they say back to us. When we say we don't need them, they say they don't need us. When we won't cooperate with them, they won't cooperate with us. When we don't accept them, they don't accept us. When we don't trust them, they don't trust us. When we isolate ourselves from them, they isolate themselves from us. When we won't work with them, they won't work with us. When we don't respect them, they don't respect us. When their ideas are not important to us, our ideas are not important to them. When we don't try to communicate with them, they don't try to communicate with us.

Our partners can say, "You get your visas; we don't need them." In earlier years many missionaries were so wanted and needed by national Baptists that the problems they encountered were common problems. Common solutions were sought. This was in some cases true of the need for visas and other legal matters. These problems are difficult and might get worse. Unity in Christ and love for each other are important elements in trying to resolve such problems.

For perhaps the first time in the history of Southern Baptist foreign missions, we are in danger of hearing many former partners in Christ in Baptist conventions or unions throughout the world who loved Southern Baptists, Southern Baptist missionaries, and the Southern Baptist Convention say to us: **"We don't want you or your missionaries. We are no longer one in Christ!"**

Even though many missionaries have deep convictions that we should be working cooperatively with Baptists overseas, they often cannot wholeheartedly do so. The position of IMB administrators and trustees seems to be: "This is the way it is! Like it or get out! If you won't do what we say, we will get other missionaries who will!"

Churches can take decisive action concerning leadership in the Southern Baptist Convention by electing leaders whose vision is for one body of Christ throughout the world, starting with Baptists. We face the gigantic task of rebuilding from the ruins of authoritative leadership. Israel faced a similar task: *"They will rebuild the ancient ruins and restore the places long devastated; they will renew the ruined cities that have been devastated for generations."* (Isaiah 61:4)

Relationships with Other Christians

We should be under no illusions concerning the historic reasons various divisions in Christianity have occurred and why many denominations have developed. Nor should we expect denominations to dismantle themselves and surrender their autonomy and convictions to others. Structures and symbols mean different things to different people and all do not agree with others on their usefulness. There have been legitimate divisions to clarify Christian doctrines and to correct false teachings. Only God knows how many divisions have occurred because of the stubbornness of some people who demanded to make their own plans and have their own way rather than follow God's plan and way. Diotrephes was such a church leader, who loved to be first, rejected even the apostle John, gossiped maliciously about others and tried to put hospitable Christians out of the church. (3 John 9-10)

The substance of Christianity, however, is the same for all Christians who believe that Jesus is God. We believe in one God, who is Father, Son and Holy Spirit. We accept the inspiration of the Bible. We believe we are saved through faith in Jesus Christ and are called to live in obedience to him. We believe we are members of the one body of Christ. The vision for our Convention should extend to a vision of our role in the larger body of Christ in our nation and throughout the world. Jesus said, *"I have other sheep that are not in this sheep pen. I must bring them also. They too will listen to my voice, and there will be one flock and one shepherd."* (John 10:16)

Christians lived and served Christ many centuries before groups were formed who called themselves Baptists and were called Baptists by others. The contributions Baptists have made to the cause of Christ in clarifying important distinctives in Christian thought are important. To date, perhaps the most easily recognized distinctive by which Baptists are known is a dogged determination to be free. We claim this freedom not only for ourselves but for all people. The next step beyond an individual's freedom is a church's freedom. Baptists have contributed greatly to the "free church" movement. Many free and evangelical churches likely have historic roots with Baptists, even though they do not identify themselves as Baptists and do not claim close ties with Baptists.

Individual freedom and church freedom do not imply that there are not important connections with others. The foundation on which freedom is built is love. We are connected to each other by love, the first and most important gift of the Spirit. We are connected by the teachings, commandments and great commission of Jesus. We are connected by the continuing debt to love one another as Christ loved us. (Rom. 13:8) All Christians are part of the body of Christ and should be concerned about the connections with all parts of his body. Since we belong to Christ and his one body, we belong also to each other. (Rom. 12:5)

Relationships with Christians other than Baptists are especially important for Christian missionaries. They arrive on fields of service from different backgrounds and historic differences in church life. Southern Baptist missionaries are sponsored by a very large Convention. Historically, Southern Baptist missionaries have viewed a Convention of churches doing mission work together as a healthy expression of the body of Christ and of church life. This has meant that many churches working together can accomplish more than what a few churches or a single church can do.

Other Christians send missionaries. Baptists, Methodists, Presbyterians, other denominations and many evangelicals without any denominational identity send missionaries. They have been in existence for many years and have quite a healthy understanding of each other. They know there are some differences between them, but normally they do not engage in spiritual warfare against each other, do not try to destroy each other and even cooperate with each other in important activities.

There are other Christians who do not attach themselves to each other in a denomination. Some of them will not cooperate or have fellowship with other Christians, especially those who belong to a denomination. Some even attack other Christians and denominations as being evil.

No Christian group or denomination has a monopoly on Christ and truth. There are many people on earth who have never known any Christian personally.

They do not know Christ or the salvation he offers. There are many people on earth who have never heard the word *Baptist*, have never met a Baptist and; if they have met one, have no idea what Baptists believe. In many places Baptists do not exist, or if they do, they number only a small minority of the population. Sometimes Baptists and other Christians are labeled by others as heretical, as belonging to a cult, and as demonic.

Devout Christians are found in other denominations and in groups that claim no denominational affiliation. All who have repented, who believe in Jesus Christ and accept his lordship belong to him and to his one body. They belong also to each other.

Most Christian groups have some sense of mission and feel responsible to send missionaries in obedience to the Great Commission. Because of the concentration of populations, movements of peoples, increased efficiency of transportation, merging economies, and increased utilization of technologies in sharing information, the world is much smaller and more crowded than ever before.

This reality should be recognized in our Convention and in our work overseas. The competitive tactics of some unscrupulous wizards in worldly affairs can become temptations to Christians too as we converge in the marketplaces of the world.

In order to appear predominant, we can engage in misrepresentations of others who belong to Christ and are engaged in his work. We might feel that we don't need them. We should remember that Christ loves, needs and wants both them and us.

There are fewer places in the world where the gospel has not been preached than ever before. Paul's ambition was *"to preach the gospel where Christ was not known, so that I would not be building on someone else's foundation."* (Rom. 15:20). That is still possible in many places. However, Paul balanced his desire to be a pioneer missionary with the desire to nurture those who had already believed so that they would become mature Christians. For this reason he retraced his steps, visited churches again and again and wrote letters to churches he could not visit.

Much missionary work is done where churches have already been planted and where Christians are living, working and doing missionary work. It is easy for missionaries and other Christians to arrive in places new to them, believing they are the first and most important Christians there. They should be careful that they do not view what others before them have done for Christ through their own eyes of arrogance, or that they with careless and loose tongues do not tear down quickly what others sacrificed over long periods of time to build.

The Christians of the first generation were hard pressed to keep believers in Christ in the one body of Christ. Satan attacked them from outside and from within the church in his desperate effort to break apart and divide Christ's one body. He has had remarkable success. Many false imitators of Christ have come along saying, "follow me" or "follow us." They have been successful in seducing many naive people to follow them rather than Christ. This, in part, accounts for the brokenness in the body of Christ.

Jesus Christ has been successful too. There are people in our generation, both Baptists and others, who give their lives for Christ. To them, Christian love is the greatest virtue. Grace abounds and the truth is told. The gospel is preached and seekers believe in him. There are people who obey God rather than men. There are people who are trying to build God's kingdom on earth. Churches are being planted on the sure foundation of Jesus Christ and his teachings. Unity in Christ remains a noble goal among many Christians.

Many Christians today grieve over the brokenness and divisions in the body of Christ. All of us today, including Baptists, were born in a generation in which the body of Christ is broken. There are many people who call themselves Baptists who will not have fellowship with each other or even admit that they are part of a larger body of Christ. While it is true that faith begins with an individual's faith in Christ, rugged individualism is blind and unhealthy if it does not see that faith is connected to Christ and to others who believe in him.

Efforts to reach people for Christ can become efforts to reach only those who are on the margins of society. Rather than having a multifaceted approach with the goal to reach all people, ours can become only a refugee ministry or only a people group focus. Jesus came to preach the gospel to the poor and oppressed. He invited also the rich young ruler to follow him. (Matt. 19:16-22) The gospel of Christ is for paupers and kings. Paul was called to carry the gospel to the Gentiles and their kings. (Acts 9:15) **The gospel of Christ is for everybody in every nation!**

Only with great damage to the cause of Christ can we compete with or ignore other Christian groups who also are trying to be obedient to the Great Commission. Among the dangers those who become believers face is confusion about the body of Christ, confusion about churches and confusion about who is sending missionaries. They should not become confused about the fact that when they believe in Christ they belong to him first. They belong also to his one great body. They belong both to Christ and to other Christians. They do not belong first to the mission-sending agency that bore Christian witness to them. Christians must not compete for their loyalty as if believers belong first to them, then to Christ. It is more than our mission to the world. It is Christ's mission to the world through us and through others.

Almost 2,000 years have passed since the disciples of Jesus in the church at Antioch were first called Christians. The meaning is clear as to why they were called Christians. **They were so much like Christ!** That is God's intention for all of the followers of Jesus throughout all ages. They are not Christ, but they have been shaped so much in his likeness that it isn't stretching the point too much for them to be called Christians.

Southern Baptists have earned a reputation for believing the Bible. The area of our nation with the greatest concentration of Baptists and Baptist churches is known as the Bible Belt. People in the Bible Belt have earned that reputation because they believe the Bible. Believing the Bible and obeying Christ are not the same thing.

The controversy in the Southern Baptist Convention is now well known throughout the Convention, among other Christians and among many people who do not claim to be Christians. Unlike the Christians in Rome who were famous all over the world because of their faith, (Rom. 1:8) Southern Baptists today are famous all over the Baptist world because of our controversy. Those on both sides of the controversy say they believe the Bible and have deep convictions about their beliefs. We have proved that we feel passionately about the Bible and what we believe about it.

What we have not yet proved is that we are truly disciples of Jesus Christ. We have not proved that our love for each other is greater than our disagreements about lesser important issues.

We have not proved that we love those who have different views from our views. We have not proved that we are even willing to try to understand why others believe as they do. The task of demonstrating that we in our generation are disciples of Jesus Christ and that we are like Christ is perhaps the greatest challenge our Convention has ever faced.

Our Lord never intended for his children to fight against each other or for his churches to fight against each other. Besides the wounds such fighting inflicts on Christ and his body, the Christians who fight are also wounded. The principle Jesus taught Peter is still in effect: "*... All who draw the sword will die by the sword.*" (Matt. 26:52) Because we have one Head, who is Christ, and belong to his one body, **Christians should love one another in obedience to Christ! Christians should not be fighting against other Christians! "By this all men will know that you are my disciples, if you love one another."** (John 13:35)

Sharing Resources

God's tenth commandment was against covetousness. Jesus had no earthly possessions. "*Foxes have holes and birds of the air have nests, but the Son of Man has no place to lay his head.*" (Matt. 8:20) Jesus warned people often of the dangers of loving and trusting in riches and other material possessions. He spoke about how difficult it is for rich people to enter heaven. Greed was viewed as idolatry by Paul. (Col. 3:5)

Following his example of poverty and expecting Jesus to return in their generation, the first believers in Jerusalem sold their possessions and goods and gave the proceeds to anyone in need. (Acts 2:45) Although their intentions were good, the utopia was shattered when greed caused Ananias and Sapphira to lie and preferential treatment occurred in the first church in the distribution of goods. Furthermore, Jesus did not return in their generation. By the time other churches were planted, church leaders appealed to love and voluntary generosity in the hearts of believers, "... *not reluctantly or under compulsion, for God loves a cheerful giver."* (2 Cor. 9:7)

Perhaps no area of life for Christians is more difficult than controlling the desire to accumulate more goods and wealth. Christians are among the most affluent people in the world. Equally problematic is the unquenched desire in the hearts of many who are not wealthy to *become* wealthy. The quest in the hearts of people for wealth and power has developed over centuries, so that now the entire world is divided along poverty lines. Much of the world is called the *Third World* in comparison to other parts of the world.

Even though Christians may contribute to the imbalance of the distribution of wealth, many rulers and wealthy people in Third World countries are even more blatant in their greed and in the oppression of their own people. The results are diseases, ignorance, corruption, poverty and wars so distressing and on such a broad scale that solutions are almost beyond reach. Images come into our homes through our televisions of people dying of disease and starvation, others freezing to death and others who spend their entire lives without shelter.

When Jesus saw the crowds of people with their sicknesses and diseases, he had compassion and helped and healed them. (Matt. 9:36) We Christians cannot afford to close our eyes and hearts to the suffering we see. Compassion for others in need is a result of God's love in people. *"If anyone has material possessions and sees his brother in need but has no pity on him, how can the love of God be in him? Dear children, let us not love* **with words or tongue but with actions and in truth."** (1 John 3:17-18 - emphasis added)

Hear What the Spirit Is Saying to the Churches

This could be the greatest generation in history for Christians to demonstrate their love and compassion for the people of the world, not only by preaching the gospel to all people but by also helping to feed, educate, provide shelter and heal their diseases. The harvest has never been more plentiful nor good shepherds more needed. There have never been more Christians scattered throughout the world with more wealth, brighter minds and better organizational and technical skills than those of our generation.

The ancient promise of God to King Solomon and the nation he ruled can be claimed by his people throughout the world today. *"If my people, who are called by my name, will humble themselves and pray and turn from their wicked ways, then will I hear from heaven and will forgive their sins and will heal their land."* (2 Chronicles 7:14) Verses 19-22 of the same chapter make it clear that if God's requirements are not met, the promised good results cannot be expected.

With the opportunities and threats both nationally and internationally so obvious to us in our generation, what is the Spirit saying to the churches? To pastors and teachers? To Convention leaders? To administrators? To lay persons, both men and women? To associations? To Baptist state conventions? To missionaries?

If we have ears, let us hear what the Spirit is saying to the churches of the Southern Baptist Convention!

Epilogue

IBTS Prague

In order to better serve the needs of European Baptists in theological education, the European Baptist Federation sold the property in Rüschlikon, Switzerland, in 1995. The one part of the property that was not sold was the chapel, which had been given by the WMU of the Southern Baptist Convention. The chapel had been the central place of worship for the seminary community for almost fifty years. It had also been the place of worship for Rüschlikon Baptist Church (German speaking with some services in English.) When the seminary moved, Rüschlikon Baptist Church disbanded, with members joining other churches in the area.

The Swiss Baptist Union, eager for a Baptist witness to remain in Rüschlikon, offered the chapel as a meeting place for the English speaking International Baptist Church of Wädenswil. The church gladly accepted the offer. After the chapel was renovated, the church moved to its new home and changed its name to International Baptist Church of Zürich. The gospel is still preached and the bells in the chapel tower still ring in Rüschlikon.

European Baptists bought property for the seminary in Prague, the Czech Republic. Prague is considered the geographical center of all of Europe. Between May 17 and July 26, 1995, the seminary moved from Rüschlikon to Prague. The move required a monumental effort on the part of all personnel associated with the seminary and almost 1,300 volunteers. One of the greatest challenges involved moving the library, which had the largest protestant and evangelical theological library in the English language in continental Europe.

In many respects, IBTS Prague has started over. No administrative or faculty personnel associated with IBTS Rüschlikon are in Prague. It is not a seminary in which a young student can begin theological studies and complete them in the same location. Students acquire basic ministerial training at the national level and in the national cultural contexts. Besides some theological education being done by extension, the number of institutions of theological education being supported by European Baptist unions has grown to 35.

IBTS seminary is fully accredited by the Czech Ministry of Education and offers a Magister (Master) in Theology equal in standing to the three theological faculties of the historic Charles University of Prague. Additionally, IBTS is a validated institution of the University of Wales and offers four advanced study degrees of Master of Theology in the areas of Baptist and Anabaptist Studies, Biblical Studies, Contextual Theology and Applied Theology. It also has rights to supervise students proceeding to a Master of Philosophy or Doctor of Philosophy degree in the theological disciplines, which was not possible in the Swiss setting. IBTS offers higher academic theological training as a support center for European Baptist seminaries to send well-prepared students for advanced academic work.

IBTS Prague is an important link between the 35 national seminaries and is the core member of a Consortium of European Baptist Theological Schools (CEBTS) that was formed in 2001. Student numbers at IBTS have continued to grow with 2002 being a record year with 95 students enrolled at the seminary. The seminary also produces the academic *Journal of European Baptist Studies*, which enjoys a good reputation. The new facilities are an important conference center for all aspects of European Baptist life, and the site of the offices of the European Baptist Federation. There is an endowment fund, which is an important part of the funding of the seminary. It does not provide all the funds that are needed, especially those needed for scholarships for eastern European students. The EBF and friends of the seminary are requested to continue to contribute to its support.

The address is:

International Baptist Theological Seminary
Nad Habrovkou 3, Jeneralka
16 400 Praha 6, Czech Republic

Keith G. Jones, Rector
E-mail: Jones@IBTS.CZ
Office phone: (from USA) 011 420 2 9639 2300
Mobile phone: (from USA) 011 420 602 219 952
Fax: (from USA) 011 420 2 9639 2370
Web Site: http://www.ibts.cz

Birgit Karlsson

Birgit Karlsson served as General Secretary of the Baptist Union of Sweden (1984-1995), as EBF Vice President (1991-1993) and President (1993-1995). She has written several books for devotional use and pastoral care, recovery and spiritual direction. She resigned as Swedish Baptists' General Secretary in 1995 to accept another position in her union. Commenting on the severe crisis regarding her nomination as EBF President, she said:

I hesitate to write about this story, anxious not to hurt where healing has taken place. A few words may, however, be said.

Some of our EBF constituency could not accept a woman in ministry who then would also serve in the leadership position. They were all persons for whom my respect ran deep and whose spirituality I did not at all question. I had anticipated some opposing reactions and had thus hesitated to agree to a nomination but had been encouraged to accept. When I learned that opposition had indeed been voiced, I again wanted to withdraw my name in order not to cause division within the Federation. Again I was assured that was not the right thing to do.

Those weeks and months in 1993 caused me to make my own inner journey to test anew my Call to ministry. I had to ask myself if I had been mistaken all these years. After all, I had served as evangelist, teacher and minister since I was 16 years of age and had been entrusted by my own Baptist Union with the role of General Secretary. Could I have been so misled and have done so going against the Bible and the Will of God?

Never shall I forget the meeting, which lasted many hours late at night during the BWA Council when "my case" was talked through in the presence of those opposing my nomination together with the leaders of both BWA and EBF. I listened carefully for a long time to all of those who spoke, feeling deeply with those who had to formulate their convictions against my nomination and moved by the warm support from others.

Finally, I asked for permission to bring the testimony of my own spiritual journey and my calling to ministry as I had understood it. The meeting ended and we prayed together. The love that poured over me from so many during those weeks while I struggled with my own Call will always remain with me as proof of the quality and depth that a Christian fellowship can hold.

Well, I was elected. I served my term, and I was even invited to visit Baptist unions where my role as a woman in a pastoral leadership role was not desirable. How much I admire them for their courage and love! My humble prayer is that some of the pain shared by all of us who took part in the events of those years will eventually be turned into blessings for many more. May it contribute to pave the way for a day when all of us everywhere will welcome a ministry in which the spiritual gifts of men and women, young and old, will be received equally. May they be accepted as God's gifts to his people for serving a world that needs a sign of hope for every kind of unity.[1]

European Baptist Convention

A. The Baptist Faith and Message of 1963

The exact time when the EBC accepted the Southern Baptist Convention's Baptist Faith and Message of 1963 as its statement of faith is unclear. Dating from the Convention annuals since 1966 to the present time, the above named statement of faith has been that of the EBC.

B. EBC Core Values

The EBC sustained strong bonds of love and unity through the years, even though much of the Christian world struggled with strife, brokenness and division. There were some good reasons for this. I called them our "Core Values," those values that were at the very heart of our work and around which relationships, service and work were built.

1. Jesus Christ is the Head of the Convention.

    Jesus Christ is the Head of local churches, just as he is the Head of the church universal. The EBC is an extension of local EBC churches, and Christ is the Head of that dimension of his church. Our service together is to be according to his purpose, done in his Spirit and for his glory.

2. Jesus Christ is the Foundation of our Fellowship.

    Christ loved, saved, forgave and accepted us. He gave us new status as kings and queens, priests and priestesses, sons and daughters, and joint heirs with him. Our fellowship with other Christians is rooted in him, who has given not only to us as individuals but to all who believe a new status in his kingdom. Normally we do not use titles among the pastoral body in the EBC. We treat all as equals, whether the pastor is called and fully supported by a local church, requested and sent by the Foreign Mission Board as a missionary or ISCer, is a bi-vocational pastor or a retired pastor. Everybody is somebody because of his status in Christ.

3. The Love of Christ Binds Us Together.

    We love each other because Christ commanded it. We love each other as he loved us. *"As I have loved you, so must you love one another."* (John 13:34b) His love for us is so great that nothing or nobody can separate us from him. Not hardship, persecution, famine, nakedness, danger, sword, death, life, angels, demons . . . nor anything else in all creation . . . (Romans 8:35-38) We are to love each other *as he loves us,* with the same depth of commitment to each other that he has made to us. Nothing can pull us apart because of our love for each other. Love binds all things together in perfect unity. (Col. 3:14) Love binds us to do service on which we agree under his leadership.

4. Administration Grows Out of the Reality of the Resurrection and Under the Leadership of the Holy Spirit.

Immediately after the Ascension of Jesus, when he was taken up out of the sight of the disciples, they gathered to pray. Gathered were the disciples (minus Judas), the women, Mary the mother of Jesus, and his brothers. During the days of prayer, Peter called a "business meeting" to elect a successor of Judas Iscariot. Imagine a "business meeting" between the Ascension and Pentecost! The one requirement of the selection of the new disciple was that he must have been a witness to the resurrection of Jesus. This says to me that the reality and the joy of the resurrection must be at the very heart of all we do, even the heart of our business meetings, our retreats, and our prayer times. I believe it is so.

5. Leadership is Rooted in Love . . . Love for God and Love for Each Other.

We practice group leadership in the EBC. Most of our work is done by volunteers who serve on about 20 committees, in Brotherhood and in EBC Women. Almost without exception, recommendations come to the Convention from these groups after they have reached consensus under what they believe is the Lordship of Christ. No coercion. No threats. Just pressing on for the common good. God gave us a beautiful model of leadership in himself. Through the prophet Hosea he said, *"I led them with cords of human kindness, with ties of love; I lifted the yoke from their neck and bent down to feed them."* (Hosea 11:4)

The Core Values were the values I believed kept the EBC united in Christ during the twenty-four years of my service as General Secretary. They were not actually presented to the Convention to be voted on. I gave them first to the Convention in my report during the Annual Meeting of 1995, then wrote them in "Merritt's Musings" in *Highlights* in the November - December issue, 1995.

The European Baptist Convention, meeting in annual session October 29-30, 2003, voted to change its name to International Baptist Convention.

Many churches of the International Baptist Convention need financial support and the Convention needs funds to start new churches. Contributions may be sent to:

Missions Endowment Fund, EBC
Baptist Foundation of Texas
1601 Elm Street, Suite 1700
Dallas, Texas 75201

or

International Baptist Church Ministries
P. O. Box 833276
Richardson, Texas 75083

or

International Baptist Convention
Am Dachsberg 98
60435 Frankfurt/Main
Germany
Jimmy Martin, General Secretary
Office phone (from US): 011 49 69 9540 8505
E-mail:gs@ibc-churches.org
Website: http://www.EBC-Churches.com

APPENDIX A

Consortium of New Baptist Seminaries

There are nearly 2,000 Baptist students now preparing for ministry at one of twelve Baptist seminaries, theological departments in universities or Baptist Houses of Study in non Baptist institutions that have been established since Southern Baptist fundamentalist leaders gained control of the SBC. The year they were founded or in which a cooperative relationship with the Cooperative Baptist Fellowship was established is in parenthesis. They are:

Baptist House of Study (1988)
The Divinity School of Duke University
Durham, North Carolina 27708-0966

Baptist Seminary of Kentucky (2002)
150 East High Street
Lexington, Kentucky 40507

Baptist Theological Seminary at
  Richmond (1991)
3400 Brook Rd.
Richmond, Virginia 23227

Brite Divinity School (1996)
Texas Christian University
TCU Box 298130
Ft. Worth, Texas 76129

Campbell University Divinity School
  (1996)
P. O. Drawer 4050
Campbell University
Buies Creek, North Carolina 27506

Candler School of Theology (1991)
Emory University
Atlanta, Georgia 30322

Central Baptist Theological
  Seminary (1994)
741 N. 31st Street
Kansas City, Kansas 66102-3964

George W. Truett Theological
  Seminary (1993)
Baylor University
P. O. Box 97126
Waco, Texas 76798-7126

Logsdon School of Theology (1995)
Hardin-Simmons University
Box 16235
Abilene, Texas 79698-6235

McAfee School of Theology (1996)
Mercer University
3001 Mercer University Drive
Atlanta, Georgia 30341-4415

M. Christopher White School of
  Divinity (1992)
Gardner-Webb University
P. O. Box 327
Boiling Springs, North Carolina 28017

The Divinity School (1996)
Wake Forest University
P. O. Box 7119, Reynolds Station
Winston-Salem, North Carolina 27109

APPENDIX B

Letter to IMB Missionaries

Re: 2000 Baptist Faith & Message

Dear Missionary:

We are encouraged to hear how God is blessing your work and how, even in the midst of global tensions and uncertainties, the gospel is multiplying and bearing fruit. I am thankful for your faithfulness to the call. We rejoice that God continues to call our Southern Baptists in unprecedented numbers and that we are seeing accelerated evangelistic response, church growth and opportunities to impact unreached people groups. We do not want anything to deter us from moving steadfastly toward completing the unfinished work of fulfilling the Great Commission.

Last year we shared with you the unanimous decision of our board with regard to the 2000 revision of the Baptist Faith & Message and the doctrinal accountability expected of us by the Southern Baptist Convention. Because of the thorough doctrinal review of each candidate in the appointment process, it was felt that those procedures were adequate and the updated BF&M would be used following its adoption. Elected administration in Richmond and regional leaders were asked and agreed to sign affirmation of the current BF&M and gave assurance that we would lead the work of the IMB consistent with the current BF&M. We already had in place a policy that if any missionary taught or practiced doctrinal positions in any way contrary to the BF&M that it would be grounds for termination. Our board felt that these policies and actions provided adequate accountability to the SBC and expressed confidence and trust in our missionaries.

However, this issue has continued to generate controversy throughout the convention and suspicion regarding some related to Southern Baptist entities who may not be in agreement with what Southern Baptists have identified as the common confession of our faith. There are many who feel strongly that those being supported by the denomination should be willing to pledge affirmation and support for the current BF&M, especially those serving with the mission boards. Failure to ask for this affirmation is creating suspicion that there are IMB personnel whose beliefs and practices are inconsistent with those represented by Southern Baptists. While we believe this is unfounded, we do not need an issue such as this to generate needless controversy, erode support and distract us from the focus on our task at such a critical time of opportunity around the world.

While there have not been major changes to the document, the statement regarding the family in 1998 and other changes in 2000 have been appropriate responses to contemporary issues and challenges that have emerged in the last 38 years since the 1963 statement was adopted. To assist our board in assuring Southern Baptists that all those who serve with the International Mission Board and supported by the convention affirm and support the current Baptist Faith and Message, I am asking that you sign the attached form indicating your affirmation and return it to your regional leader. You are welcome to note any area of disagreement with the 2000 BF&M. You should have received a copy last year or can request one from your regional office or download it from the Internet site @www.SBC.NET.

The BF&M responds to an American culture that is sliding rapidly into relativism, and it is altogether appropriate for Southern Baptists to stand for a united expression of what we believe. Signing this affirmation protects you from charges of heresy behind your back while you are overseas and cannot defend yourself. It will also disarm those who may be trying to use the BF&M to divide Southern Baptists and isolate the IMB from other agencies and state conventions that have endorsed the current revision. Since all new missionaries processed since June 2000, including the 1155 new missionaries commissioned in 2001, have affirmed the 2000 BF&M, your affirmation of this revision will assure consistency in our missionary force as we serve the Lord together. This will also clearly communicate to overseas Baptists and our Great Commission partners what we believe.

Just as we are expected to be financially accountable for the use of resources and morally circumspect in our life and witness, we who have chosen to serve with a denominational mission agency are expected to be doctrinally accountable to those who provide our support and send us out. There should be no reticence in our willingness to express agreement with what the SBC has adopted. Asking you to affirm the current BF&M has not been requested or required by the convention or our board of trustees, but our board is aware of this action and does commend and support it. We are simply seeking to move beyond a continuing and potentially damaging issue that could distract us from our mission task, unnecessarily create suspicion on the part of some and erode support of you and the IBM. I cannot over emphasize how important your cooperation is in order for us to move forward in fulfilling the Great Commission.

Thank you for your understanding and cooperation in this request. Your regional leader is prepared to follow up with you personally concerning your questions or personal clarifications. We are grateful for your dedication and are praying God would richly bless you, your ministry and family as we move into a new year.

Sincerely yours,
Jerry Rankin

Name _____

I have read and am in agreement with the current *Baptist Faith and Message.*

❏ Yes

❏ No. Please cite any area of difference.

_____
_____
_____
_____

In accountability to the International Mission Board and Southern Baptists, I agree to carry out my responsibilities in accordance with and not contrary to the current *Baptist Faith and Message* as adopted by the Southern Baptist Convention.

Signature _____

Date _____

Notes

Chapter 1

1. H. Leon McBeth. *The Baptist Heritage — Four Centuries of Baptist Witness,* (Broadman Press, 1987), 239-42.
2. William R. Estep. *Whole Gospel, Whole World — The Foreign Mission Board of the Southern Baptist Convention 1845-1995* (Nashville: Broadman and Holman, 1994), 51.
3. Jesse C. Fletcher. *The Southern Baptist Convention — A Sesquicentennial History* (Nashville: Broadman and Holman, 1994), 33.
4. Estep, 56-57.
5. Ibid.
6. Ibid., 58.
7. Fletcher, 11.
8. Ibid., 53.
9. Ibid., 54.
10. Ibid., 56.
11. Ibid., 10-11.
12. Bernard Green. *Crossing the Boundaries: A History of the European Baptist Federation* (The Baptist Historical Society: Didcot, England, 1999), 2.
13. Fletcher, 51.
14. Ibid., 67-68.
15. Ibid., 62.
16. Estep, 68-69.
17. Fletcher, 55.
18. Estep, 71-72.
19. Ibid., 73.
20. Fletcher, 55.
21. Ibid., 68.
22. Estep. 114.
23. Estep, 118.
24. Ibid., 121.
25. Fletcher, 131-132.
26. Estep, 122
27. Fletcher, 132.
28. Estep, 122-123.
29. Ibid., 150.
30. Ibid. 149.
31. Fletcher, 97, 99.
32. Fletcher, 121.
33. Green, 2.
34. Fletcher, 121-122.
35. Ibid., 127.
36. Ibid., 122-123.
37. Ibid., 129.
38. Ibid., 130.
39. Ibid., 136-37.
40. Ibid., 120
41. Ibid. 138-40.
42. Ibid., 142, 43.
43. McBeth, 686-87.
44. Fletcher, 144.
45. Ibid., 145-46.
46. Ibid., 148-50.
47. Ibid., 158-59.
48. Ibid., 161, 170.
49. Ibid., 172.
50. Ibid., 178.
51. Yona Pusey. *European Baptist Women's Union: Our Story 1948-1998* (Impressions: Oakham, England, 1998), 7-8.
52. Green, 7.
53. Ibid., 12-14.
54. Grady C. Cothen. *What Happened to the Southern Baptist Convention: A Memoir of the Controversy* (Macon, Georgia: Smyth & Helwys Publishing, 1993), 68.
55. Fletcher, 208.
56. Ibid.
57. Ibid., 209.
58. Ibid., 226.
59. Cothen, 69.
60. Fletcher, 238-39.
61. Ibid., 334.
62. Ibid., 253-54.

Chapter 2

1. Herschel H. Hobbs. *The Baptist Faith and Message* (Nashville: Convention Press, 1971), 24, 28.
2. David S. Dockery. *The Doctrine of the Bible* (Nashville: Convention Press, 1991), 100
3. Hobbs, 28-30.
4. Russell H. Dilday, Jr. *The Doctrine of Biblical Authority* (Nashville: Convention Press, 1982), 39.
5. Williston Walker. *A History of the Christian Church*, Revised Edition (Charles Scribner's Sons, Published simultaneously in the United States and Canada under the Berne Convention), 60.
6. Dockery, 106-107.
7. Ibid., 101.
8. Ibid., 89.
9. Ibid., 89-90.
10. Dilday, 97-98.
11. Erickson, Millard, J. "Problem Areas Related to Biblical Inerrancy," *The Proceedings of the Conference on Biblical Inerrancy*, (Nashville: Proadman Press, 1987), 175.
12. Ibid., 189.
13. Ibid., 175.
14. Ibid., 178.
15. Ibid., 183.
16. Ibid., 184.
17. Paker, J. I. "Problem Areas Related to Biblical Inerrancy," *The Proceedings of the Conference on Biblical Inerrancy*, (Nashville: Broadman Press, 1987), 205.
18. Patterson, Paige. "Response to Robert Preus presentation of 'The Inerrancy of Scripture.' " Ibid., 68.
19. Jones, Peter Rhea. "Response to Millard Erickson's Presentation of 'Problem Areas Related to Biblical Inerrancy.'" Ibid., 197.
20. Humphrey, Fisher. "The Baptist Faith and Message and the Chicago Statement on Biblical Inerrancy." Ibid., 329.
21. Dockery, 86-88.
22. Dilday, 96.
23. Ibid., 108.
24. Paul Pressler, *A Hill On Which To Die* (Nashville: Broadman and Holman, 1999), x.
25. Cothen, 172.
26. Ibid., 173-174.
27. Ibid., 174.
28. Ibid., 126-127.
29. Ibid., 208.
30. Ibid., 209.
31. Ibid., 212.
32. Ibid., 213.
33. Ibid., 214.
34. Ibid., 216-217.
35. Ibid., 221-222, 226.
36. Fletcher., 271-272.
37. Ibid., 291-292.
38. Ibid., 294.
39. Cothen, 232.
40. Ibid., 242-244.
41. Fletcher, 272.
42. Cothen, 245.
43. Ibid., 247.
44. *Highlights*, Newsjournal of the European Baptist Convention (July 1989).
45. Cothen, 260-261.
46. Fletcher, 308.
47. Ibid., 310
48. Ibid., 312
49. Cothen, 248.

Chapter 3

1. Cothen, 142-143.
2. *European Baptist Convention Annual, 1991*, 25.
3. Ibid.
4. *The Baptist Record,* Mississippi Baptist Convention, October 31, 1991.

Chapter 4

1. Minutes of EBF Consultation on Baptist Mission in Europe, Dorfweil, Germany, January 28, 1992.
2. Ibid.
3. Ibid.
4. "Currency Trading," *The Wall Street Journal.* January 28, 1992.
5. Transcript of Audio Tape of Minutes of Business Meeting; International Baptist Church, Brussels,Belgium; January 26, 1992.
6. Ibid.

7. Ibid.
8. Ibid.
9. Letter from FMB to all SBC missionaries in Europe, Middle East and North Africa, February 11, 1992.
10. Ibid.
11. EBPS. February 17, 1992.
12. Ibid.
13. Letter to Gerd Rudzio (GBU) from John Jackson, Winston Crawley and Don Kammerdiener (FMB), May 28, 1992.
14. EBPS. March 2, 1992.
15. Ibid.
16. Ibid. March 7, 1992.
17. Ibid., April 16, 1992.
18. Ibid., April 29, 1992.
19. EBF General Council Minutes. September 28 - October 1, 1992.
20. Ibid.
21. Archives, Baptist Union of Scotland.
22. Estep, 364.
23. Fletcher, 335.

Chapter 5

1. *EBPS*, September 15, 1993.
2. Ibid.
3. Green, 70.
4. Article 4, Hamburg Agreement.
5. Article 5, Hamburg Agreement.

Chapter 6

1. *The Biblical Recorder*, June 26, 1999.
2. Ibid.
3. Ibid., February 3, 2001.
4. *Intercom*, February, 2001.

Chapter 7

1. "What Is Biblical Inerrancy?" by Clark Pinnock, (Paige Patterson's Response to the Presentation), *The Proceedings of the Conference on Biblical Inerrancy* (Nashville: Broadman Press, 1987), 93-94.
2. Machievelli, Niccolo'. *The Prince* (Chicago: The University of Chicago Press, 1985), vii.
3. Ibid., 70-71
4. Ibid., 34-35.

5. Ibid., 68-69.
6. Peck, M. Scott. *People of the Lie: The Hope for Healing Human Evil*, (New York: Simon and Shuster,1983), 72-79.
7. Ibid., 79.
8. Ibid., 66.
9. Ibid., 67.
10. Ibid., 75.
11. Ibid., 76-77.
12. Ibid., 58.
13. Ibid., 66-67.
14. Ibid., 65-66.
15. Ibid., 70.
16. Ibid., 20, 38.
17. Ibid., 83.

Chapter 8

1. McBeth, 64-65.

Chapter 9

1. Wasserman, Dale. *Man of La Mancha*, (New York: Dell Publishing Co., Inc.), 99
2. "IMB Fires Missionaries," *Associated Baptist Press. May 10, 2003.*
3. *The Baptist Standard,* August 25, 2003.
4. *The Biblical Recorder*, June 28, 2003.
5. Ibid. July 5, 2003.
6. Ibid.
7. Wendy Ryan, "Baptist World Alliance Accepts Cooperative Baptist Fellowship," Article from BWA, July 11, 2003.
8. *The Biblical Recorder*, January 3, 2004.
9. Ibid.
10. "SBC Executive Committee Votes for BWA Withdrawal," *Associated Baptist Press*, February 18, 2004.

Epilogue

1. Crabb, Stanley. *Our Favorite Memories*: *European Baptist Federation 1949-1999*, (compiled by the European Baptist Federation, Hamburg, Germany, 1999), 134-135.

Additional Recommended Reading

Copeland, Luther. *The Southern Baptist Convention and the Judgment of History: The Taint of Original Sin.* Lanham, MD: University Press of America, 2002.

Gourley, Bruce T. *The Godmakers.* Franklin: Providence House Publishers, 1996.

Humphreys, Fisher. *The Way We Were: How Southern Baptist Theology Has Changed and What It Means to Us All.* Macon: Smyth & Helwys, 2002.

James, Robison B. *The Unfettered Word: Southern Baptists Confront the Authority-Inerrancy Question.* Waco, TX: Word Books, 1987.

Kell, Carl L., and Camp, L. Raymond. *In the Name of the Father . . . The Rhetoric of the New Southern Baptist Convention.* Carbondale: Southern Illinois University Press, 1999.

Kimball, Charles. *When Religion Becomes Evil.* San Francisco: Harper San Francisco, 2002.

O'Brien, Robert. *Stand With Christ . . . Why Missionaries Can't Sign the Baptist Faith And Message 2000.* Macon: Smyth & Helwys, 2002.

Neely, Alan. *A New Call To Mission . . . Help for Perplexed Churches.* Macon: Smyth & Helwys, 2000.

Shurden, Walter B., *The Baptist Identity . . . Four Fragile Freedoms*. Macon: Smyth & Helwys, 1993.

Index

A

Accountability, 176, 183–84
Actions for SBC churches, 179–86
  accountability of church leaders, 183–84
  investigate the Bible, 179–82
  investigate Cooperative Program, 184–85
  investigate your church, 182–83
  open discussion forums, 185–86
Adams, Theodore, 13
Allen, Clifton, 23
Allen, Jimmy, 53
Allison, Gray, 23
Anabaptists, 5
Angelov, Theo, 92, 98
Annual meetings (SBC), 154–60
Annuity Board, 15
"Another gospel"
  in SBC fundamentalist movement, 163–64, 166–75
  warnings against, 151–52
Apocrypha, 30, 32
Apology by FMB, 91, 98–101, 105–7
Armstrong, Annie, 10, 11, 69
"Articles of Religious Belief," 14
Associated Baptist Press, 54, 106
Athanasius, Bishop, 30
Authority, 33
  and Bible as weapon of attack, 27
  of fundamentalists over Convention, 55
  over information, 49–50
  over Jesus Christ, 156–60
  over missionaries, 162–63
  of pastors, 50–51
  as theological issue, 25
  of trustees over president of board/staff, 70
Autographs, 34–36, 42

B

Backus, Isaac, 2
Baker, Harriet A., 7–8
Baker, Larry, 53
Ballenger, Isam, 58, 59, 64, 86, 87, 105
Baptist Bible Institute (BBI) (New Orleans), 14
Baptist Bible Union of America, 16
Baptist Brotherhood of the South, 13
Baptist colleges and universities, 6, 55. *See also* specific institutions
Baptist Cooperative Missions Program, Inc., 54
Baptist Faith and Message, 22–23, 156, 161–63, 172, 216, 220–22
Baptist General Convention of Texas, 11, 200
Baptist Hundred Thousand Club, 18
Baptist Missionary Society, 3
Baptist Press, 49–50, 54
Baptists
  associations of, 1
  and Landmarkers, 6–7
  missions issues for, 3–5
  religious freedom of, 2
  SBC partnerships with, 204–6
Baptists Committed to the SBC, 49, 54
Baptist Standard (Texas), 10
Baptist State Convention of North Carolina, 119–20
Baptist Student Missionary Movement, 14
Baptist World Alliance (BWA)
  CBF in, 201–2
  EBC in, 118
  EBC support for, 90
  and EBF, 20
  and European Baptist Women's Union, 19–20
  organization of, 13
  SBC defunding of, 201
  SBC withdrawal from, 202–4
Barber, Peter, 59, 61, 92, 95–101, 104, 105, 120, 132
Bates, Carl, 23
Baylor University (Texas), 12, 55
Bazaar Chapel (China), 7
Bellevue Baptist Church (Memphis), 23
Benfield, Ray, 131, 140
Bennett, Harold, 53
The Bible, 27–32. *See also* Gospel of Jesus Christ
  acceptance of canon, 30–31
  accusations of not believing, 41–42
  authority and theory about, 27
  fundamentalist interpretations of, 157–60

The Bible—*Cont.*
   as fundamentalist weapon of attack, 27
   inerrancy of, 34–40
   Jesus as criterion for interpretation of, 22, 29, 156–57
   languages of, 29, 30
   manuscripts of, 28–29
   purpose of, 34
   studying/asking questions about, 179–82
   translations of, 31–32
Bichkov, Alexei, 125
Blanchard, William, 67, 94, 105
Bold Mission Thrust, 24
Bowen, Thomas J., 7
Boyce, James P., 6
British Baptists, 5
Broadman Press, 21
Broadus, John A., 6
Brooks, E. B., 200–201
Brotherhood Commission, 53
Bruster, Bill, 54
Bullock, Pat, 67

C

Canon, 30–31
Carey, Lott, 7
Carey, William, 3
Carroll, B. H., 40, 165–66
Cauthen, Baker James, 66, 111, 115
Central (First) Baptist Church (Moscow), 118, 130
Charleston Association, 1
Chicago Statement on Biblical Inerrancy, 39
China, 7, 10
Christian Life Commission, 53
Christians, SBC relationships with, 206–10
Churches of SBC
   actions for, 179–86
   appeal to, 165–77
Civil Rights Movement, 21
Civil War, 8–9
Clarke, John, 2
Claytor, Bob, 67
Clopton, S. C., 4
Coffey, David, 61, 92, 95, 98, 124
Coleman, R. H., 15
Commandments, rebellion against, 166–67
Conference on Biblical Inerrancy, 36–40
Confession of Faith Versus a Creed, 16
Conservative Resurgence movement, 24–25
Conservatives, 23–24, 42
Consultation on Baptist Mission in Europe, 86–88
Continental Baptists, 5

Cooperative Baptist Fellowship (CBF), 54
   BWA membership of, 201–2
   origin of, 54, 85–86
   and Rüschlikon funding, 62, 101
   SBC repudiation of, 138–44
Cooperative Program, 17, 43, 83, 90, 184–85
Consortium of New Baptist Theological Schools, 219
Copying of Bible, 31–33
Core Values, EBC, 216–17
Corts, Mark, 65
Cote, W. D., 8
Cottle, Charles, 134
Council of Carthage, 30
Covetousness, 210–11
Crabb, Stanley, 92, 95
Crawley, Winston, 86, 92
Creedalism, 6, 16
Creswell, Mike, 92, 95
Criswell, W. A., 22–24, 39, 50
Criswell Institute of Biblical Studies (Texas), 23
Crouch, Henry, 48
Currie, David, 49
Czech Republic Baptist Union, 140

D

Davis, Ralph and Cora Joyce, 110, 113
Day, John, 7
Dayton, B. J., 7
Deacons, women as, 22, 57
Dead Sea scrolls, 29
DeMent, B. H., 14
Dilday, Russell, 35, 39, 40, 141
Dill, Rick and Nancy, 119
Disobedience, warnings against, 174–75
Division, 191
   legitimate, 175–76
   in SBC, 153
   warnings against, 173
Dockery, David, 34–35, 39, 96
Domestic Missions Board, 3
Domestic Slavery Considered as a Scriptural Institution, 4
Don Quixote, 190
The Dorfweil Statement, 87–88, 94, 97
Draper, James, 44
Dutch Mennonites, 5

E

Eagle, James P., 13
Elder, Lloyd, 53
Elliott, Ralph, 21
English language churches, 7, 120–22
Erickson, Millard J., 36–38
Error (in Bible), definitions of, 35, 37

Estep, William R., 106, 107
Euro-Asiatic Federation, 123–24
European Baptist Convention (EBC), 131
  author's work in, *See* Merritt, John
  Baptist Faith and Message (1963), 216
  Core Values of, 216–17
  countries in, 116–17
  IBC defunding of, 88–92
  IBTS resolution passed by, 61–62
  Italian churches in, 113, 115
  partnerships of, 119–20
European Baptist Federation (EBF)
  Consultation with FMB, 1992, 94–101
  EBC in, 117–18
  EBC support for, 90
  and Hamburg Agreement, 101–4
  organization of, 20
  Rüschlikon IBTS given to, 52, *See also* International Baptist Theological Seminary (Rüschlikon, Switzerland)
  sale of Rüschlikon property, 213
  and women in leadership, 123–27
European Baptist Press Service (EBPS), 60–61, 93
European Baptists, 167–68
  and defunding of IBTS, *See* International Baptist Theological Seminary (Rüschlikon, Switzerland)
  and Dorfweil Statement, 87–88, 97
  and interpretation of Scripture, 124–26
  post-World War II developments, 19–22
  relationship with FMB, 85
  Rüschlikon IBTS given to, 52
European Baptist Women's Union, 19–20
Eusebius, 30
Evangelism, 21
Executive Committee, SBC, 49, 53, 54

F

False witness, 83
Fiddes, Paul, 93
Firisiuk, Alexander, 126
First African Baptist Church (Richmond), 5
First Baptist Church (Monrovia), 7
First Baptist Church of Dallas, Texas, 12, 23
First Baptist Church of Vicenza, Italy, 113–14
Fletcher, Jesse C., 106, 107
Floyd, John and Helen, 123, 140–41
Foreign Mission Board (FMB)
  African field, 7
  Consultation with EBF, 1992, 94–101
  early receipts to, 4
  establishment of, 3–5
  during Great Depression, 18
  and Hamburg Agreement, 101–4

Foreign Mission Board—*Cont.*
  policy on work in Europe, 123
  as resource for EBC pastors, 119
  and Rüschlikon IBTS, 19, 52, *See also* International Baptist Theological Seminary (Rüschlikon, Switzerland)
  J. B. Taylor on, 8, 9
  H. A. Tupper on, 8, 9
  and women in leadership, 59
Foreign missions. *See also* International Baptist Theological Seminary, Rüschlikon, Switzerland; Missionaries
  Lottie Moon offering for, 11–12
  H. A. Tupper's "cherished plan" for, 9
  Wilson—Hancock letter on FMB, 64–71
  women in, 7–11
Fort Worth Pastors' Conference, 15
The Forum, 54
Francisco, Clyde, 21
Freedom, 2, 171–72, 174–75, 198–99
Frost, J. M., 12
"The Fruits of Norrism" (Lee Scarborough), 16
Fuller, Charles, 46
Fuller, Richard, 3–4
Fundamentalist movement in SBC, 27–56
  accusations of not believing the Bible, 41–42
  aspects of "another gospel" in, 166–75
  and authority over information, 49–50
  Bible as weapon of attack in, 27
  and call for parity, 44–45
  and Conference on Biblical Inerrancy, 36–40
  Conservative Resurgence, 24–25
  crisis of conscience engendered by, 42–43
  early peace initiatives, 44
  and inerrancy of the Bible, 34–35
  and language of church cultures/Bible, 40–41
  and lay leadership, 50–51
  and leadership of SBC agencies/institutions, 53–54
  J. Frank Norris in, 15–16
  and Peace Committee, 45–48
  responses to, 48–49, 54–56
  and women in pastoral leadership, 50
Furman, Richard, 17
Furman Baptist College (South Carolina), 6
Furman University (South Carolina), 55

G

Gambrell, J. B., 14
Gender inclusiveness, 159, 193–98
Genesis Crisis, 21
Georgetown Baptist College, 6
German Baptists, 5
German Baptist Union (GBU), 92, 100
Germany Baptist Mission, 136

Gero, Julia, 125
Gheorghita, Nic, 92, 124, 126
Golden Gate Baptist Theological Seminary (California), 18, 53
Gospel of Jesus Christ, 145–64, 160–62, 209
    authority of Jesus Christ in, 147
    authority of Jesus in other scriptures, 147–49
    defined, 145
    inclusiveness of, 209
    love in, 149–51
    and state of SBC, 153–64
    unity in Christ, 152
    voice of Jesus Christ, 146
    warnings against "another gospel," 151–52
Gould, Thomas, 2
Governance by consensus, 6
Graham, Billy, 20–21
Graves, J. R., 6
Gray, Bill, 132
Great Commission, 69, 209
Great Depression, 18
Guderian, Hans, 92, 98
Gutenberg, Johannes, 32
Gutenberg Bible, 32
Guy, Cal, 75

H

Hamburg Agreement, 96, 100–104, 106, 138–39, 142
Hancock, William, 62, 64, 86, 90
Haralson, Jonathan, 13
Hardy, Steve, 67
Hart, Oliver, 1
Hartfield, Jimmy and Susie, 110
Harwell, Jack, 65
Hayner, George, 134
Henry, Jim, 138
Herchenhahn, C. O., 110
Hester, Jim and Gene, 114
Hewett, John, 62, 76, 77, 92
Hine, Nick, 89–90
Hinson, E. Glenn, 63, 74, 75, 78, 82
Historical Commission, 19
History of Southern Baptist Convention (A Summary), 1–25
    Annuity Board, 15
    Baptist Faith and Message, 22–23
    Baptist student movement, 14
    and BWA, 13
    Christian education, 5–7
    and Civil War, 8–9
    Confession of Faith vs. a creed, 16–17
    Conservative Resurgence movement, 24–25
    Cooperative Program, 17
    early fundamentalist issues, 15–16

History of Southern Baptist Convention—*Cont.*
    establishment of SBC, 1–5
    European developments after World War II, 19–22
    foreign and home missions, 3–5
    and Great Depression, 18
    lay leadership, 13–14
    Lottie Moon Christmas offering, 11–12
    mission expansion to Europe, 5
    modern conservatives vs. moderates, 23–24
    state conventions, 8
    Sunday School Board, 12
    women in foreign missions, 7–8, 10–11
    women's missionary societies, 9–10
    and World War II, 18–19
Hobbs, Herschel, 22, 39
Hogue, Calvin and Betty, 136
Holcomb, Dan, 110
Holmes, Obadiah, 2
Holy Spirit, 157, 168, 194–95
    and authenticity of books of Bible, 30
    Bible inspired by, 28
    gift of, 180
    hearing, 211–12
    ministry of, 146
    quenching, 171
    and study/application of Scripture, 152
    and translations of Bible, 31
Home Mission Board, 14, 18, 53, 57–58
Hopper, Jo Ann, 93
Hopper, John D., 59, 64, 75, 78–81, 92, 93, 97
Hughey, J. D., 114–16
Humphreys, Fisher, 39

I

Indian Mission Association, 5
Inerrancy, 34–35
    of autographs, 34–35
    of Bible, 35
    Conference on Biblical Inerrancy, 36–40
    and copying of the Bible, 32–33
    defined, 34, 37
    two meanings of, 36
Information, authority over, 49–50
Inguanti, Carmelo, 114–15
Integrity, 78–80, 86–87
International Baptist churches, 120–22
International Baptist Church of Brussels, Belgium, 88–92
International Baptist Theological Seminary (Prague, Czech Republic), 213–14
International Baptist Theological Seminary (Rüschlikon, Switzerland), 19
    and authority of trustees over president of board/staff, 70

International Baptist Theological
    Seminary—*Cont.*
  and birth of CBF, 85–86
  CBF support for, 92–93
  defunding decision, 59–64
  FMB representatives' apology for defunding,
    98–100, 104–8
  and IBC's defunding of EBC, 88–92
  original gift of, 52
  reconsideration of defunding, 71–80
  refusal to reverse defunding, 81–84
  Summary of Doctrinal Principles of, 80–81
International Mission Board (IMB), 58, 153,
    162–63, 172, 173, 200–201, 203, 220, 221
Italian Baptist Mission, 113, 114, 128
Italian Baptist Union, 115, 116

J

Jackson, John, 67, 92, 94, 96, 98, 105
James, I, King of England, 32
James, Samuel M., 92, 93, 96, 98, 101, 102,
    106, 107
Jefferson, Thomas, 2
Jesus Christ. *See also* Gospel of Jesus Christ
  authority of, 147–49
  Christians as copies of, 33
  as criterion by which Bible is interpreted,
    22, 29
  Great Commission given by, 69
  and importance of truth, 108
  inclusion of everyone by, 195–97
  language used by, 41
  only division authorized by, 175–76
  SBC and authority over, 156–60
  Scriptures of, 33
  teachings of, 29
  unchanging nature of, 194–95
  vision of, 187–89
  voice of, 146
Jeter, J. B., 5
Johnson, W. B., 2–3, 5, 17
Jones, Keith G., 214
Jones, Peter Rhea, 38–39
Judson, Adoniram, 3, 4
Judson College (Alabama), 5

K

Kammerdiener, Don, 92, 94
Karlsson, Birgit, 61, 123–27, 214–15
Kennedy, J. Hardee, 111
Kim, Billy, 202
King, Martin Luther, Jr., 21
King James Version (KJV), 32
Komendant, Gregory, 134
Kulbich, Victor, 134

L

Landmarkism, 6–7
Language(s)
  of the Bible, 29, 30, 40–41
  of church cultures, 40–41
Lay leadership, 13–14, 50–51
Laymen's Missionary Movement, 13
Leavell, Frank H., 14, 111
Lee, Hal, 92, 93, 98
Legitimate division, 175–76
Leland, John, 2
Lewis, C. S., 176
Lewis, Larry, 57–58
Liberalism, 22, 23, 45, 59
Liberia, 7
LifeWay Christian Resources, 12
Lolley, Randall, 51, 53
Lorenzen, Thorwald, 59
Lottie Moon Offering for Foreign Missions,
    11–12, 69
Lotz, Denton, 124, 126, 201, 202
Love, 149–51, 199–200
Lunsford, William, 15
Luther, Martin, 31

M

Machievelli, Niccolo, 166–67, 169, 172, 174, 176
Maddry, Charles E., 19
Madison, James, 2
Mainstream Baptists, 154
Mallau, Hans Harald, 59
Manly, Basil, 3
Manly, Basil, Jr., 6
Mantz, Felix, 63
Manuscripts of Bible, 28–29, 35
Marshall, Martha Stears, 4
Martin, Dan, 49
Mary Hardin-Baylor College (Texas), 5
Masino, Luigi, 115
Massey, Newell, 110
McBeth, Leon, 16–17
McCall, Duke, 13
McClellan, Albert, 47
McIntosh, Martha, 10
Mercer Baptist College (Georgia), 6
Meredith College (North Carolina), 55
Merritt, Cora Joyce, 109
Merritt, Dewey, 110, 113
Merritt, Elizabeth Pope, 112, 113, 115, 116, 128,
    134, 136, 141
Merritt, Inman, 109
Merritt, James Philip, 112, 113, 128
Merritt, James Polk (grandfather), 109
Merritt, James Polk (J. P.), 109

Index

Merritt, John, 62, 92, 94, 95, 96, 98, 106, 109–43
  (One Missionary's Journey)
  call to foreign mission service, 112–13
  and controversy over women in leadership, 123–27
  and EBC—Baptist State Convention of North Carolina partnership, 119–20
  as EBC General Secretary, 115–20
  and EBC in EBF, 117–18
  as EBF President, 122–23
  as EBF Vice President, 120–21
  education, 111
  and English language churches, 120–22
  family background, 109
  first pastorate, 111–12
  and FMB's decision on work in Europe, 123
  home church education/evangelism/missions, 110
  and Interlaken Baptist Assembly of 1994, 140
  Milan, Italy, church, 114–15
  Moscow visit with EBF, 118–19
  and SBC decision concerning CBF, 138–44
  Sneads, Florida, pastorate, 112–13
  Vicenza, Italy, church, 113–14
Merritt, John Mark, 112, 113, 128
Merritt, Lucy Walters, 109
Merritt, Mary Katherine, 109
Merritt, Michael Paul, 112, 113, 128
The Message of Genesis (Ralph Elliott), 21
Mid-America Baptist Theological Seminary (Tennessee), 23
Midteide, Per, 61
Midwestern Baptist Theological Seminary (Missouri), 20
Milan Baptist Church, 114, 115
Missionaries. *See also* Foreign missions
  to Africa, 7
  authority over, 162–63
  fired by IMB, 200–201
  "liberation" of, 203–4
  Jerry Rankin's letter to, 220–22
  slave owners as, 2
  Ron Wilson's accusations against, 70–71
  women as, 9, 10
Missions. *See also* Domestic Missions Board; Foreign missions
  Cooperative Program funding for, 17
  EBC support for, 90
  as issue in establishment of SBC, 2–5
  role of women in, 7–11
  women's missionary societies, 9–10
Mississippi College, 6, 111
Moderates, 23–24, 48
Moon, Charlotte (Lottie), 10–12
Moon, Edmonia, 10

Moore, Alice, 20
Moore, John A., 115
Moore, Rayford and Lorinne, 110
Moore, Winfred, 45, 46, 49
Moss, Zeb, 69
Mullins, E. Y., 13

N

Negrut, Paul, 124, 126
New International Version (NIV), 32
New King James Version (NKJV), 32
New Orleans Baptist Theological Seminary (NOBTS), 14
New Testament, 29
Nigeria, 7
Nobel, Alfred, 124
Norris, J. Frank, 15–16
Northen, W. J., 13

O

O'Brien, Bill, 69
Old Testament, 29, 33
Oncken, Johann Gerhard, 5, 20
Oradea, Romania, 67, 70

P

Pace, Bill, 67
Packer, J. I., 38
Parallelism, 204–5
Parity, call for, 44–45
Parker, Keith, 64, 86, 87, 105
Parks, Keith, 52, 58, 60–61, 64, 68, 91, 93
Partiality, 159–62, 173
Pastors
  authority of, 50–51
  disparity in education of, 6
  women as, 22, 50, 57
Pastor's Conference (1962), 21
Patterson, Paige, 23–25, 38, 66, 67, 89, 90
Peace Committee, 45–48
Peck, M. Scott, 169–70, 176
People of the Lie (M. Scott Peck), 169–70
Philadelphia Association, 1
Pinkston, Glen and Nina, 119
Pollard, Frank, 45, 53
Popkes, Wiard, 59, 60, 62, 80, 81, 86, 92, 95, 97, 98
Prague Seminary. *See* International Baptist Theological Seminary (Prague, Czech Republic)
Pressler, Paul, 24–25, 41–42, 106, 107, 156
Press Service, 19
Priesthood of all believers, 50–51
The Prince (Niccolo Machievelli), 166–67, 169
Providence Baptist Association (Liberia), 7

Q

Queen's Road Baptist Church (China), 7

R

Radio and Television Commission, 19, 53
Randall, Phyllis, 66, 67
Rankin, Jerry, 163, 220–22
Ray, Willis J., 18
Religious freedom, 2
Reynolds, Ray and Helen, 121, 136
Rice, Luther, 3
Richmond Baptist College (Virginia), 6
Riggins, Hunter, 66
Roberts, I. J., 4, 7, 8
Roberts, Phil, 66, 67, 75–76, 89
Robertson, George and Carolyn, 131
Rogers, Adrian, 23, 24, 155, 156
Romania, 53
Romanian Baptist Union, 102, 104, 123, 124, 126–27
Rome Baptist Church, 114
Ruchti, Helen and Dub, 114
Ruden, Eric, 125
Ruden, Kerstin, 125
Rudzio, Gerd, 92
Rüschlikon Seminary. *See* International Baptist Theological Seminary (Rüschlikon, Switzerland)
Rushbrooke, J. H., 20
Russian Baptists, 118, 130
Rutledge, Kevin, 140

S

Sandy Creek movement, 4
Satan, 188, 208–9
SBC Today, 54
Scarborough, L. R., 165–66
Scarborough, Lee, 16
Schuetz, Eduard, 70
Scientific study, 21
Scott, Catherine, 4
Sehested, Nancy, 48
Self exaltation, 174
Seminaries, 20. *See also specific seminaries*
 contact information for, 219
 and fundamentalist control, 55
 parity on faculties of, 44–45
 Peace Committee visits to, 46
Septuagint, 29
Seventh Baptist Church (Baltimore), 4
Shackleford, Al, 49, 54
Shakespeare, William, 168
Sherman, Cecil, 44, 46
Shuck, Henrietta Hall, 4
Shuck, J. Lewis, 4, 7

Sims, John, 67
Slavery, 2, 4
Smith, Bailey, 44
Smith, Becky, 119
Smith, James, 53, 119
Smith, Skip, 67, 94, 99, 104, 105
Sophie Newcomb College (New Orleans), 14
Soul freedom, 2
Southeastern Baptist Theological Seminary (North Carolina), 20, 53
Southern Baptist Alliance (SBA), 48
The Southern Baptist Convention—A Sesquicentennial History (Jesse C. Fletcher), 106
Southern Baptist Convention (SBC)
 appeal to churches in, 165–77
 BWA defunded by, 201
 current state of, 153–64
 fundamentalist takeover of, 27–56
 and Hamburg Agreement, 142
 history of (A Summary), 1–25
 leadership of agencies/institutions of, 53–54
 new vision for future of, 187–212
 repudiation of CBF by, 138–44
 suggested actions for churches in, 179–86
 withdrawal from BWA, 202–4
Southern Baptist Foundation, 19
Southern Baptist Press Association (SBPA), 49–50
Southern Baptist Theological Seminary (SBTS) (Kentucky), 6
Southwestern Baptist Theological Seminary (Texas), 12, 44–45
Spezzacatena, Antonio, 133
Stanley, Charles, 45, 46
State convention Baptist papers, 49–50
State conventions, 8
Statement of Faith (1925), 22
Statement of Principles (SBC, 1946), 19
Stetson University (Florida), 55
Stewardship Commission, 19
Stout, Herbert, 137
Sullivan, James, 21, 23
"The Summary of Doctrinal Principles" (Rüschlikon), 80–81
Sunday School Board, 12, 14, 18, 21, 53
Sutton, Bill, 66, 67
Swiss Baptist Union, 213, 214

T

Talos, Vasile, 92
Talpos, Vasile, 125
Tanner, William, 53
Taylor, George B., 8
Taylor, James B., 8, 9

Theological schools, 23, 55, 154
Tichenor, I. T., 12
Translations of the Bible, 31–32, 35
Triennial Convention, 1–5
Tripp, Frank Edward, 18
Truett, George W., 12, 13, 15–17, 20
Truth, failure to live by, 168–70
Tupper, Henry Allen, 8, 9, 11–12
Turner, Lydia, 5
Tyndale, William, 32

U
Unity, 152, 190–91, 205–6

V
Vestal, Dan, 54
Vision for future of SBC, 187–212
    for inclusiveness of genders/generations, 193–98
    for the nations, 198–200
    for new leadership, 189–90
    for potential within ourselves, 188–89
    for relationships with Baptist partners, 204–6
    for relationships with other Christians, 206–10
    for sharing resources, 210–11
    two potential destinies, 191–93
    for unity, 190–91
Vulgate, 31

W
Wagner, Guenter, 59
Walter, Karl Heinz, 59–61, 80, 81, 92, 93, 96–98, 105, 106, 120, 122, 124, 126, 132
Walters, Harold, 110
Walters, Joe, Jr., 110
Walters, John Wesley, 109
Watts, J. Wash, 111

Watts, John D. W., 74
Wayland, Francis, 4
Weatherford, Carolyn, 53
Webb, Mary, 5
White, K. Owen, 22
Whole Gospel—Whole World (William R. Estep), 106
Williams, Roger, 2, 4
Williams, William, 6
Willingham, J. R., 12
Wilson, Ron, 64–70, 87, 182
Woman's Missionary Union, 9, 10, 13–14, 19–20, 53, 73
Woman's Missionary Union Training School (Louisville), 13–14
Women
    Biblical status of, 159–61
    as deacons, 22
    in early Baptist life, 45
    European Baptist Women's Union, 19–20
    in foreign missions, 7–11
    and gender inclusiveness, 159, 193–98
    Jesus' treatment of, 195–97, 200
    in leadership roles, 27, 123–27
    as messengers, 10, 11
    ordination of, 22, 57
    in pastoral leadership, 50
    and SBC partiality toward men, 159–62
    vision for, 200
Women in Ministry, 48, 54
Women's missionary societies, 9–10
World War II, 18–19
Wumpelmann, Knud, 52, 124
Wycliffe, John, 32

Z
Zeschky, Walter, 61